Language and Culture in

PERSIAN

Bibliotheca Iranica
Literature Series No. 7

No. 1
Once a Dewdrop
Essays on the Poetry of Parvin E'tesami
Edited by Heshmat Moayyad

No. 2
Suppressed Persian
An Anthology of Forbidden Literature
Paul Sprachman

No.3
Reading Nastaʿliq
Persian and Urdu Hands from 1500 to the Present
William L. Hanaway and Brian Spooner

No. 4
Conversations with Emperor Jahangir
by
"Mutribi" al-Asamm of Samarqand
Translated from the Persian with an Introduction by
Richard C. Foltz

No. 5
Welcoming Fighānī
Imitation and Poetic Individuality in
the Safavid-Mughal Ghazal
Paul E. Losensky

No. 6
The Sands of Oxus
Boyhood Reminiscences of Sadriddin Aini
John Perry

Language and Culture in

PERSIAN

Paul Sprachman

MAZDA PUBLISHERS, Inc. ◆ Costa Mesa, California ◆ 2002

The publication of this volume was made possible by a grant from the Iranica Institute

Mazda Publishers, Inc.
Academic publishers since 1980
P.O. Box 2603, Costa Mesa, California 92628 U.S.A.
www.mazdapub.com

Library of Congress Cataloging-in-Publication Data
Sprachman, Paul.
Language and Culture in Persian/ Paul Sprachman.
p.cm—(Bibliotheca Iranica: Literature Series; no. 7)
In English with some text in Persian.
Includes bibliographical references (p.) and index.

ISBN: 1-56859-144-6
(Softcover, alk. paper)

1. Persian language—Social aspects. 2. Persian language—Political aspects. 3. Language and culture—Iran. 4. Persian language—Style. 5. Persian language—Alphabet. I. Title. II. Series.
PK6224.75.S68 2002
491'.55—dc21
2002033676

To him, the artist known as Isac زال
And her, the *fleur de lis* that grew in Gaule.

Contents

Romanization

Vowels

Short		*Long*		*Diphthongs*	
ـَ	a	آ	ā	ـَیْ	ey
ـُ	o	ـُو	u	ـَوْ	ow
ـِ	e	ـِی	i		

Consonants

b	ب	r	ر	f	ف
p	پ	z	ز	q	ق
t	ت	s	س	k	ك
th	ث	sh	ش	g	گ
j	ج	ṣ	ص	l	ل
ch	چ	ḍ	ض	m	م
ḥ	ح	ṭ	ط	n	ن
kh	خ	ẓ	ظ	v/w	و
d	د	ʿ	ع	h	ه
d̲	ذ	gh	غ	y	ی
eh	ـه (*silent h*)	‘ *or* ’	ء	kh^{v}ā	خوا

Quirks. Certain names with common English spellings like Mohammad (the Prophet), Elahi, Amirshahi, Khomeini, Saddam Hussein, etc. “And” (و) is usually *va* (Iran) or *wa* (Afghanistan, Tajikistan), but is sometimes shortened to *o* as in *jān-o kherad* (see introduction).

The Names of Signs Used in Writing

Eleven rhyme with "hey":

ه	ژ	ز	ر	خ	ح	چ	ث	ت	پ	ب
hey	*zhey*	*zey*	*rey*	*khey*	*hey*	*chey*	*sey*	*tey*	*pey*	*bey*

Four with "saw":

ط	ظ	ف	ی
tā	*zā*	*fā*	*yā*

Three with "cough":

ق	ك	گ
qāf	*kāf*	*gāf*

Two with "I'll"

ذ	د
zāl	*dāl*

Two with "lean":

ش	س
shin	*sin*

Two with "team":

م	ج
mim	*jim*

Two with "cod"

ص	ض
sād	*zād*

Two with "gain":

ع	غ
eyn	*gheyn*

One with "Tom":

ل

lām

One with "tune":

ن

nun

One with "mauve":

و

wāw/vāv

One with "Al F.":

ا

alef

One with "Tom's eh":

ـئـ ؤ أ ء

hamzeh

Introduction

There is a stunning case of illiteracy in Alberto Manguel's *A History of Reading*— stunning because it comes in a book devoted to the "craft of deciphering and translating signs" (Manguel 1997:7). Page twenty-six, which introduces a chapter about how "reading begins with the eyes," contains an illustration from a manuscript kept in the Istanbul University Library. Manguel has labeled the illustration "teaching optics and the laws of perception in a sixteenth century Islamic school." The illustration serves the purposes of *A History of Reading* well, but Manguel's caption ignores a Persian inscription that appears above the classroom where five scholars are discussing optics. Had he been able to read the inscription, he would have changed the caption. It is the most famous invocation in all Persian literature and looks like this:

بنام خداوند جان و خرد

These words are the first half-line of Ferdowsi's *Shahnameh*, an epic poem that tells the history of Iran from its beginnings in myth to the Arab invasion in the seventh century. This hemistich says a lot about Persian. Like two other languages that use this alphabet, Arabic and Urdu, written Persian is a string of consonants and long vowels processed from right to left:

←

بـنـام خـداونـد جـان و خـرد

d r   kh u n ā j d n vā d kh m ā n b

Unwritten, but evident when the verse is read aloud, are short vowels which can be shown by adding above- and below-the-line marks to the unvoweled text:

← بِنامِ خُداوَنْدِ جانُ و خِرَد

In left-to-right transliteration, the Persian reads *be-nām-e khodāvand-e jān-o kherad* or "in the name of the God of soul and intellect." The hemistich also reveals an important way Persian consonants are distinguished from one another. The first two elements, *be-nām* ("in [the] name"; yes, Persian *nām* and English "name" are related), begin with two "teeth," slight upward projections from the baseline:

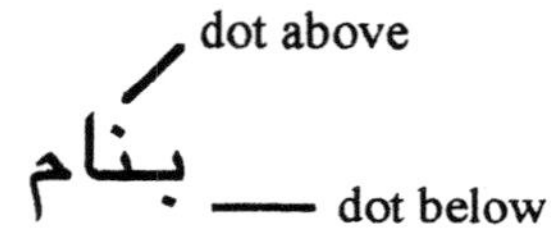

The teeth are the same except that the first has a dot below and the second a dot above. A dot below makes the tooth sound like English b, and a dot above like English n. Dotting plays the same role in the next three nouns in the verse, all of which begin with the same triangular shape:

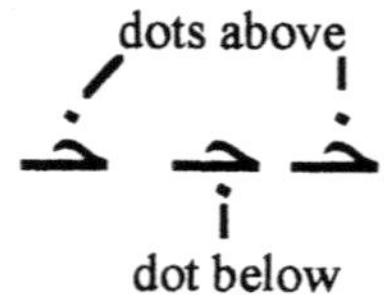

A dot above the triangle yields kh, a guttural sound found in English imports from Yiddish like "chutzpah" and "chanukah." A dot below the triangle makes it sound like English j in "jar."

As vital as these facts of Persian are to the craft of deciphering the inscription, to interpret it one needs to know its origin, Ferdowsi's *Shahnameh*. This knowledge allows the reader to infer more than Manguel did from the illustration, to speculate about the illustrator's intentions. By using a Persian inscription rather than a passage in Arabic from the Qoran, for example, the illustrator was not indicating an "Islamic" school, as the caption explains, but an Iranian one, or, at least, one influenced by Iranian culture. Perhaps the choice of inscription shows that the students used Persian to study optics.

Knowing the meaning and provenance of the verse leads to other speculations. One scholar reads it as emblematic of Ferdowsi's adherence to a particular form of Islam: Ismaili Shi'ism (Zaryāb Kho'i 1992:17). In Ismaili thought, intellect is the First Cause and soul the First Effect of that Cause. There is nothing definitively Islamic about this thought; it came to Islam from a form of Greek philosophy known as Neoplatonism. Did the illustrator use Ferdowsi's invocation to suggest that the school was not governed by the majority (Sunni) views on philosophy and science? Was it meant to proclaim the privileged position of intellect and reason in the curriculum?

Of course, one could not expect the Persian-less Manguel to speculate this way. He used the illustration because it served the purposes of his history. The misleading nature of his caption is obvious only to those who know Persian. For other readers "a sixteenth century Islamic school" suffices.

Language and Culture in Persian is about what readers of Persian know. It asks the question: What understandings do readers share that enable them to comprehend skillful writing in the language? Common knowledge of this sort comes in two ways:

explicitly in the form of the alphabet, morphology, syntax, punctuation, and other obvious aspects of writing, and

implicitly in the form of a shared set of basic facts and ideas that allows readers to construct the meanings of texts.

Who is a skilled writer of Persian? Opinions vary considerably. Anthologists have always had aesthetic and stylistic criteria that define a canon of one sort or another. These concerns tend to exclude more writers than they include. *Language and Culture in Persian* is less discriminating than an anthology. To judge the skillfulness of Persian it asks: Does the writing convey a message that is readily apparent to many users of the language? While such a standard can never yield something worthy of the title "masterpieces of modern Persian Literature," it will expose readers of this book to a wide variety of contemporary writing.

The materials in the book are topically arranged readings and translations selected specifically because they illustrate key features of the language and culture of literate Persian-users. They appear not only because they include all the orthographic and grammatical features of Persian, but also because they implicate ideas that, properly explored, lead to important insights about the shared culture of those who speak and read the language. While there is little disagreement about the mechanics of modern written Persian, the assumptions that most readers of the language bring to a text are very difficult to define because they are rarely explicit and rarely uniform. Users of Persian already "know" these assumptions so there is no need to spell them out. Those unfamiliar with the language have no choice but to discover them. They have to digest many good texts and discard many more poor ones before a pattern of ideas emerges that competent readers would term characteristic of their community.

What makes a topic useful? My experience teaching English as a second language is material here. Responsible for classes composed of adult native speakers of five to ten different languages, I often struggle to find topics that will engage students in common conversation. The utility of a topic in such classes relates to its capacity to engross students so much they need to stretch, or even burst, their competence in English to explain it. The topic proves even more useful if it resonates in the cultures of the student's classmates, so that it invites "That's like what we call..."-type comments. In a class of East Asian students, for example, I discovered that the Korean word *han* epitomizes such a topic. Not only is there no ready synonym for it in English, Koreans sometimes write it with the Chinese character *hen*; thus not only is *han* meaningful in Korean culture, it is also familiar to students from the People's Republic of China, Taiwan, and Japan.

Korean	Chinese/Japanese
han 한	*hen* 恨

Like all good topics of conversation *han* is at the center of a complex semantic web. Many young Koreans will say that it is characteristic of the World War II and Korean War generations. Those who experienced Japanese colonization can have *han* for the colonizers. The post-WWII division of Korea and hopelessness about reunification also arouse *han*. There is even an expression that most Koreans I have asked know: "When a woman has *han*, she can make frost in the summer." This word evokes history and a mixed brew of feelings akin to dislike, remorse, despair, and grief. *Han* is a good topic for Korean speakers in conversation and culture classes because it requires explanation. Koreans often have to stretch their English to define the term for *han*less classmates, and even after they achieve a working definition, they often amend it because the meaning of *han* varies from individual to individual. Chinese readers, by contrast, can translate *han* as "hate," and therefore do not have to push their English as a second language beyond the facile equivalence of dictionary definition.[1]

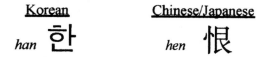

Language and Culture in Persian explores writing that expresses *han*-like topics. The book views written Persian first as a medium of ideas, and, second, as a system of expression. Its sixteen chapters present topics that invite scrutiny, provoke discussion, and characterize a common culture drive its contents. It begins at the beginning with the Persian alphabet. The first chapter, Persianizing English, introduces basic Persian sounds and their written representation with English analogs. This chapter goes into the unstable orthography of foreign words in the language. It also shows how Persianizing, rather than being haphazard, at times can be systematically hostile to English.

What is topical about an alphabet? First, there is the issue of the Arabic letters in Persian. Those who speak the language very well, but not have read widely in the language, are often in doubt about the correct spelling of its Arabic elements. As the alphabetic tables at the beginning of this book show, four separate letters represent the "z" as in "zoo." Language reformers want to facilitate literacy by reducing "redundant" letters to one "pure" Persian character. Traditionalists resist this simplification, because it would distance learners of the modified alphabet from their literary heritage. Like learners of the simplified characters of China, the users of the simplified Persian alphabet might not be able to understand texts in the old alphabet. Chapters II and III, History in the Alphabet and The Politics of the Alphabet, contain excerpts that address these issues.

As the book progresses, the topics grow more complex, implicating more and more historical, religious, social, and cultural information, and thus become more and more lexically and structurally difficult. By going from literal, interlinear translations to idiomatic English, the book focuses on the untranslatable, on types of cultural information that rarely become explicit. Ancillary explanations and notes guide the reader to fundamental relationships between language and culture in Persian. Chapter IV, The Pleasures of the Alphabet, explores a facet of the language that the linguistic engineers mentioned in Chapter III ignore: calligraphy. Persian has always been the medium of a fierce iconoclasm, which is why writing in the language is a fully developed art. In calligraphic Persian, the shapes of consonants and long vowels are more meaningful than the sounds they represent.

From the alphabet and orthography, the book proceeds to topics that form the first chapters of traditional grammars and readers: formal and informal introductions, courtesy, marriage, and eating. Chapter V, Naming and Interrogation, combines the questioning of political prisoners and how people get acquainted under less punitive circumstances. It also explores politeness in

Persian, the language's "double-you" nature and its honorifics. Humility, Chapter VI, introduces other honorifics in systematic Persian politeness and ends with an excerpt in which one speaker goes so far in flattering that he insults. Acquaintance and familiarity lead to Marriage and Mating in Persian, Chapter VII. This chapter presents materials on wooing and suitors, marital law, and failed marriage. That even the simplest legal language in Persian is couched in Arabisms tells us that the language is still as dependent on Arabic to lay down the law as English is on Latin for the same purpose. Chapter VIII, Eating, introduces the omnivorous Persian verb *khordan*, which is at the heart of so many gut feelings in the language.

The next two chapters of *Language and Culture in Persian* deal with movement and change of one sort or another. Chapter IX, Estrangement and Nostalgia, is about exile, dislocation, and homesickness. It also considers the Persian New Year celebration Now Ruz in its capacity to unite expatriate communities no matter how divergent their views. Chapter X, Coming of Age, studies how the language expresses the journey from youth to adulthood.

Strong feelings make the topics of the next two chapters very rich. One of the texts in Love and Eroticism, Chapter XI, is a poem that, though published almost fifty years ago, is still unsettling for its unmistakable expression of a woman's sexual pleasure. This chapter also addresses the widening gap between the modest Persian of the older societies of Asia and the libidinous language of the westernized diaspora. Death at Karbala, Chapter XII, is about mortality and transfiguration. It focuses on texts about the central passion of many Persian-users—the martyrdom of Imam Hoseyn. The rich topic in this chapter is the persistence of martyr culture among Persian-users. A losing battle that took place near a date palm grove on the west bank of the Euphrates almost fifteen centuries ago lives in the language of modern politics and warfare.

Even stronger feelings surface in the last chapter. Chapter XIII, Us/Them, looks at the language of ethnic identity. The first excerpt in this chapter is about a loosely defined Aryanism that the many Persian-users share. This constructed identity became particularly compelling during World War II when the armies of the Third Reich were "liberating" British colonies. The Aryanism and Islam the majority shares often cause minorities to stand out more than they want to. The other two texts in the chapter—one about Jews, the other about Christians—describe the consequences of being conspicuous.

To summarize: *Language and Culture in Persian* is a pre-reader. It assumes no prior knowledge of the language. The book introduces basic linguistic and cultural information users of the language share. Relying on concise texts from many types of writing, it is a guide to the mechanics and fundamental ideas, inferences, assumptions, understandings, opinions, and judgments that are characteristic of the community of Persian-users. One of the book's principal purposes is to discover the culture of this community without requiring an appreciation of the language that results from years of laborious study. The texts and accompanying analyses are designed to encourage discussion and further exploration. Though they are representative, in many cases well-known, these texts appear in the book specifically because they mean more than they say, require explanation, and avoid cliches, simplifications, and stereotypes.

---

[1] Michael Agar (1994:100) calls these ideas "rich points."

Chapter I

Persianizing English

Basics

Writers often Persianize non-Persian names and expressions. This chapter examines some of these Persianizations, because an effective way of discovering the Persian alphabet and how the language sounds is through analogy. The method uses what readers of this book already know, English spelling and pronunciation, to help them find out what they do not know, Persian orthography and phonology.

English expressions enter Persian in various guises. Though the Persianization of English is not consistent, the written forms of these words reveal how the language assimilates non-Persian in writing and in speaking.[1] The first part of this chapter presents twelve examples that help users discover the basic forms of the letters and the sounds those forms represent. The twelve examples that follow come from Moṣāḥeb (1966), a Persian version of the *Columbia Desk Encyclopedia* that approaches the Persianizing of countless foreign words in a systematic way.

example 1: "atom"

m t a ←

اتـــم

"Atom" shows that Persian does not have symbols for short vowels, except at the beginning of a word. Faced with the form *atm*, the reader must supply one of three short vowels: a, e, o, or Ø. Thus اتم can be *atam*, *atem*, *atom*, or *atm*. Context plays a big part in determining what fits; because in this case the reader is looking for an English analog, the choice is obvious. "Atom" also shows how Persian represents English a and t in the middle of a word and م with its long "tail" at the end.

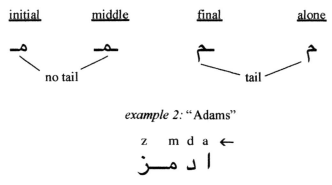

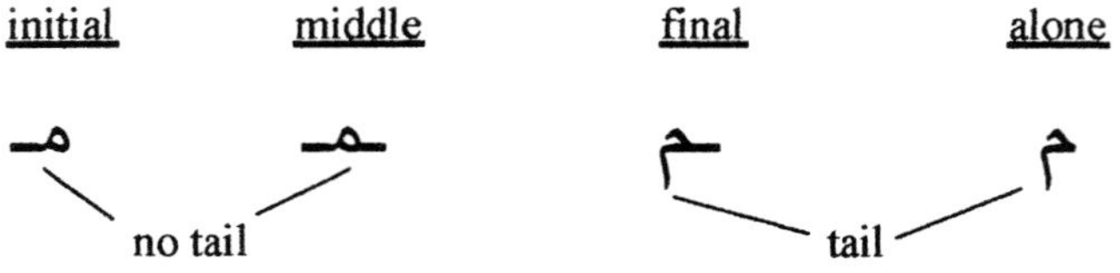

example 2: "Adams"

z m d a ←

ا د مـــز

The name "Adams" repeats some of the lessons of "atom." It also shows how English d and z appear in Persian. Here م appears without a tail in the middle of a word. "Atom" and "Adams" show that some letters like ت and م join the letters that follow them, while others like ا and د do not.

example 3: "Edison"

n s i d e ←

ادیسن

The inventor's name brings new wrinkles. "Edison" teaches that besides representing a, the vertical line ا can also be English e (it can also be o as shown in the next example). "Edison" also introduces three new letters: the vowel long i ی , and the consonants ـسـ (s in the middle of two letters) and ن (n at the end of a word). All three letters, where permitted, attach to the letters that precede and come after them.

initial	middle	final	alone
یـ	ـیـ	ـی	ی
سـ	ـسـ	ـس	س
نـ	ـنـ	ـن	ن

example 4: "offset"

t s f o ←

افست

In "offset," we see a new consonant ف, which is not doubled; i.e., written اففست. We also find ت in the form it takes at the end of a word.

initial	middle	final	alone
فـ	ـفـ	ـف	ف
تـ	ـتـ	ـت	ت

example 5: "Oxford"

d r f s k ā ←

آکسفرد

"Oxford" illustrates something new about the vertical line ا; it can be doubled. In this case then ا + ا = آ or long a, which comes closest in Persian phonology to the first sound in the English word. "Oxford" also introduces the letters ک, which attaches to the letter after it and ر , which does not. ر looks and behaves exactly like ز (example 2) without a dot above. A few more words will be enough to show the bulk of the Persian letters used to Persianize English.

example 6: "Alabama"

ā m ā b ā l ā ←

آلاباما

"Alabama" introduces the way Persian represents l and b. ل is like آ and ك, because it rises above the other letters. ب behaves like toothy and dotted ت and ن, except ب's dot is below the line. "Alabama" also shows something "Edison" says about Persianization: namely, that it tends to make short vowels long. The second vowel in Edison, which is not long in English, pronounced like the "i" in "bit," becomes "ee" as in "see" in Persian. Likewise the "a"s in "Alabama" rather than sounding like the "a" in "cat," are like the *ah*s a doctors requests when examining the throat.

example 7: "Bridgeport"

t r ow p j i r b ←

بریجپورت

The Persianizing of "Bridgeport" needs two new consonants, ج and پ, and a new vowel: long و. ج is a triangular shape with a dot below, and پ belongs to same family as ب , ن , ت , and ی. It also reveals another pattern: to reproduce English "o" in "port" Persian resorts to a diphthong ـَو or ow.

initial	middle	final	alone
جـ	ـجـ	ـج	ج
پـ	ـپـ	ـپ	پ

example 8: “Cheshire”

r sh ch ←

چشـر

“Cheshire” introduces the consonants ch and sh. چ has the same shape as ج and two more dots. ش behaves exactly like س juggling three dots above its teeth.

example 9: “Gettysburg”

g r b z i t g ←

گتیزبرگ

In “Gettysburg” one finds two forms of the consonant گ (always pronounced as “g” in “get”): connected and unconnected. گ looks like ک with an extra “hat.” Like ک and ل , گ belongs to the family of letters that rise above the baseline to tower over other letters.

initial	middle	final	alone
کـ	ـکـ	ـک	ک
گـ	ـگـ	ـگ	گ
لـ	ـلـ	ـل	ل

example 10: “Harvard”

d r ā v r ā h ←

هاروارد

"Harvard" introduces two letters, ـهـ and ـو. Like ر and ز , و connects only to the right; ـهـ can connect on either side. Because ر , و , آ , and د do not attach to the letters that follow them, the last five letters of "Harvard" appear as if they were written separately. Middle ـهـ can also look like an electrocardiographic downblip ـهـ

<u>initial</u>	<u>middle</u>	<u>final</u>	<u>alone</u>
	ـهـ		
هـ	ـهـ	ـه	ه
و	ـو	ـو	و

example 11: "Utah"

h ā t u y ←

يـوتاه

In Persian the sound that begins "Utah" or y is written with the same letter that represents ـيـ , the long i in "Bridgeport." This means that the letter can be read three different ways. Just as "y" in English can be a vowel ("myth," "party") or a diphthong ("try") or a consonant ("yard," "beyond"), Persian ی functions in three ways. One may ask why this Persianization of "Utah" ends in ـه , which is silent in English. Apparently the form of the word in English was more important than the sound. Many Persianizings that similarly prefer the written form of a word to its pronunciation come later in this chapter.

example 12: "Death Valley"

i l v   th d ←

دث ولی

Although spoken Persian does not have the th (θ) sound, the way it assimilates "Death Valley " in this instance introduces one simulation of the English sound in "think," "toothy," and "faith." Persian ث is like ت with an extra dot on top. This example completes the introduction of virtually all of the letters Persian uses to write English.

Dotting

In many cases, dotting above or below a shape distinguishes one letter from another. Six letters introduced in this chapter, namely ن , ت , ث , ب , ی , and پ , have one or more dots. At the beginning of a word and when connected on both sides, these letters share the basic shapes:

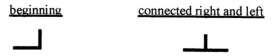

beginning	connected right and left

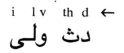

The final forms of these letters vary, but in all cases, the two factors that determine what letter those shapes become are:

1. number of dots and
2. their placement (above the tooth or below it).

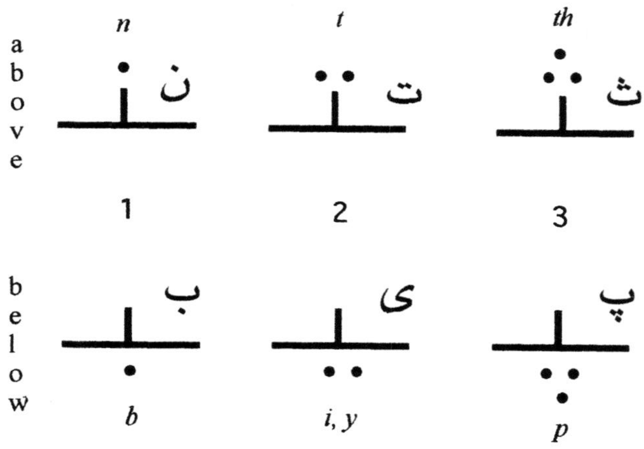

The six letters ن , ت , ث , ب , ی , and پ , must be dotted. Other dotted letters presented thus far are: ج and چ. These two letters share the basic shapes:

initial	middle	final	alone
ﺣ	ﺤ	ﺢ	ح

The only thing that distinguishes them is dotting. ر / ز and س / ش are other pairs of letters introduced in this chapter and differentiated by the presence or absence of dotting:

no dots	dots
s = ﺲ ﺴ ﺳ س	sh = ﺶ ﺸ ﺷ ش
r = ﺮ ر	z = ﺰ ز

Dotting and Dyslexia

Readers of Persian must be able to distinguish dots to decode words. Slight variations in the number and/or position of dots have profound effects on what words and phrases mean and how they sound. Because of the important role dotted consonants play in the writing system, the classic symptom of dyslexia in Persian is the misplacement of dots. Usually contextual clues and other inferences are enough to help readers identify the proper dottings; however, as the examples below suggest, when written in isolation, many words that have wholly different meanings and pronunciations look almost the same in writing.

To appreciate the challenges subtle differences in dotting present, one needs to look at word skeletons, the undotted outlines of words. For example, the basic shape سٮٮ , depending on the number and position of dots, yields five words with at least five distinct meanings and pronunciations:

سٮٮ	سبب	sabab	"cause, reason"
	سبت	sabt	"Sabbath"
	سیب	sib	"apple"
	سنت	sonnat	"tradition, custom"
	شیب	shib	"slope, downgrade"

Another skeleton that is the basis of five separate words is ٮسٮ:

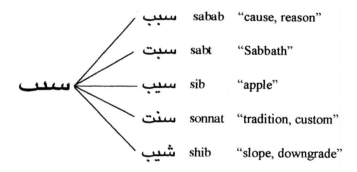

ٮٮسٮٮ	بیست	bist	"twenty"
	پیست	pist	"track, trail, *piste*"
	پیشت	pisht	sound made to cats
	نبست	nabast	"s/he, it didn't close"
	نیست	nist	"s/he, it is not"

A very productive, yet deceptively simple shape that can be five separate words, many of which bear multiple and unrelated meanings, is ٮار:

ٮار	بار	bār	"time, occasion," "load"
	باز	bāz	"again," "falcon"
	تار	tār	"thread," "dark"
	ناز	nāz	"wile, coyness," "luxury"
	یار	yār	"friend, lover"

Fortunately most skeletons are not as prolific as ٮٮس, ٮٮسٮٮ, and ٮار; however, because of the width of the semantic fields of the words they support, even they can be challenging.

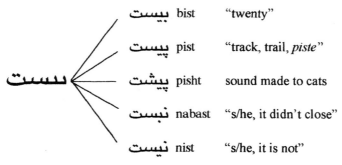

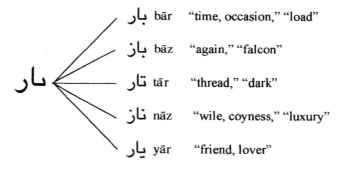

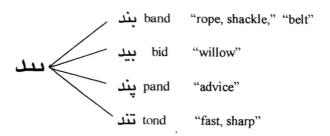

ٮٮد	بند	band	"rope, shackle," "belt"
	بید	bid	"willow"
	پند	pand	"advice"
	تند	tond	"fast, sharp"

Skeleton	Word	Transliteration	Meaning
سـر	سبز	sabz	"green"
	سیر	sir/seyr	"garlic," "full"
	شتر	shotor	"camel"
	شیر	shir	"milk, " "lion"

Skeleton	Word	Transliteration	Meaning
ربان	زبان	zabān	"tongue, language"
	زنان	zanān	sufix & "women"
	زیان	ziān	"damage, hurt, loss"

ٮا , a very simple skeleton, is the basis of at least five key terms that readers easily confuse:

Skeleton	Word	Transliteration	Meaning
ٮا	با	ba	"with"
	نا	nā	prefix: "non-/un-"
	پا	pā	"foot," "basis"
	تا	ta	"to, until"
	یا	yā	"or"

Not only do Persian readers have to mind their dots, they also must differentiate between two consonants (contrasted in example 9 above) that are distinguished by a line or "hat," namely ک and گ:

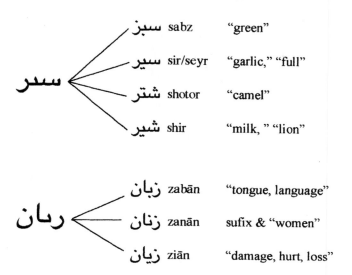

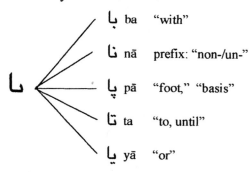

کور
- کور kur "blind"
- گور gur "grave"
- گوز guz "walnut, " "audible fart"
- گوژ guzh "bent, curved, hunched"

کىر
- کبر kebr, kebar "pomp, pride," "old age"
- کیر kir "penis"
- گبر gabr "infidel," "Zoroastrian"
- گیر gir "hold, catch, block"

سىك
- سبك sabk, sabok "style" "light"
- سنگ sang "stone, gem"
- شيك shik "stylish, chic"

Principled Chaos

The second part of this chapter examines various examples of Persianized English drawn from many texts and suggests certain reasons behind the authors' choices. While what follows is hardly a general theory of Persianization, it elicits important recurring patterns. It also reinforces principles introduced in the first part of the chapter.

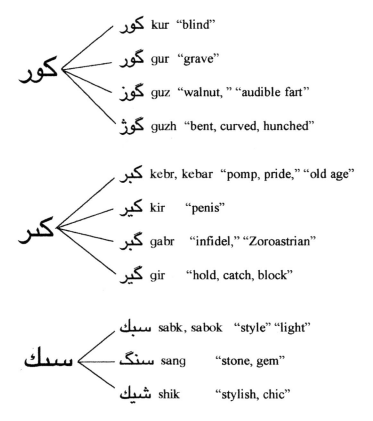

Everyone who has examined the Persianizing of English systematically, finds that the process is not stable. For professional reasons, the librarians F. Tehrani and M. Behzādi demand uniformity in Persianization; but, as Behzādi sadly notes, as far as the transliterating of names and expressions into Persian, "no special rules exist and anyone, from translators, writers, researchers to journalists, etc. according to her/his own personal taste, bent, or level of ignorance and understanding has Persianized the written form of words from various foreign languages in a different way" (Behzādi 1993:104-05).

But is Persianization as haphazard as Behzādi asserts? The following examples suggest that it is not. While she is certainly right that there are no widely accepted rules or regulations comparable to Library of Congress romanization tables (Tehrani 1991:44-45), for example, in the vast majority of cases there are at most two versions of the Persianized English words and phrases.

The best place to start is with "Persian" itself. The word has reentered the language through the Persianization of "Anglo-Persian":

آنگلو پرشین

[Irāni 1992:25] n i sh r p owl g n ā ←

The Persianizer began with the long a used in "Oxford," so his "Ang" rhymes with "gong" rather than the American "bang." The next three consonants do not present problems because they have, more or less, Persian equivalents. But ow in "lo" like the three short vowels (a, e, o) and the other vowel-consonant combination (ey) is problematic. Luckily the Persian diphthong ـَو is close enough. The language also readily supplies the next two consonants p پ and r ر , and the author has chosen sh ش for the s in the last syllable, so that his "Pers" rhymes with "Hersh." He could have chosen ژ the zh sound found in English "treasure" and "measure." The Persianization of the last syllable "sian" illustrates a common tendency. Instead of the short vowel that rhymes with "shun," the author stretches the sound into i ـیـ , making the Persianized "Persian" rhyme with "her sheen." In a related example, the Persianizer of "Persianist" follows the same path:

پرشیانیست

[Golestān 1996:18] t s i n ā i sh r p ←

As noted above, the Persianization of English vowels, especially the short vowels e and o, typically alternates between two possibilities. In both cases there is a short form and a long one:

short		*long*	*short*		*long*
e	◄——►	i	o	◄——►	u

There are two forms of "Rochester," for example. One reproduces the e in the second syllable, the second lengthens it into i, making the word rhyme with "raw keister":

[Moṣāḥeb 1966] راچستر 1

e

r t s | ch ā r ←

i

[Moṣāḥeb 1966] راچیستر 2

Two Persianizations of "son," the last syllable in "Madison" and "Nixon," show how the short vowel o can stretch into the "oo" u making the syllable sound like "soon":

مدیسن

o

[Nodushan 1973:56] n | s i d m ←

نیکسون

[Irāni 1989:29] n u s k i n ←

The lengthening of vowels also occurs at the beginning of words like "internet":

اینترنت

[Bāshgāh-e Ketāb] t n'r t n i ←

Here the vertical line ا *alef* comes before the i ﯾ to prevent the reading "yenternet." The lengthening of e to i also appears in both syllables of the first word in "British Airways":

بریتیش ارویز

z i v r a sh i t i r b ←

[*Payām-e Emruz* 1998]

The Persianization of "ways" reveals how the lack of a w sound in Iranian Persian transforms English words. In this form, "Airways" rhymes with the standard American dictionary pronunciation of "vase." Occasionally lengthening a vowel turns a proper English name into a common Persian noun. For example, the novelist Jane Austen becomes Jane " the sleeve" (āstin):

جین آستین

[Yunesi 1973:39] n i t s ā n i j ←

"Jane" illustrates how Persian produces the ey sound in "hey."

Persianization purists insist upon representing every sound of English even if their language lacks them. This kind of fidelity to the original can take Persianized English to absurd extremes. Examples come in a guide to publishing manuscripts that first appeared in 1986. The author is so faithful to English phonology in Persian, he invents a way of representing the w sound in "Wade":

وٗید ← *invented w*

[Samiʿi 1987:44] dey '

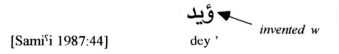

Rather than having readers round their lips to produce an English w, however, this Persianization makes them contort the voice box into an initial glottal stop (in English, the slight catch of air in the throat that often occurs between syllables in "uhoh" or "Long Island") and follow that with ey. The result is something like "o'eyd." All this effort merely to avoid admitting that w-less Iranian Persian normally substitutes veyd (as in "conveyed") for weyd. Though most Persianizers do not go to these extremes, mute English consonants often speak in Persian. For example, the preference of the written to the spoken form is clear in the following "Lincoln":

extra "l" →

لینکلن

[Irāni 1987:24] n l k n i l ←

Clearly the "l" in "coln" is more faithful to the form than the sound of the name. This "extra l" combined with the lengthening of the vowel in the first syllable makes the president's name "lean colon." The same fidelity to English orthography is in this Persianization of "Lloyd":

extra "l" →

للوید

[Golestān 1996:18] d i owl l ←

This example also shows the way the language assimilates "oy," the Yiddish interjection. In Persian, "Lloyd" becomes two syllables, sounding a little like "low weed."

Persian also has at least two "Saul Bellow's." The first simply converts the English diphthong "au" (ɔ) of "Saul" to long a, which makes it a homograph of Persian *sāl* or "year." Persianizers are unanimous on the author's last name: both English b and l have Persian equivalents and "ow" repeats the lesson learned from the "o" in "Anglo" above.

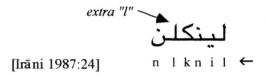

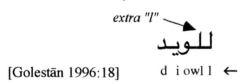

سال بلو

[Golshiri 1977:230] ow l b l ā s ←

The second Persianization of "Saul" is more complex. It begins as the first, but then adds ئ , the glottal stop and و , long u. This Persianization is traditional in two ways: it is more faithful to the spelling of the original, and it reflects the form of the name as it appears in Persian translations of the Bible:

long u *glottal stop*

[Homāyun Pur 2000:388]

سائول بلو

ow l b l u ' ā s ←

Both authors have avoided the false fidelity of an "extra l" to Persian the author's last name. An intersyllabic glottal stop is common in Persian. One author uses it to represent "Boeing" in Persian:

بوئینگ

[Bahār 1976:151] g n i ' ow b ←

There is nothing biblical about this Persianization. The glottal stop merely prepares Persian speakers to pronounce "ing" after the diphthong ow.

More reductions. To Persianize the "th" (θ) in "Death Valley" (example 12 above), one authoritative source used ث , which sounds like English "s" in "son." This is another example of the tyranny of the written over the spoken. My survey of the Persianization of this th shows that ث is not used often. Most authors are like the Persianizer of "Bethlehem Steel"; they reduce the non-existent-in-Persian th to its nearest equivalent: ت (t):

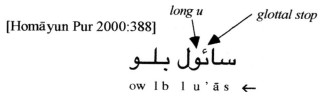

[Bahār 1976:151] *prosthetic alef* th → t

بتلهم استیل

l i t s m h l t b ←

The Persianization of "Steel" shows how the language handles English words beginning with s followed by c, ch, k, m, n, p, q, or t. Like Spanish, Persian abhors the initial clusters "st" or the "sp" in "Sprachman," the "sch" in "school," etc. Persianizings of such words begin with a helping (prosthetic) vowel represented by the vertical line ا *alef*. Another example is "Stephan," which in Persian sounds like "Estefan":

prosthetic alef

استفن

[Irāni 1987:24] n f t s ←

Motivated Persianizations

Occasionally resentment determines how English looks in Persian. Some writers' dislike of certain words and the people who use them is so strong that it blinds them to the librarians' need for uniformity in transliteration or to the purists' preoccupation with fidelity to the original. Motivated Persianizations purposely pun on existing words (often vulgar or obscene) to suggest unpleasant associations that are impossible in the original. Angry Persianizers are indifferent to phonology and spelling, they want revenge. The next three examples are from the works of well-known authors who express distaste for English-speaking cultures in their Persianizations.

The first example comes from the satirical writings of Ḏabiḥ Allāh Behruz, who made no secret of his disdain for English Orientalists. His sense of his own superiority probably stems from when he served as teaching assistant to the renowned

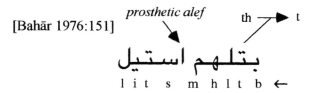

Cambridge Persianist Edward G. Browne (1862-1926). Behruz was the model Iranian chauvinist. He wanted to purge all Arabic words from Persian and invented a new alphabet to replace the one used in this book; his ornery treatises on pre-Islamic chronology and etymology contradicted the views of virtually all other scholars; and he wrote blasphemous satires of fundamental Islamic beliefs in retaliation for the Arab conquest of Iran that took place some thirteen centuries before he wrote. Behruz's excessive regard for his own opinions complemented his contempt for European Orientalists and their "non-native" Orientalism. His Persianization of "British Museum" is contemptuous in this way. An unmotivated version of the phrase based on rules derived from the examples in this chapter is:

بریتیش میوزیوم

m u i z u i m sh i t i r b ←

To demean the museum, Behruz resorts to bathroom humor (Behruz 1931:8):

audible fart *beard* *on*

بریشش گوزیم

m i z u g sh sh i r b ←

The new version, *be-rish-ash guziam*, meaning "[may/that] I fart on his beard," takes advantage of chance harmonies between innocent English sounds and Persian scatology:

beritish (British) → *be-rish-ash* (on his beard)
miuzium (museum) → *guziam* (I audibly fart)

Behruz was not the only Anglophobe to deflate English with flatulence. In Simin Dāneshvar's novel *Savushun*, one of the main characters, who is jealous of his brother's Western education, mangles the names of two universities: "Manchester" and "Massachusetts." An unmotivated version of the first is:

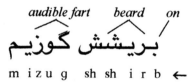

منچستر

r t s ch n m ←

To take the shine off a Western doctorate in agriculture, the jealous brother exploits the similarity between the second syllable of the name and *chos*, Persian for "silent fart":

silent fart

من چس تر

r t s ch n m ←

Dāneshvar (1974:126) writes the name out in three separate syllables to make the pun more obvious. Another example: an unmotivated Persianizer would write "Massachusetts":

ماساچستس

s t s ch ā s ā m ←

Predictably the novel's envious brother replaces the third syllable with the same audible fart heard in Behruz's British Museum:

audible fart

ماساگوزت

t z u g ā s ā m ←

which makes the name "Masaguzat." Though both puns are impossible in English, one translation of the novel tries to recover the flavor of the original by extemporizing "Hardfart" (Ghanoonparvar 1990:167).

The third example of motivated Persianization leaves the bathroom and enters the den. It comes in an essay by ʿAli Akbar Saʿidi Sirjāni, an outspoken critic of the superficial westernization of Iran. A noted scholar of Persian literature, Saʿidi Sirjāni mourned the death of traditional culture and despised its successor: the seductive entertainment of American television and cinema.

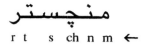

Normally the author wrote "television" in the accepted Persian way, which makes it sound like French *télévision*, the likely source (Saʕidi Sirjāni 1994:206):

تلویزیون

n u iz i v l t ←

But, when one of his essays warns of the dangers of the "satanic device," Saʕidi Sirjāni (1992:2) rewrites the first syllable to make it read *taleh*, Persian for "trap":

trap

تله ویزیون

n u i z i v h l t ←

As this brief survey of Persianizing—both principled and ulteriorly motivated—shows, certain fathomable rules determine how English words and names appear in the language. Principled Persianization usually yields no more than two basic forms of foreign expressions. In all cases, cross-referencing from one form to the other can satisfy—at least in part—librarians' and researchers' need for uniformity and consistency. When non-linguistic concerns influence how English looks, however, Persianization becomes culturally revealing, close to the subject of this book. The difference between the principled forms and those motivated by strong feelings are rich points, complex ideas embedded in "simple" spelling conventions.

---

[1] On inconsistencies in transliterating in Persian see Behzādi (1993). For guidelines on how to Persianize English forms, see Tehrani (1991) and Tavakkoli (1994).

Chapter II

History in the Alphabet

Arabic Letters

Chapter I introduced letters that allow Persian to represent English words and expressions. Needless to say, these letters are not the entire alphabet. This chapter presents eleven others that complete the Persian writing system. It also shows how the choice of one form over another is not merely a convention of spelling, but a rich point in Persian culture.

The following eight letters entered Persian in the seventh century when a new religion, Islam, and new conquerors, Arabic-users, moved eastward to Central and Southwest Asia.

ق	غ	ع	ظ	ط	ض	ص	ح
q	gh	ʕ	ẓ	ṭ	ḍ	ṣ	ḥ

These letters survive in the language because Persian has had to assimilate many Arabic words and expressions. Unable to pronounce them in Arabic, Persian speakers reduced them to the nearest familiar phoneme. As a result, various letters can stand for a particular sound. For example, four letters sound like English "z," three like "s," and two each like "t" and "h."

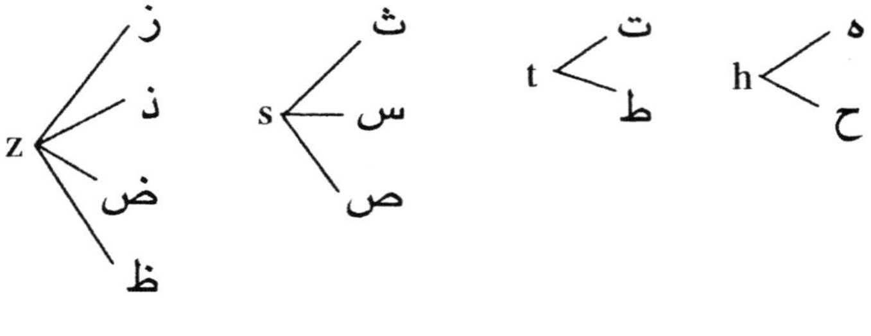

There are no English equivalents of غ and ق. In Iranian Persian they sound the same, close to the "r" in the standard French pronunciation of "Paris." In Afghanistan and Tajikistan, they are differentiated, pronounced more like their Arabic ancestors. There is no English equivalent for ع also, but it exists as the Hebrew letter (not sound) ע, as does ق, Hebrew ק.

The letters that Persian and Arabic shared at the time of the invasion are:

ذ خ ء
ḏ kh '

As noted in Chapter I, ء is a glottal stop, the minuscule pause that some people make to keep "g" and "I" in "Long Island" from eliding, or the sound that separates the two syllables of "uhoh." The form خ, as mentioned in the Introduction, sounds like ch in "chutzpah." The letter ذ is merely د with a dot on top. Like the letters that the language uses to Persianize English, the form of each Persian symbol used to accommodate Arabic words changes depending on its position (alone, connected right *or* left, connected right *and* left).

Certain patterns emerge when readers collate the eleven "Arabic" letters in this chapter with those introduced in the first chapter. They can readily identify families of letters that share the same basic form but differ in the ways they are dotted. For example, the ح family is composed of the basic form ح (no dots), ج (one dot below), چ (three dots below), and خ (one dot above). Similarly, one dot above makes the letter د differ from ذ ; ص from ض ; ط from ظ ; and ع from غ. The two "loop and tail" letters ف and ق, though differing by one dot above, and similar in shape, are not full siblings:

initial	middle	final	alone
ئـ	ـئـ	ـأ ـؤ ـئ ء	ء
خـ	ـخـ	ـخ	خ
ذ	ـذ	ـذ	ذ
صـ	ـصـ	ـص	ص
ضـ	ـضـ	ـض	ض
طـ	ـطـ	ـط	ط
ظـ	ـظـ	ـظ	ظ
عـ	ـعـ	ـع	ع
غـ	ـغـ	ـغ	غ
فـ	ـفـ	ـف	ف
قـ	ـقـ	ـق	ق

Arabization and De-Arabization

After the Arab invasion of Iran, Arabic versions of place and personal names replaced Persian ones. Many people not only converted to Islam, the new religion, they also rushed to make the names of their families and their home towns Arabic to show their allegiance to the conquerors. In the absence of an Arabic name, the conquerors or their Persian allies and clients Arabized. This process, called *taʿrib*, changed the map of the Persian world forever. To take one famous example: before the Arab invasion, the lowlands of the Tigris and Euphrates (today southern Iraq) was known in Persian as *irāg*. After the rise of the Arab empire, geographers replaced the *irāg* with Arabic *ʿerāq*, the name of the modern state (Moḥammadi Malāyeri 1996:79):

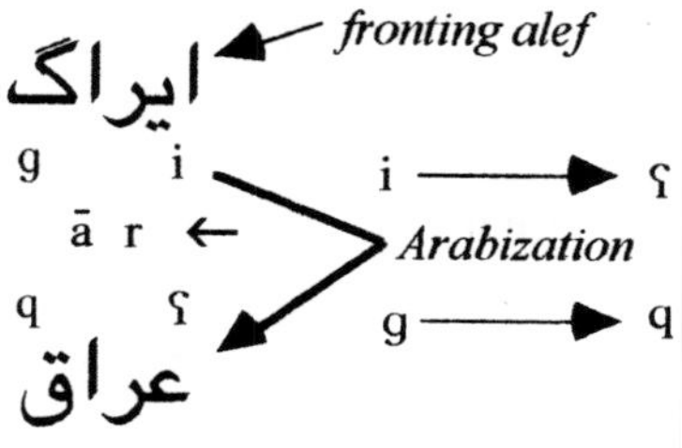

Not having گ , Arabic speakers substituted ق , a likely analog. For the “fronting alef,” which prevented the readings *yerāq*, for example, Arabic inserted Semitic ع.

Another example of Arabization that has survived is the name of Iran’s third largest city and former capital *eṣfahān*. The second letter in the name, ص , did not exist in Persian until the Arabs invaded. The “p” in the old name, *espahān*, was new to Arabic speakers so they changed it to the closest familiar sound, “f”:

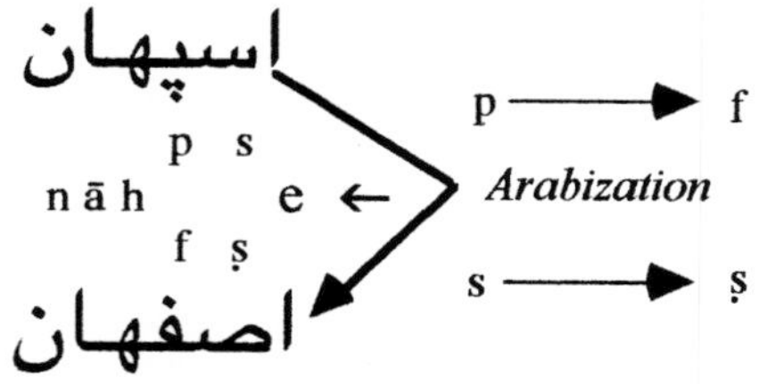

This Arabization suggests that the two languages had ا , ه , and ن in common.

Less enduring has been the Arabization of Iran’s present capital: Tehran. Until relatively recently most Persian texts used the Arabic form *ṭehrān*; however, today the spelling *tehrān* is almost universal. This change reflects a process of de-Arabization or re-Persianizing that came with the rise of nationalist sentiment in the region. Linguistic nationalism, incidentally, also accounts for the most famous change: “Persia” to “Iran” in 1934. The government of Reza Shah (r. 1925-41) reasoned that “Pers” or “Pars” applied to Fars province, which was only part of Iran (Makki 1983:6:199).

t ◄——————— ṭ

تهران *de-Arabization* طهران

The change from ط to ت coincided with the rise of Iranian nationalism in the early twentieth century (Eqbāl 1971:541; Kasravi 1973:383), when writers expressed their nativism by re-Persianizing the old Arabized forms. A new dynasty in Iran, the Pahlavi, institutionalized this policy by creating a Persian Academy, the *farhangestān* (Ghani, C. 1998:400). The process continues under the Islamic Republican Academy of Language and Literature. Alphabetical nationalists in and out of the Academy wanted to push de-Arabization as far as it would go. They proposed purging all "Arabic" and "Turkish" words from Persian and changing the writing system. The next chapter discusses these changes and the reasons why they have failed.

Familiar (Traditional) Words with

ء ح خ ذ ص ض ط ظ ع غ ق

The traditional expressions that appear in this chapter entered Persian long before those in Chapter I. They are useful in two ways: first, they show how the eleven letters above appear in writing; second, they are convenient handles for topics that are vital to an understanding of the shared culture of Persian-users. Readers should not assume, however, that the examples taken as a whole, represent an integrated or systematic view of that culture. They appear here through accidents of Arabic orthography. But, despite the arbitrary nature of their selection, they are, more or less, like the Korean word *han* mentioned in the Introduction. They require explanations that rooted in the politics, cultures, and societies of those who use Persian.

example 1: mo'ad̲d̲en ad̲ān

doubling sign ⟶ اذان مؤذّن

n d̲d̲ 'm n ā d̲ a ←

The call to prayer is an اذان which a crier مؤذّن ("muezzin" in English) delivers. Both words relate to the Semitic word "ear": in Arabic اذن (*od̲n, od̲on*), Hebrew אזן. The birdlike sign over ذ in مؤذّن indicates a doubled consonant. Traditionally in places where Persian-users lived, the مؤذّن would climb to the top of a minaret to deliver the call; however, in modern times loudspeakers have taken his place. Whether live or taped, the اذان sets the rhythm of life in Persian culture. They divide the day into five times that require cleanliness and conversation with God. In their regularity and ubiquity, they are like the church bells of Christianity or the prayer wheels of Tibetan Buddhism.

At times the اذان interrupts the flow of daily life. The crier who calls out of tune or who disturbs people's sleep with his call is a common figure in Persian literature, the butt of many jokes. In Saʿdi's *Golestān,* which has been a model for Persian prose since it appeared in 1258, he is a nuisance:

مؤذّن بانگ بی هنگام برداشت

t sh ā d r b m ā gnh i b g n ā b n d̲d̲ ' m ←

نمی داند که چند از شب گذشته است

t s a he t sh d̲ g b sh za dn ch hek d nād i m n ←

The Muezzin raised the untimely cry;

He knows not how much of the night has passed.

[Saʿdi 1984:81]

Part of the اذان is an Arabic phrase that means "hasten to prayer," and that contains three letters introduced in this chapter:

حيّ على صلاة

t ā l ṣ ā l ʕ yy ḥ ←

Note that ل + ا, written "u-shaped" ـا in Chapter I ("Alabama"), is the more standard لا here. The Arabic word على (ʕalā) demonstrates a feature of the language that is also found in Persian. Although the ى in على looks exactly like the Persian ى (long i or y), it is actually read ī or long a. The final letter in this phrase is ة which represents a "tied up" ت. Like ت it is pronounced t.

example 2: ramaḍān

رمضان

n ā ḍ m r ←

The ninth month of the Islamic calendar is رمضان. According to the Qoran (2: 185), the Prophet Mohammad received the revelations of God during this month. Muslims celebrate the lunar month by fasting from dawn to dusk. Like the اذان , رمضان contours the pace of life in places where people use Persian. Because lunar and solar years do not coincide, رمضان can come during any season. When it occurs in the summer, the fast is often a difficult twelve hours. Mid-winter fasting is easier, but, no matter what the season, رمضان is a time of sleeplessness. The fasters wake up long before sunrise to prepare and eat the predawn meal and must stay up until dawn celebrating with relatives and friends.

The Qoran allows those who are ill or journeying to postpone the fast. They must make up the days they miss when no longer ill or not traveling. This feature of fasting has led to the anagrammatic Persian saying (Dehkhodā 1973:2:872):

رمضان را مرضان خواند حکیمی دانا

ānād i m i k ḥ d nā kh n ā ḍ r m ā r n ā ḍ m r ←

Literally: "A savvy physician reads *ramaḍān maraḍān*," or, when رمضان comes around the doctor sees many "patients."

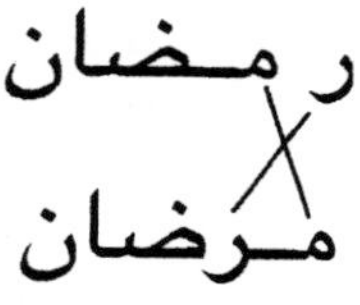

Anagrammatically: "A sly doctor plays the RAMADAN ANGLE: he charges AN ARM AND A LEG."

example 3: qorbān

قربان

n āb r q ←

In the Qoran (5: 27), قربان is the "sacrifice" or "offering" the devout present to God. In this respect it is loan-word from Hebrew: קרבן (Klein 1987:591). Though قـربان retains this meaning in Persian, it is far more common to use it figuratively in daily conversation. Speakers use the non-literal قربان to refer to themselves in polite speech and writing. For example, the phrase قربان شما (*qorbān-e shomā*) , literally "[may I be] your sacrifice," is a common way to express appreciation. قربان is part of a system of politeness in Persian (called *taʿārof,* see Beeman 1986:50-60, 141-162) that obliges speakers and writers to avoid referring to themselves as "I" or "me." Politeness in Persian, a recurring topic in this book, requires control of many words like قـــربان that allow speakers and writers to esteem those whom they address by belittling themselves.

example 4: ʕajami

عجمی

i m j ʕ ←

عجمی, also أعجمی, illustrates the relationship between language and nationality. The word derives from an Arabic verb meaning "to be a non-Arab" or "to speak with an accent." The adjective أعجمی in the Qoran (41: 44) refers to any language but Arabic. The Qoran (16: 103) also privileges "pure and clear" Arabic over any "foreign" (i.e. أعجمی) tongue.

Soon after the Arab conquest, the sense of the word narrowed to "Persian speakers," because of their inability to produce certain sounds the way their masters pronounced them. But despite the phonological challenges spoken Arabic posed for Persians, not only did many of them master the written language, they codified its grammar. They were also primarily responsible for compiling the first scientific dictionaries and grammars of the language, and some even became famous for their Arabic poetry. Nevertheless the narrow sense of the word prevailed, and it became an ethnic slur. No matter how well Persians wrote Arabic and no matter how much they Arabized in other ways, Arabs used عجمی to stigmatize them as servile posers, Semitic wannabees.

The case of Ziād b. Salmā (or Soleymān, d. ca. 704) is instructive in this respect. He was a *mowlā*, a Persian client or affiliate of a powerful Arab tribe that invaded Iran. The Persian speaking Ziād was so good at defamation and insult poetry in Arabic that skilled native writers dared not satirize his adoptive tribe for fear of retaliation. Despite his mastery of written Arabic, Ziād was known as the أعجمی because he said Persian ت instead of Arabic ط (Goldziher 1977:113). Thus, when Ziād tried to say the Arabic word *solṭān* meaning "ruler," he used ت for ط making his accent unmistakably عجمی (Ebn Qotayba 1966:1: 430):

Proper Arabic		ʿajami
سلطان	→ 'Ajamization	سلتان
n ā ṭ l s		n ā t l s ←

example 5: ṣigheh

صيغه

he gh i ṣ ←

Literally "rule" or "paradigm," صيغه is an Iranian Persian term for "temporary wife." The final letter is actually the "tied up" Arabic ة , which in Persian is reduced to something like "eh." While most Muslims do not practice temporary marriage (*motʿa* in Arabic), many Shiites consider it lawful. They believe that Qoran 4:24 allows men to use their wealth to acquire temporary companionship.

Though temporary marriage has not been common in Iran (Haeri 1989:14), the Islamic Republic officially endorses the practice. Some theologians argue that a temporary marriage, which is subject to civil and religious laws, is far more enlightened than the unregulated pre- and extramarital sex of the West (Haeri 1989:97).

In effect, the practice of temporary marriage commodifies a woman's capacity to gratify the sexual needs of men. Like any other commodity, this capacity is subject to the laws of supply and demand. During peak travel periods, when many men are on pilgrimages or business trips without their wives, the price of a temporary marriage goes up. Conversely, during wars or as a result of an easing of divorce laws, when the number of "surplus" women rises, a buyers' صيغه market occurs.

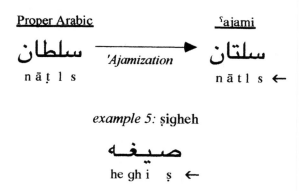

example 6: bāṭen ẓāher

ظاهر باطن

n ṭ ā b r h ā ẓ ←

Literally "inside" and "outside," باطن and ظاهر lie at the polar ends of a range with infinite intermediate gradations. They can refer to two sides of a complex issue: باطن with undotted ط represents the "heart" of the matter, while ظاهر with a dotted ظ is the sum of its surface features. The two antonyms also reflect a reality that is apparent to many Persian-users: namely, not everything is what it appears to be (Beeman 1986:11-12, 70-72, 107-108). Persian mysticism or تصوّف (*taṣavvof*) teaches not to look at the beguiling surfaces of reality but to hunt for truths that lie hidden beneath them.

One of the sublime features of classical Persian poetry is its fluent expression of the ineffable. To show the relationship between the easily graspable outside to the obscure inside, the greatest mystical poet in Persian, Jalal al-Din Rumi (b. Balkh 1207), often paired the words باطن and ظاهر. His epic poem *Masnavi* (Rumi 1971:593) refers to the dual nature of the Qoran: its cloak of simple letters (*ḥarf*) that masks a compelling inner significance:

حرف قرآن را بدان که ظاهریست

t s i r h ā ẓ hek n ā d b ā r n ā r q f r ḥ ←

زیر ظاهر باطنی بس قاهریست

t s i r h ā q s b i n ṭ ā b r h ā ẓ r i z ←

Know that the word of the Qoran is a surface;
Beneath the surface is a very mighty interior.

In this line, ظاهر becomes "exoteric," the vulgar meaning that all apprehend, while باطن is the "esoteric" interpretation evident only to a select few.

example 7: ḥāfeẓ

حافظ

ẓ f ā ḥ ←

A حافظ is literally "one who remembers." The term derives from the Arabic verb meaning "protect, preserve." In Persian a حافظ is one who knows the Qoran by heart, who preserves it as a living book, as God's Mind made manifest. The most famous حافظ in Persian literature was a poet born in Shiraz around 1325. He is not famous for his ability to recite the Qoran, but for a type of lyric poem known as the غزل (*ghazal*).

It is difficult to overestimate the importance of Hafez in and to Persian. One contemporary writer goes so far as to say that when Persian-users know Hafez they know themselves (Ḥaqqshenās 1991:169). Many users of the language know him as the "Tongue of the Unseen," لسان الغیب (*lesān al-gheyb*), owing to his ability to express the hidden truths of Sufism mentioned in the previous example. Hafez's influence on Persian as a language is comparable to Shakespeare's influence on English. Just as English speakers are so familiar with the phrase "to be or not to be" that it is difficult for actors playing Hamlet to say it unselfconsciously, those who know Persian have marked the end of رمضان so often with the following line that it too has worn out its welcome in the language:

ساقی بیار باده که ماه صیام رفت

t f r m ā i ṣ h ām hek hed ā b r ā i b i q ā s ←

"Saki [cup-bearer], bring on the wine for the month of fasting has gone" (Hafez 1983:1:184). Because Hafez's poetry reaches unattainable heights in Persian, very few translators have been able to convey its greatness in other languages.

example 8: sharq gharb

شرق غرب

q r sh b r gh ←

Like باطن and ظاهر, شرق and غرب express two ends of a range of meanings. شرق is "east" and غرب is "west." In Qoran 24: 35, they do not signify particular directions but encompass the totality of location or "creation," from sunrise in the East to sunset in the West. In this way, شرق and غرب are like the "Alpha and Omega" in the Bible (Rev. 1: 8), which do not refer to the letters that begin and end the Greek alphabet but to the gamut of being.

ω ←——————→ α

غرب شرق

Contemporary events have widened the divide between شرق and غرب. Because of Persian-users' increased sensitivity to a shared past of colonialism and post-colonial present, the language pits one against the other. Until recently شرق and غرب meant the hostile blocs of the Cold War. Now they represent the two sides in the modern antagonism between the traditional cultures of the Middle East and parts of Asia and the technologically advanced societies of the United States, Europe, and other parts of Asia, between spirituality and materialism, between the post-colonized and the post-colonizers. In these confrontations, extremists gather at the ends of the east-west range. Those who champion modernism and secularism are often said to be suffering from غربزدگی (*gharbzadegi* "Westitis"), while those who prefer returning to a purist form of Islam are afflicted with عربزدهگی (*ʿarabzadegi* retro- "Arabitis"). In Persian the difference between the two is one dot:

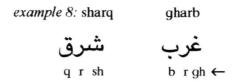

Dotted and Undotted Pathologies

Ø dot ———————— *dot*

عربزدگی غربزدگی

i g d z b r ʕ   i g d z r gh ←

Those who wish a pox on both ends of the spectrum have revived the qoranic expression via a line from Jalāl al-Din Rumi (Rumi 1976:1:46 quoted by Zarrinkub 1974:27):

نه شرقی، نه غربی – انسانی

i n ā s n e   i b r gh he n   i q r sh he n ←

"Neither Eastern, nor Western—Human." During the Islamic Revolution, this became the slogan:

نه شرقی، نه غربی جمهوری اسلامی

i m ā l s   i r u h m j   i b r gh he n   i q r sh he n←

"Neither Eastern, nor Western—Islamic Republican."

Islamic Republican Jargon: Unfamiliar Terms with

ء ح خ ذ ص ض ط ظ ع غ ق

Because the Persian writing system has remained more or less the same for fifteen centuries, whenever a traditional word was needed for a new meaning, a deep well of Arabic vocabulary was always available. The Islamic Revolution in 1979 and, more recently, the rise of the Taliban in Afghanistan made the revival of Arabic vocabulary inevitable. In Iran a secularizing, Western-oriented monarchy that encouraged the study of European languages suddenly fell, and a theocracy founded on the Qoran and the principles of Islam took its place. Secularism was suddenly out and religion was in. In the last two decades, Islamic Republican language-makers and ideologues have gone to the Arabic well frequently. The next part of this chapter introduces some of the Arabic jargon of Islamic Republicanism. Some of this jargon can also be found in Afghan Persian as well. These are terms that, unlike those in the first part of this chapter, had never been part of common Persian usage or had been dormant for centuries. While secularists ruled, many of these terms were locked in the Qoran or consigned to the arcana of theology, far from the discourse of the westernized elites. They came to life with the Revolution and spread quickly as tokens of the desecularization of Persian culture. A few of these terms have supplanted the jargon that Western-oriented elites borrowed from French and English. Some have stuck while others, like many Persian neologisms, have disappeared.

At the beginning of the Revolution, anti-monarchists and desecularizers needed a term to demonize those who had prospered under the previous monarchy. For this purpose they revived *ṭāghut*, an Arabic word from the Qoran (2: 256) that was wholly new to modern, secular Persian. The traditional meaning of the word is "evil," "that which people worship in place of God."

example 9: ṭāghut

طاغوت

t ugh ā ṭ ←

Though طاغوت had been part of the vocabulary of classical poets like Rumi, when it reappeared in newspapers and in posters, it took contemporary writers by surprise. Since the beginning of the Revolution, طاغوت has been a code word for Pahlavi period corruption and slavish imitation of the West. In Islamic Republican-speak, any form of blatant Westernism or secularism is *ṭāghuti*. A revolutionary slogan contrasts the term to *mellat*, "Muslim people, nation":

ز طاغوت گسستیم به ملت پیوستیم

m i t s v ey p t ll m heb m i t s s g t ugh ā ṭ z ←

"From the طاغوت ourselves we have freed / And joined the folk of godly creed" [*Hamgam* 1978:39].

طاغوت also became part of the graffiti of Tehran. When she saw it written on a wall, the writer Mahshid Amirshahi asked what it meant. Her companion, a well educated native user of Persian, replied, "How do you spell it?" (Amirshahi 1995:59). The friend's confusion was understandable; because of the overlap of letters and sounds outlined at the beginning of this chapter, the word can be written eight different ways, all pronounced the same in Iranian Persian but differentiated in Afghanistan and Tajikistan. As Chapter III discusses in detail, the alphabetic ambiguity the eight possible spellings of طاغوت exemplify has led to calls for language reforms that range from simplification of the existing alphabet to abandoning it altogether for a European one. The eight Iranian Persian طاغوتs are:

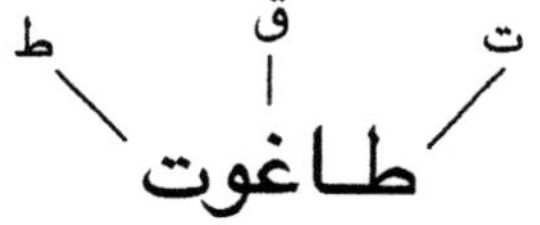

1. طاقوت	2. تاغوط	3. تاقوت	4. تاغوت
5. طاقوط	6. طاغوط	7. تاقوط	8. طاغوت

Another word that left religious discourse and entered Islamic Republican speech is *mostaḍʿafin*. The term originally appeared in the chapter of the Qorān called "Women" as "those that are deemed weak and are therefore oppressed by the strong" (4:97, 98). It also refers to "[orphan] children and women who are weak and oppressed" (4:127). In seventh century Arabia, the coinage *mostaḍʿafin* was an important break with the past. It gave religious, social, and legal status to those who had had no rights before the Prophet Mohammad (also an orphan) began his mission. In its new sense, *mostaḍˤafin* is analogous to "proletariat."

example 10: mostaḍˤafin

مستضعفين

n i f ʕ ḍ t s m ←

During the period 1978-79 , the revived مستضعفين started appearing in modern Persian as the politically and economically "oppressed." The term first became current in this sense in the writings of ˤAli Shariˤati, whose essays, books, and sermons attracted faithful audiences in the late 1960s and early 1970s (Arjomand 1988:93). In March of 1979, both the term and those to whom it referred were entirely alien to western-educated observers of the early Revolution:

> You have to see these revolutionary مستضعفين to appreciate the true meaning of 'deranged' and 'demented.' For the life of me, I can't tell what hole they've crawled out of or what hell they're headed for. All I know is that they don't bear the slightest resemblance to me or you" [Amirshahi 1995:235-36].

Be that as it may, after twenty years of Islamic Republican Persian, the term مستضعفين has become integral to the language. Many readers know the word in its institutionalized sense as part of the name of a charity conglomerate, the "Foundation for the Oppressed" *bonyād-e mostaḍˤafin.* Readers of contemporary Persian will also recognize two Persianizations of the Arabic form. In the first, *mostaḍˤafān* مستضعفان (Amuzegār 1995:242), the Arabic plural suffix ين has been replaced by the Persian ان. The second is the adjective مستضعف , found in a phrase used in many standard biographies of young people martyred at the Iran-

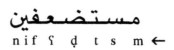

Iraq War front: "an oppressed household" *khānavādeh-ye mostaḍʿaf* (خانوادهٔ مستضعف Faṣiḥ 1989:183). Needless to say, after the Revolution, coming from a خانوادهٔ مستضعف was better than having *ṭāghuti* roots.

مستضعفین has an evil counterpart formed on the basis of the same paradigm: *mostakbarin* مستکبرین , another Arabic word that derives from the Qoran (16:23 and 23:67). In scripture, *mostakbarin* refers to the "arrogant," those who put on airs, pretending to know something that others do not. Theo-political usage puts the terms at opposite ends of the social spectrum:

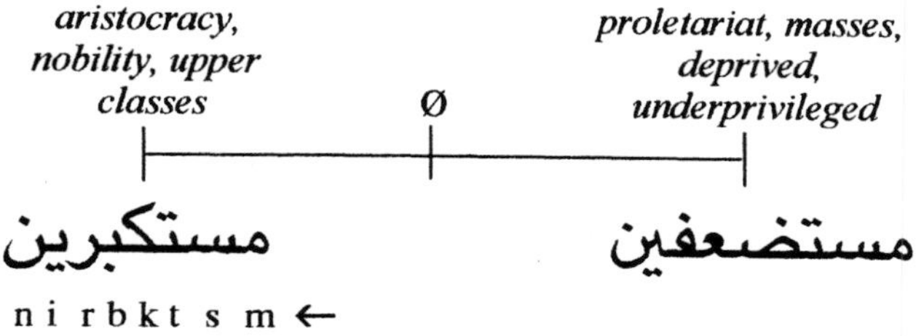

Unlike the range bounded by غرب / شرق , there are no gradations on this scale, no middle ground between the two warring words.

Initially Islamic Republican social and cultural policies were adamantly anti-*ṭāghuti*. In time these policies unified into a cultural revolution the purpose of which has been to eliminate any vestige of secular thought or behavior. The revolution reversed social changes that the first Pahlavi ruler Reza Shah brought about in the late 1920s and that intensified under his son. The rulers of Iran have employed official and vigilante desecularization squads to enforce the revolution throughout the country. Squad members have insisted that men dress modestly and abandon western ties for buttoned collars. The tie, in pre-Revolutionary Persian *kerāvāt* (French *cravate*), became an *afsār-e ṭāghuti* افسار طاغوتی a "طاغوتی bridle" (Pārsipur 2000:103).

They also have made sure that women cover themselves by wearing veils that many had never worn. The desecularizing linguistic climate that the cultural revolution fostered became the context for a number of neo-Arabic expressions that relate to the dress and appearance of women and girls. For example, newly minted Perso-Arabic that describes a woman whose hair showed from beneath her veil is بد حجابی or "badly veiled," which is composed of Persian *bad* (related to English "bad") and the Arabic *ḥejāb* (a "screen" or "curtain" that originally shielded the wives and women of the Prophet from the prying eyes of his followers in Qoran 33:53). The qoranic notion is the basis for the revival of veiling in Iran, but vigilantes known variously as "the sisters of Zeynab (in honor of the revered sister of Imam Hoseyn)" *khᵛāharān-e zeynab* خواهران زینب and *gasht-e thār allāh* (example 12) that punish women for being badly veiled are Islamic Republican innovations.

example 11: bad ḥejābi

بد حجابی

i b ā j ḥ d b ←

At times the cultural revolutionaries enforced the anti-Western dress codes with some brutality. The severe nature of their enforcement is reflected in the Arabic terms they revived to name the enforcers. *Thār* ثار or "vengeance" is not found in the Qoran, but it is a Semitic word meaning "flesh" and, by extension, "retaliation" for an insult to one's blood relative (related to Hebrew שאר; Klein 1987). Among the squads that regularly arrested or punished the poorly veiled and immodest was the "vengeance of Allah patrol" (Ṣayyād 1996:451), a bilingual phrase that joins Persian *gasht* گشت, "patrol," to the neo-Arabic *thār allāh*:

example 12: gasht-e thār allāh

گشت ثار اللّه

ā ll a r ā th t sh g ←

Like the combination ثار الله , innovations and revived terms are not as common in modern Arabic as they are in Persian. This imaginative use of Arabic shows that not only does Persian borrow from qoranic language, it revitalizes it by extending the semantic fields of words to areas that rarely occur to native users.

Another example of the imaginative, non-native application of Arabic is the political use of the phrase "sower of corruption on earth" *mofsed fi al-arḍ*, the Islamic Republican term for gross offenders of the moral order. In the Qoran (18:94), the phrase refers to the "Gog and Magog" people, whom some commentators identify as the nomadic tribes of Central Asia.

In Islamic Republican Persian, the phrase became more inclusive. For example, in the eyes of the leaders of the Islamic Republic, the signers of the first Camp David accords, Jimmy Carter, Menachem Begin, and Anwar Sadat, were *mofsed fi al-arḍ* (*Jomhuri-e Eslāmi* 14 Khordād, 1358/4 June, 1979).

example 13: mofsed fi al-arḍ

مفسد فی الأرض

ḍ r'la i f d s f m ←

To sanctify the cause of Islamic Republicanism and thereby demonize political opponents of the regime, word makers revived the qoranic (58:22) phrase "party of God," *ḥezb allāh*. Prior to the Revolution, most users of modern Persian would have defined *ḥezb* as a political "party" in the Western sense: for example, the Iran Party, *ḥezb*-e *irān*; the Communist Party, *ḥezb-e tudeh*, etc. Political parties in this sense first entered Persian usage during the latter half of the nineteenth century. By the late twentieth century, the modern Persian term had long since lost its qoranic connotation, namely “those whom God favored with Faith and admitted to heaven.” The revival of the phrase served the cultural revolutionary purpose of re-Islamizing political discourse. *Ḥezb* was once again with “God” in Persian, and parties that did not have the deity in their names were secular and therefore vulnerable to charges of طاغوتیism.

example 14: ḥezb allāh

حزب الله

ā ll a b z ḥ ←

Like مستضعفین , *ḥezb allāh* has an evil opposite: the “Party of Satan,” *ḥezb-e sheyṭān*, which also comes from the Qoran (58:19). The Persianized form of the phrase drops the Arabic article *al-* ال from *sheyṭān* becoming:

example 15: ḥezb-e sheyṭān

حزب شیطان

The two parties sit at opposite ends of the Islamic Republican political spectrum:

absolute fidelity to the principle of the rule of the supreme cleric; belief in Islam as the universal and timeless answer to society's needs; no taint of Eastness or Westness in the struggle against the arrogant	*loyalty to non-Islamic groups: liberals, secularists, leftists, royalists, agents of the former secret police, Freemasons, the purged members of royalist military and government organizations*
حزب الله	حزب شیطان

[Moḥammadi 1987:134]

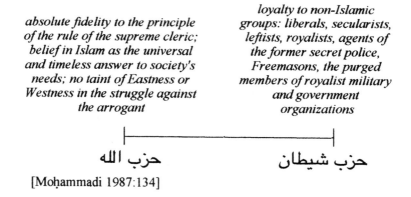

As in the case of the مستضعف / مستکبر polarity, there is no middle ground between the two terms. One is either a member of the Party of God or the Party of the Devil. These revived Arabic phrases thus erased the shades of difference among the various political factions that surfaced during the Revolution. The result was the muting of political debate.

Islamic Republican Persian has also taken advantage of two qoranic words built on the same Arabic paradigm to demonize an important opposition group. The first of the two words, *mojāhedin*, appears in the Qoran (4: 95) as "those who strive in the path of God." It became part of the Persian political lexicon in the late 1960s when the Islamic Marxist "People's Crusaders" *mojāhedin-e khalq* began to fight the Pahlavi regime. The use of the term in those days was clearly an attempt to base partisan attacks on the regime and its allies in Islam. The loose confederation known as *mojāhedin* also fought in Afghanistan as anti-Soviet and, later, anti-Taliban forces.

example 16: mojāhedin

مـجـاهـديـن

n i d h ā j m ←

The مجاهدين fought in the Revolution but quickly broke with Khomeini and his allies. To characterize this betrayal, Islamic Republicans used a rhyming term from the Qoran (4: 61): *monāfeqin* or "Waverers, Doubters, Hypocrites." In the original context, the *mojāhedin* were followers of the Prophet Mohammad who deserted him when a crucial battle went wrong.

example 17: monāfeqin

مـنـافـقـين

n i q f ā n m ←

The substitution, منافقين for مجاهدين, was essential to Islamic Republican Persian. Like many other dichotomies in this chapter, the two words represent the ends of an ideological spectrum that contains no middle ground. Nearly ten years after the Revolution, one of V. S. Naipaul's Iranian informants was slapped because he failed to make the substitution (Naipaul 1998:186).

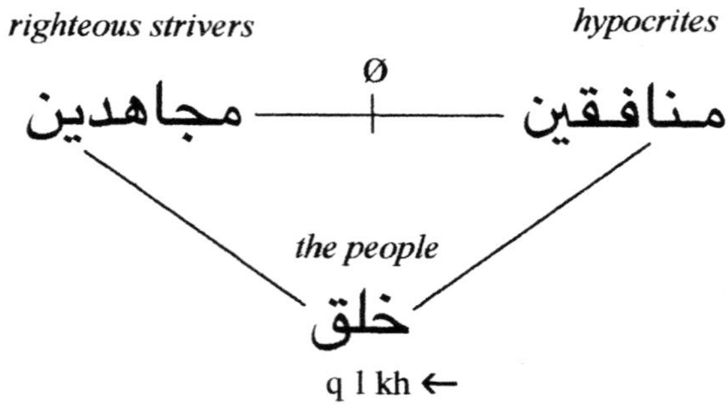

This brief survey of the Islamic Republican lexicon reveals an important function of newly-minted Arabic vocabulary in modern Persian. These terms, which often contain the non-Persian letters introduced in this chapter, serve as signposts to the past. Often the terms and phrases themselves or the way neologists have employed them are obscure to many secular users of the language. This obscurity drives users back to the sources to discover the origins and contexts of the Arabic terms. Once they establish the provenance of the terms (usually the Qoran or qoranic commentary), there can be no doubt about their spellings or original intents. Unlike the Persianizations of the English terms in Chapter I, the revived Arabic words and phrases have found a welcome and unambiguous home in Persian.

The neo-Arabic of Islamic Republicanism differs from Persianized English terminology in a politically significant way. The Persianized Western terms are not only difficult to process for monolingual Persian readers, who obviously do not know the original European words, they also can be challenging to those who do. More used to seeing them in their original Roman alphabetic dress, the latter stumble when sounding out the Persianized forms. After a pause, they often recognize them with "Of course, that's ...."

The revived Arabic terms of revolutionary or radical Persian, by contrast, are "foreign" in a different way. Because the Persian writing system accommodates them naturally, even readers who have never seen these terms before have the vague notion that they have or, more importantly, that they should have. The evocative Arabic terminology reminds the non-traditional of a past that their secular or non-native educations obscured. Like the two ways of writing Chinese, the traditional system of Taiwan and the simplified characters of Communist China, the Persian of Iran, Afghanistan, and Tajikistan, under secularizing regimes and the revived Arabic of re-Islamization are tokens of political, cultural, and social schisms. They divide Persian-users into two incompatible groups: the Arabized and the Westernized. The former have revived traditional language to return to a salutary past, while the latter have encouraged the Persianization of European words to attain a form of modernity identified with the West.

Chapter III

The Politics of the Alphabet

Curing Ambiguity

Chapter II introduced letters that entered Persian due to the Arabization of the seventh century. In the classical period, writers never, as far as I know, questioned the imposition of the Arabic writing system on Persian. However in recent times, especially after 1928 when Turkey discarded its Arabic-based alphabet for a European one, complaints about these letters have grown louder and louder. Alphabetic nationalists have championed a "pure" form of writing that uses words, some of which were and are obscure, to avoid Arabic and other "foreign" words (Karimi-Hakkak 1989; Gheissari 1998:81-2). Other writers have called for alphabetic reform according to the "principles of modern linguistics" (Bāṭeni 1970:57-62; Khayyām 1994:72-96). The reformers often point out that Persian is inefficient because as many as four letters can represent one sound. They contrast the syllabic system of the Arabic alphabet, which ordinarily does not mark short vowels, to the fully voweled systems of European languages and find Persian wanting.

Bāṭeni (1970:58) complains that grammar school students waste a great deal of time trying to remember whether a particular word is written with س or ص ; ز or ظ, etc. To hasten literacy, he recommends that the Arabic letters leave Persian and that writers spell words with the remaining "pure" Persian forms. Thus, he would change the Arabic name مصطفی (*moṣṭafā*) to مستفا (*mostafā*). This suggestion makes perfect linguistic sense.

In Persian phonology, the consonants ص and س — ط and ت are the same and, though the last letter in مصطفی looks like long i, because of the requirements of the Arabic writing system it is pronounced long a. Persian speakers can say the name because it entered the language centuries ago, but they need to know Arabic to write it.

simplification

ص ———► س

ط ———► ت

ی ———► ا

مصطفی ———► مستفا

ā f ṭ ṣ m ā ft s m ←

Bāṭeni does not dwell on the cultural and historical consequences of alphabetic reform. His example, however, is very instructive along these lines. Not only is مصطفی a name, signifying "chosen," or "select" in Arabic, *al-moṣṭafā* ("the one chosen by God to receive the message") is a universally recognized epithet of the Prophet Mohammad. Owing to مصطفی 's religious significance, many Persian speakers give the name to their sons (Ershādi 1993:86-87).

Reducing مصطفی to مستفا would also displace the word from a tangle of lexical associations that binds a great deal of Persian vocabulary. Many modern Persian words are related to the name مصطفی , because they share the three "root" letters of the word: ص , ف , and ا. This illustrates something that almost all Arabic words share; no matter how long, they boil down to roots of three letters. Knowing the basic meaning of the root helps Persian readers guess the meanings of unfamiliar words that make use of it. The tree that grows from ا , ف , and ص reveals how many Persian words are related to مصطفی.

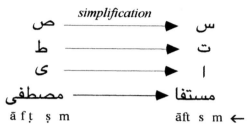

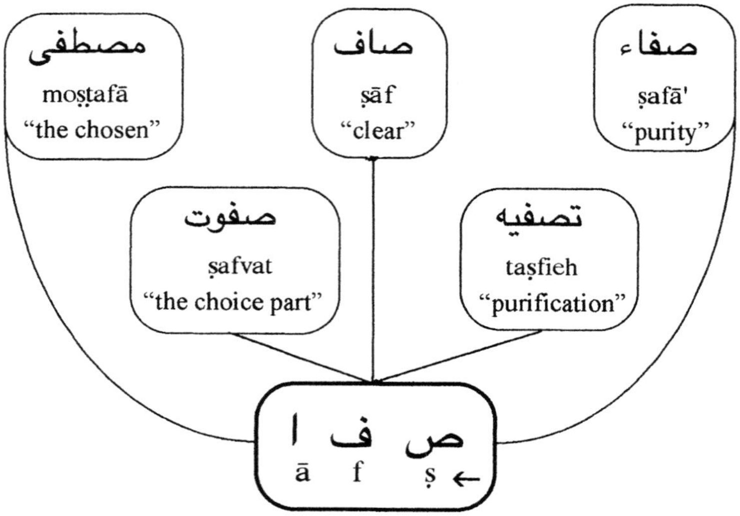

All five terms stem from three letters, the basic meaning of which is "to be pure, select."

Bāṭeni would uproot the tree that grows from the root *ṣ f ā*. Though his reforms would make the language more phonetic and thus easier to learn, they would also alter it other ways. They would deny readers the system of three-letter Arabic roots that allows intelligent guesses about the meanings of words (Rāhjiri 1970:139). Were Bāṭeni's proposals implemented, texts written before simplification would have to be "re-Persianized" and heavily footnoted. Otherwise Persian-users that become literate after their implementation would be cut off from their literary heritage. Does such a sacrifice justify the gains of quicker literacy? So far, most Persian users have resisted drastic alphabetic reform. The only people to use a non-Arabic alphabet to write Persian are the Tajiks of the former Soviet Republic, who write Persian in Cyrillic and know the language as Таджики "Tojiki." In the case of Tojiki, political rather than linguistic considerations motivated the change from Arabic writing system to the Russian one. Despite the change, however, many Tajik speakers can also read Persian works in the Arabic script.

Persian is not the only language that uses several letters to represent one sound. Modern English, which one alphabetic reformer (Khayyām 1994:26) considers superior to Persian as a computer language, for example, has four ways of indicating "f" as in fluff: *f*, *ff*, *ph*, and *gh*:

fight (faɪt) *off* (ɔf) *photograph* (foʊtoʊgɹæf) *enough* (inəf)

The ambiguity generally does not lead to calls for reform. This is because making all English spellings phonetic, that is to decree that all fs should be written *f*, would impoverish the language. English uses alphabetic ambiguity imaginatively. Alternate spellings often become trademark names of products, franchises, bands, etc.:

Fotomart	>	photo + mart
Kwik-Fill	>	quick + fill
Shoprite	>	shop + right
Phish	>	fish
phat	>	fat

Bāṭeni's call for alphabetic reform is like the Europeanization of Turkish or the simplification of Chinese—it argues cogently for change on linguistic grounds, but is silent about the historical, political, and cultural implications of such change. The truth is, however, alphabetic reform is never purely linguistic. In 1928 Atatürk used it to dislodge his country from the "backward" Middle East and integrate it into "modern" Europe. Changing the Turkish system from Arabic to a modified German and creating "pure" Turkish words to replace Arabic and Persian vocabulary oriented educated students toward Europe, on one hand, and made them Turkish nationalists on the other. The languages of science and technology became privileged over the language of the Qoran.

In China, Mao Zedong ordered the simplification of Chinese characters. While reducing the number of strokes in a word from seventeen to seven, for example, facilitated Chinese literacy, it also sharpened the cultural divide between mainland China and Taiwan, which continues to use the older system. Thus the two ways of writing Chinese have become emblematic of the political distinctions between the two Chinas—one nominally communist, the other capitalist; one claiming to be the only China, the other defiantly nationalistic. More significantly, both the Turkish and the Chinese experiences show that changing a writing system separates readers from the written works of the past. After 1928, centuries of Ottoman and Persian literature, history, philosophy, etc., expressed in the Arabic alphabet, became obsolete in Turkey, known only to a few scholars of language, history, and religion called "Ottomanists." Likewise, generations of readers cannot fully understand thousands of classical Chinese works because they only know the simplified characters. There is no reason to believe that if reformers were to change Persian along Ata Türkian or Maoist lines, the same kind of cultural dislocation would not ensue.

Trees that Grow from Familiar Roots

To illustrate how Arabic operates in Persian, one can trace the roots of two words introduced in Chapter II: *ẓāher* (ظاهر) or "outside, appearance" and *ḥāfez* (حافظ) "preserver." Like the name مصطفی , both stem from three basic Arabic letters that are very productive in Persian. Ẓāher (Chapter II, example 6), is made up of the Arabic letters ظ , ه , and ر , a root whose basic meaning is "to become visible." In addition to *ẓāher*, these letters in various combinations form at least five other words used in contemporary Persian:

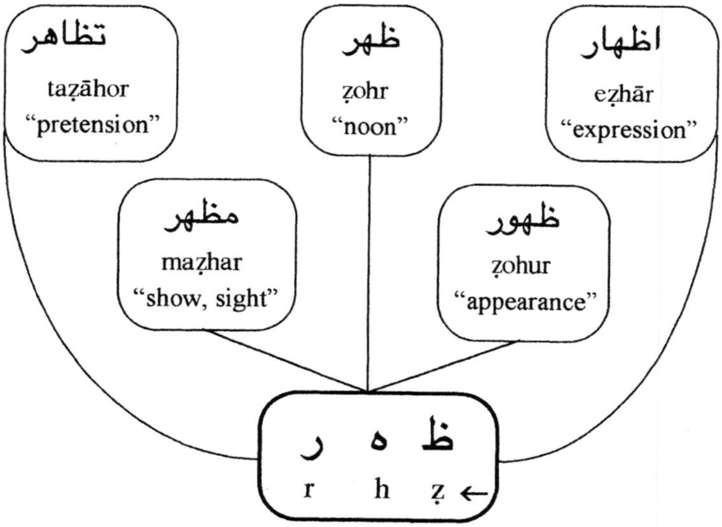

Four of the derived words are synonymous with their Arabic cognates. One, *maẓhar*, in Arabic is "looks, appearance," not "place where one must appear," its meaning in Persian. This divergence illustrates how Persian infuses new meanings into traditional Arabic, a process that some of the revived Arabic words and phrases in Chapter II also evince.

The next tree shows that Hafez (Chapter II, example 7) stems from the root letters ح , ف , and ظ , which like ظ , ه , and ر are also the basis of at least five other current Persian words. The basic meaning of the root is "to preserve, guard, defend." All of the words are also found in Arabic, but *moḥāfaẓeh-kār* shows another common way Persian borrows from that language. The Persian suffix *-kār* "work, doing" attaches to محافظه . The Perso-Arabic hybrid is then susceptible to further affixation. For example, the Persian suffix *-āneh* attaches to کار turning the word into the adverb *moḥāfeẓeh-kārāneh* or "conservatively." محافظه کار also admits the suffix ان to become *moḥāfeẓeh-kārān* "conservatives."

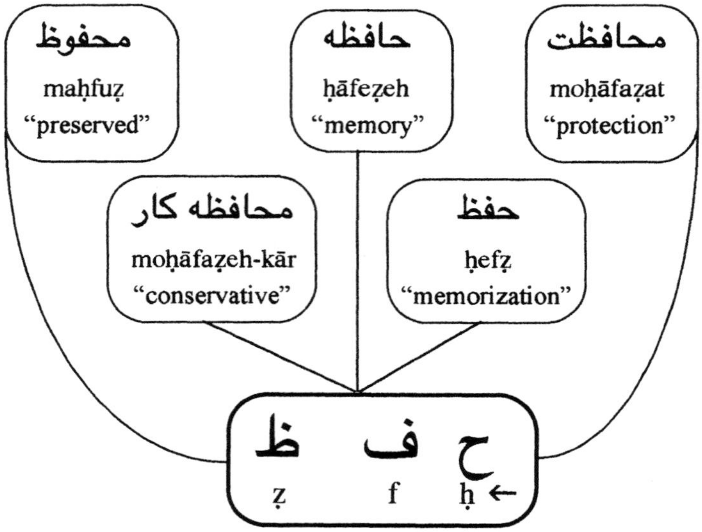

Latin : English :: Arabic : Persian

Many writers think that Persian's reliance on Arabic morphology is a liability. At the extreme end of the anti-Arabic spectrum, is the Persian purist Dāryush Āshuri (1993:110), who sees the "limitless and inappropriate mixing of Arabic and Persian" as the principle problem of the language. ʿAli Ḥaqqshenās (1991:254), a linguist, says that profligate borrowing from Arabic imposes foreign pluralization and spellings on the language. This "exo-morphology" makes Persian unnecessarily complex, and therefore difficult to learn. Furthermore, argues Ḥaqqshenās, the complexity robs the language of its uniformity and weakens its innate ability to form new words and phrases. In this view, the Arabic elements in Persian bear a very heavy burden. But is the way Persian has assimilated Arabic materially different from the way Japanese, for example, has nativized many Chinese elements or the way English has borrowed from Latin?

Consider how Latin roots function in English. English words derived from Latin are so plentiful, form such a significant part of the language's lexicon, that most users are unaware of their presence. Ḥaqqshenās' argument is analogous to faulting English for its reliance on Latin and Latin morphology. He would say, for example, that the large number of "port" words, i.e., those words that contain the Latin root *port*, all having something to do with the basic meaning "carry," make English unnecessarily difficult to learn:

Base	*Suffixes*
deport	-able, ability, -ation, -ed, -ee, -er, -ing, -s
export	-able, ability, -ation, -ed, -er, -ing, -s
import	-able, ability, -ant, -ation, -ed, -er, -ing, -s
porter	-s
portable	-ility, -s
report	-able, ability, -ed, -er, -ing, -s
transport	-able, -ability, -ation, -ed, -er, -ing, -s

But does the ubiquity of these Latin borrowings rob English of its originality, its Anglo-Saxon "creativity"? Are students who have not studied Latin formally at a disadvantage when they have to learn these borrowings? If they do not know Latin but know the meaning of some of the "port" words, can't they infer the meanings of unfamiliar ones? Very few users of English have called for purging the language of words derived wholly or in part from Latin. Rather than decrying the influence of non-native words and exo-morphology, users of English study Latin either for the general betterment of their vocabularies or for standardized tests that focus on nuances of word meaning like the Scholastic Aptitude Test.

Clearly, just as Latin and the way that Latin words are formed have become integral to English (becoming, in many cases, "Anglicized"), so too have certain Arabic elements become inseparable from Persian. Though this sentiment has appeared in Persian many times (e.g., Khānlari 1944:162), writers restate it every generation (e.g., Samiʿi 2000:167). Even contemporary Persian assimilates Arabic expressions whole. For example, the Arabic phrase *ḍarbo-l-ajal*, literally "the striking of the deadline" or "immediately" is found in a newly published dictionary of vernacular Persian (Najafi 1999). If purists were to purge all Arabic and even the neo-Arabic terms from Persian like those in Chapter II, the anti-reformers argue, the language would be unrecognizable.

The Current Level of Arabic in Persian

To illustrate the extent to which originally Arabic expressions are native to modern Persian, I have chosen to annotate writing from a book that advocates wholesale alphabetic reform to make Persian a language that meets the needs of computer programming. In the book, "The Coming Script," Masʿud Khayyām, favors three basic modifications that make Persian resemble a European language. First, he would reverse the direction of the language, changing it from right-to-left language to left-to-right like English. Second, he would add three symbols to the traditional system to represent the short vowels a, e, and, o. Finally, he would write Persian with only the independent forms of letters, making it appear as it does in crossword puzzles. This would facilitate literacy, because learners would not have to master the initial, medial, and final forms of letters. At the end of his book, Khayyām applies the first and third modifications to a poem by Hafez, the great Persian poet introduced in Chapter II. Here is the first hemistich of the original (Hafez 1983:1:288) followed by Khayyām's (1994:97) version.

سـالـهـا دل طـلـب جـام جـم از مـا مـی کـرد

d r k i m ā m z a m j mā j b l ṭ l d ā' h l ā s

درك ی م ام زا م ج ماج ب ل ط ل د اه ل ا س

s ā l hā d l ṭ l b jā m j m āz mā m i kr d

There are many things at work here. Persian readers, conditioned to process right-to-left, can misread the familiar word *dark* درك ("realization"), which by chance forms the last three, unconnected letters of *mi-kard* می کرد at the end of Khayyām's Hafez. It takes a moment for left-to-right Persian vision to reverse direction and see the intended version. Khayyām's choice of poetry, one of the most familiar of the poet's familiar lyrics, serves several purposes. By modifying the most authentic of texts, one that scholars have debated for centuries, Khayyām asserts that even the Persian of Persians is susceptible to alphabetic reform. He also uses this particular poem for what it means to contemporary readers.

The entire line contains an idea that Hafez expresses often:

سالها دل طلب جام جم از ما می کرد   آنچه خود داشت ز بیگانه تمنا می کرد

"For years the heart was seeking the cup of Jamshid from us,
Begging the outsider for what the self already possessed."

In other words, without being aware of it, the human heart intuits understandings that elude reason. In this line the symbol of the unknowable is the magic goblet that showed Jam, a mythical king of ancient Persia, everything in the world. Of course, this reading conforms to the poet's own particular form of mysticism; but, because the poetry of Hafez like the plays of Shakespeare is timeless and placeless, it admits many readings. Recently the second hemistich served as the title of a book on Iran (Narāqi

1976). In the contemporary setting, "outsider" became "foreigner," and the line alludes to the slavish imitation of the West, the modern malady *gharbzadegi* (see Chapter II) that causes Iranians to seek abroad what they already possess at home.

Given its advocacy of alphabetic reform, Khayyām's book might be expected to be free of words with the Arabic letters that overlap with pure Persian: namely, ث ح ذ ص ض ط ظ. Khayyām might have even resorted to the archaic Persian style of Aḥmad Kasravi (1976) to nativize his writing. But, as is clear from these excerpts, Khayyām does not follow the purist path. To show this, I have reproduced passages from "The Coming Script," annotating some of the Arabic-derived terms with their three-letter roots and italicizing all of them in the English translations that follow.

<u>Passage 1</u>

ا س ف   ق د ر
متاسفانه اما همان قدر که زبان ما خوب

ق و ی   ض ع ف
و قوی است بد و ضعیف است. نارسائی

های این خط که بخش هائی از آن در

ح ض ر
دفتر حاضر عنوان شده چنان است که به

ن ظ ر   ع م ل   و ق ف
نظر می رسد عملاً در حال توقف است و

ك م ل
تا فلج کاملش راه زیادی باقی نمانده.

> *Unfortunately, however*, to the *extent* that our language is good and *strong*, so is it poor and *weak*. The insufficiencies of this *script*, some of which have been *outlined* in this book, are such that it *seems* [the writing system] is *effectively* in a *suspended state*, and it won't be long before *complete paralysis* sets in [Khayyām 1994:2].

Rather than shunning Arabic in this passage, Khayyām uses it to good purpose. The first sentence contains a kind of parallelism that characterizes a great deal of Persian prose. Two pairs of adjectives, each consisting of a pure Persian word and an Arabic word, give the sentence its rhetorical force:

Persian	*Arabic*
khub خوب	qavi قوی
"good"	"strong"
bad بد	ẓa$^{?}$if ضعیف
"poor"	"weak"

Khayyām could just as easily have used Persian words meaning "strong" and "weak," but this would not have had the same effect, which is only possible *because* of the Arabic in Persian. There is only one small concession to pure Persian in this passage: the use of *daftar* instead of the semitic *ketāb* (Hebrew כתב), which the translation cannot capture with "book." In English, some writers and speakers make a rhetorical distinction between "tome" and "book." The former, which is Latin in origin, is somehow higher in status, more scholarly, heavier than the Ango-Saxon equivalent.

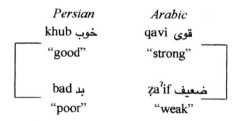

In the next excerpt, Khayyām explains that he cannot address the objections traditionalists might raise to his proposed modifications.

Passage 2

س أ ل   أ ص ل

مسالهٔ اصلی این است که نمی توانیم

ع ص ب   ع ص ب

پاسخ گوی عصبیت ها تعصب ها و

ع ص ب

عصبانیت هائی باشم که این سخن بر

می انگیزد.

The *basic issue* is that we cannot respond to the *penchants, prejudices,* and *peeves* that this discussion provokes [Khayyām 1994:27-28].

Here the author makes fine distinctions in meaning with three Persianized Arabic words, *ˁaṣabiat, taˁaṣṣob, ˁaṣabāniat,* all of which share the same Arabic root letters: ع , ص , and ب . The rhetorical effect, suggested in translation with alliteration, would have been impossible had there been no Arabic to exploit.

In the next passage Khayyām mentions one reason why many Persian writers resist alphabetic reform so strongly. It begins with a Persian aphorism, three of the five words of which are originally Arabic. This produces the kind of rhetorical effect found in the previous two passages.

<u>Passage 3</u>

ع و د ع ش ق ق و م
عادت از عشق قوی تر است و این خود
د ل ل
بهترین دلیل مقاومت در برابر پیشنهاد
ع و د
های عادت شکن است. اما این بار چاره
ع و د
ای جز عادت شکنی متعادان نیست زیرا
ح د د م د ن
ما از قافلهٔ تمدن اتوماتیزه به حد کافی
ف ی د
دور هستیم و با ادامهٔ استفاده از خط
کنونی به مراتب دورتر هم می مانیم.

> *Habit* is *stronger* than *love*, which itself best *explains* the *opposition* to *ground-breaking* proposals. But this time there is no remedy but to break the *habits* of the *habituated*, for we are far *enough* behind the caravan of automated *civilization*, and by *continuing* to *use* the present script we will fall *even further* behind [Khayyām 1994:96].

Khayyām uses two Persian words from the same Arabic root to rhetorical effect. As in the case of the previous passages, without Arabic the effect is impossible:

habit : the habituated :: *ʿādat* عادت : *moʿtād* معتاد.

To explain the resistance to alphabetic change in Persian as an inability to break a bad habit is to avoid the political and cultural nature of the battle between reformers and conservatives. As

Khayyām says, his ninety-six page "tome" would have been much longer had he broadened his discussion to include the relationship between the Persian language and Persian identity.

Persian and National Identity

The close relationship between language and nationality in Persian often sharpens the debate over alphabetic change. Some of the fiercest objections to the simplification or wholesale change of the traditional writing system are made on nationalistic grounds. Because many writers associate being Iranian and Persian, they see alphabetic reform, no matter the motive, as an attack on their selfhood. The cultural historian Shahrokh Meskoob believes Persian to be the sole agent of historical continuity, "We maintained one nationality or, perhaps better put, our national identity, our Iranianness, through the blessing of language, by means of the vitality of Persian as a refuge" (Meskoob 1992:31). Another influential writer values language in general because it is "in reality the sole agent connecting the various individuals from diverse classes" (Dustdār 1991:xxii). The notion of language as cultural glue applies specifically to Persian, because according to the translator Najaf Daryābandari (1989:678), it is "responsible for uniting the disparate elements that make up the Iranian national identity." Persian, asserts an article by the scholar Jalāl Matini (1982:127), "documents the independence and survival of the [Iranian] nation." By "Iranian," these writers generally do not mean the people living within the present boundaries of Iran. To them the Iranian nation encompasses any people who speak or read Persian, who participate in its rich literary culture. Such people live in present-day Iran, Tajikistan, Afghanistan, Pakistan, and India. The identification of "Persian" and "nationality" is so natural that even a strong critic of the language-as-nationality school (Vaziri 1993:4-5) uses the terms "Farsi" and "Farsi Language" instead of "Persian."

Holders of the transnational view of Persian detest the current fashion of calling it *fārsi* فارسی (e.g., Matini 1988). They argue that this confines the language to one province of present-day Iran (fārs فارس) and encourages nationalists in Afghanistan and former Soviet Tajikistan to use their own terms for the same language. Afghans who want to distinguish the Persian they use from Iranian forms of the language call it *dari* دری, while Tajiks favor the term تاجیکی Таджики "Tojiki." Brian Spooner (1994) argues that this linguistic nationalism marginalizes Persian in universities that offer it as a "less commonly taught language." Alphabetic reformers tend to encourage the separatists who want to divide Persian along political and national lines.

Persians			
ایران	fārsi	فارسی "Farsi Language" [Vaziri 1993:176]	**Iran**
افغانستان	dari	دری	**Afghanistan**
تاجکستان	tājiki	تاجیکی / Таджики	**Former Soviet Union**

Threats to Traditional Literacy

Modifications based on linguistic principles or motivated by purism are not the only threats to the Persian writing system. The education of Persian teachers is in a poor state. According to the former University of Tehran professor of literature ʿAli Akbar Saʿidi Sirjāni (1994:30), Persian language and literature departments have become dumping grounds for undergraduates who get the lowest grades on the national college entrance examination. Instead of entering the most "difficult and engaging" of disciplines, studying and teaching Persian, the skilled users of the language test into medicine, engineering, law etc. This leaves a generally unqualified and unmotivated pool of applicants to become Persian instructors. The academic devaluation of the language will lead to generations of students who unknowingly mistake مهافزه کار and محافظه کار or مستقا and مصطفی. Allowing this to happen, says Saʿidi Sirjāni, is a form of sedition, for it robs the Persian-using people of their cultural heritage, one of the few things that defines national identity when (as had been the case in Iran for many years) modernization is synonymous with Westernization. The denaturing of language then would make the nation of its users vulnerable to "imperialism." An accidental decline in Persian language education, according to Saʿidi Sirjāni, is merely "idiocy" *ḥamāqat*; while an intentional one is "treachery" *khiānat*. In this view, insisting that students know the difference between ه and ح, and ض and ظ, etc. is not pedantry but patriotism.

Higher Persian education outside of Iran does not promote writing in the language either. Matini (1995), who has surveyed North American and European universities that offer Persian studies on the graduate level, finds that students are required to read others' works rather than express themselves in Persian. The demands on graduate students' time at these universities, five or six or even seven years for a Ph. D., are severe. They have to study at least one other Middle Eastern language (Arabic, Hebrew, Turkish) as well as European languages like Russian and German that are the media of a great deal of scholarship on Persian. While this education enables students to master non-vernacular studies of Persian, it does not lead to active participation in scholarly discourse in the language. It also forces non-native Persian literature specialists to rely more on European scholarship than on the work of experts whose first language is Persian. Matini contrasts higher Persian education in Europe and North America to graduate studies in more commonly taught languages like French, German, Spanish, and Italian. A Ph. D. in one of these languages usually certifies that the holder can, for example, write an academic article in it, a task that, according to Matini, is beyond the capabilities of almost all non-native graduates in Persian literature.

The sorry state of Persian studies in the United States played an important role in the academic career of the Iranian historian ʿAbd al-Hādi Ḥā'eri. In "What Went On" (1993), a thinly veiled *roman à clef*, Ḥā'eri tells the story of Omid ("hope"), a seminary student of little promise from a prominent clerical family. Having failed as a seminarian, Omid apprenticed as a weaver, but the love of reading soon brought him back to school. Hard work and passion made Omid a confident writer of Persian; family connections helped him to get his writings into print. Every turn in Omid's Horatio Alger tale restates Ḥā'eri's credo: "the only things that warrant success in life are: belief in the justness of one's path; unstinting effort in reaching one's goal; consultation with right-thinking and well-meaning people; and indifference to what defeatists and the malicious say" (Ḥā'eri, ʿA. 1993:7). Eventually Omid, like the author of his tale, graduated from the University of Tehran and obtained a scholarship to study abroad.

In 1970 Omid became a graduate student and teaching assistant at an unnamed Canadian university. His graduate student days coincided with the Imperial Iranian government's efforts to showcase its version of the Persian heritage. During his graduate student days, Omid developed a "scholarly tie" with a professor from a prestigious university in the United States.

Omid's encounters with North American Orientalism put Ḥā'eri's credo to a severe test. Before leaving Iran, he seems to have been under the impression that the study of the Middle East in the West was free of prejudice and politics. Omid had thought that a reputable university in the United States would be a place where scholars could work hard, publish the fruits of their research without fear of reprisal, and advance. But, after becoming an assistant professor at the American university, he soon learned how naive his impression of American academia was.

The politics of Persian literacy entered Omid's story, when he (like his creator) accepted an invitation to review a work by a well-known professor of history. True to his credo, Omid wrote candidly. Although the review concluded that the book was "a welcome and thought-provoking contribution, Omid's candor did not please the author, who wrote to the editor of the journal that the reviewer was not tenured, implying that his opinion of the book was not authoritative. Omid then criticized the famous professor's pretense of knowing enough Persian to conduct the research presented in her books, while exploiting anonymous graduate students to make up for her inadequacy (Ḥā'eri, ˁA. 1993:479). The discrepancy between the level of the professor's Persian literacy (low) and her academic status (high) led Omid/Ḥā'eri to conclude "even at an important American university...one can spend a lifetime in ignorance, yet at the same time enjoy an international reputation for scholarship" (Ḥā'eri, ˁA. 1993:480).

In Iran, literacy alone can be emblematic of a good education. The sentiments Saˁidi Sirjāni expressed in his lament about the decline of Persian literacy often become the topic of casual conversation. The newspaper columnist and novelist Abu al-Qāsem Ḥālat reported that he was once at a social gathering where the subject of higher education came up. Parents of college students were complaining about the arbitrary nature of the *konkur* (French *concours*), the national college entrance examination that not only determines who enters but what entrants study once enrolled. One parent confirmed the pessimistic view discussed at the beginning of this chapter. He reported that his son got a degree in literature without having the slightest interest in the subject. The son's indifference to Persian spelling worries the father, who tells Ḥālat the following story:

> One of my friends by the name of Ghaḍanfari, after waiting eight years for a phone, finally got one and called to tell me his number. I said to my son, 'Take this number down and put it in the phone book.' A few days later when I needed to call Ghaḍanfari for something, I looked in the book but the number wasn't there. I said to my son, 'Didn't I tell your to write it down and put it in the book?' 'Sure,' he said. Then he paged through the book and, instead of stopping at غ , he reached the ق section and

showed me the number. Then I realized that after fifteen years of formal education, he wrote Ghaḍanfari as 'Qazan Fari' [Ḥālat 1997:1:350].

Literate *Illiterate*

غضنفری قزن فری

i r f n ḍ gh i r f n z q ←

This is an obvious example of the alphabetic ambiguity Bāṭeni would cure with simplification In Iranian dialects, غ and ق sound exactly alike, and ض and ز are pronounced the same way in all Persians. Unaware of the Arabic word *ghaḍanfar* (literally "lion"), the son made a natural mistake. Because a threshold score on the college entrance examination consigned him to Persian literature, he remained indifferent to the actual spelling. Naturally his version of the name was phonetic. To Ḥālat, an elegant satirist who often seasoned his prose with allusions to Persian literature and ironic bits of Arabic, the son's misspelling signified the poverty of higher education.

Ironic Arabic

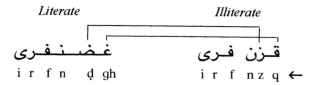

As the examples discussed in Chapter II show, what had been a light dusting of Arabic before the Islamic Revolution has become a storm of Arabisms after it. All writers are aware of this Arabization, but very few dare exploit its satirical possibilities overtly in Iran. This leaves the field open today to the pseudonymous and the exiled. One work that grew from this field in Paris is a collection of letters written during the period 1988-1995 contains many examples of ironic Arabic. In his letters, Behrouz Emdàdi-ye Asl, describes the social, economic, and cultural conditions of post-Iraqi war, post-Khomeini Iran. His descriptions of the Cultural Revolution give him ample opportunity to mimic the hyper-Arabized Persian of the political classes in the Islamic Republic. He takes the opportunity so often that the reader senses irony, rather than critical analysis, is driving the contents of his letters.

Emdàdi-ye Asl, who is very sensitive to language in general, is especially attentive to the forced re-Arabization of Persian education. He notices the change in primary schools where they

> place too much emphasis on Arabic, the language of the glorious Qoran and apparently the language that angels speak, and [where] students in some Arabic classes are forced to speak the language with one another. Ludicrous, isn't it [Emdàdi-ye Asl 1996:136]?

Even more ludicrous to him is when Arabic in the form of the Qoran enters classes on presumably secular subjects at the University of Tehran. He mentions reading in the newspaper of

> one worthy professor who explained to his students that once he had to go on an errand when traffic was not permitted. He evaded the traffic police by reciting the verse 'and We have put a bar in front of them and a bar behind them, and further, We have covered them up; so that they cannot see' [Qoran 36:9]. He added that this holy verse also worked for a young man that wanted to visit his fiancee and consummate their betrothal without her father seeing them [Emdàdi-ye Asl 1996:137].

Emdàdi-ye Asl fears that the Arabization of public school discourse from the elementary grades to the university will desecularize education in Iran. This will reduce all scientific and cultural debates to the controversies that had preoccupied the clergy in Medieval Islam and that have resurfaced in political discourse under Islamic Republican theocracy. To characterize these debates Emdàdi-ye Asl uses a phrase composed of three Arabic nouns joined by Persian syntax:

3 2 1

دعوای بول و غایط

ṭ y ā gh u l u b i ā v ʕ d ←

or "the argument between urine and defecation" (Emdàdi-ye Asl 1996:74, 101). In the anti-clerical view, most response literature in Shiite jurisprudence (a genre with the Arabic rubric *towḍiḥ al-masāyel* "the resolution of questions") is concerned with matters of personal hygiene and sanitation.

Emdàdi-ye Asl also deplores the Arabization of the names of streets, public places, and businesses in Tehran. He blames the late twentieth-century Arab cultural aggression, which has been "more savage than the Mongol invasion," for enterprises like "The Islamic Sandwich Shop, *Ḥadith* Shirtmakers, Zeynab's Kindergarten, and the ʕAli Aṣghar Hospital" (Emdàdi-ye Asl 1996:19). He also reports that vital statistics offices throughout Iran refuse to register newborns with non-Islamic names.

Whenever secular writers like Emdàdi-ye Asl take an educated swipe at Arabic, they almost always appeal to the great novelist and essayist Ṣādeq Hedāyat. One of Emdàdi-ye Asl's letters from Tehran begins with a poem by Hedāyat that epitomizes the hip, secular, theology-is-scatology view and with an allusion to his surrealist novel *Buf-e Kur* ("The Blind Owl"):

We have a country like a head; کشوری داریم مانند خلا
In it we're just like Hoseyn: dead. ما در آن همچون حسین در کربلا

> Certainly there were wounds in the life of Ṣādeq Hedāyat that ate at and eroded his soul like leprosy, which is why he complained and railed the way he did. But were that dear savant to return from the grave today and favor our homeland with a glance, he would undoubtedly avow that 'our' condition is even worse than that of Hoseyn at Karbala [Emdàdi-ye Asl 1996:89; the first sentence alludes to Hedāyat 1965a:9].

Hedāyat was the champion of anti-Arabic irony in modern Persian. Because this clergy-undermining irony served the cultural policies of the Westernizing Pahlavi regimes, many of his works reached the reading public uncensored during the nearly three decades after his suicide in 1951. However, even the secularizers found his attack on religious superstitions and folk beliefs *Tup-e Morvāri* ("The Pearl Cannon") too irreverent to allow its publication. Though everyone knew Hedāyat to be the author, clandestine printings attribute the work to the anagrammatic Hādi Ṣedāqat:

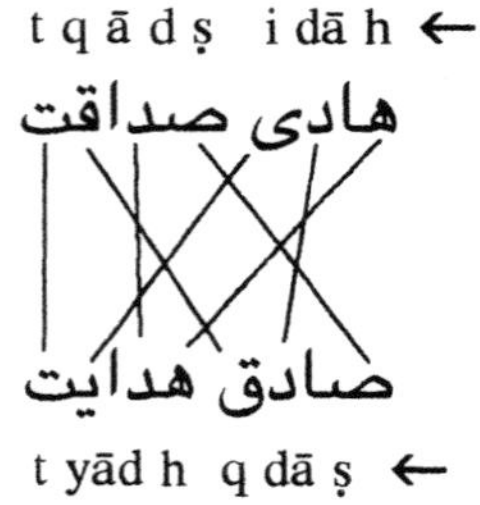

Emdàdi-ye Asl would naturally invoke Hedāyat or Ṣedāqat, who was at his most vituperative when describing the Arabic conquest of Iran. The arch-secularist thought it was worse than the cataclysmic Mongol invasions of the twelfth and thirteenth centuries. In "The Pearl Cannon," Hedāyat describes Arabic as a "bastard, ponderous language they [the Arabs] foisted on the conquered nations as an international medium for the exchange of ideas like Esperanto, which feat is considered Islam's only miracle" (Hedāyat sd:21-22). When a lingam-worshipping queen converts to Islam, she declares war on the Latin alphabet, which in Hedāyat's Arabophobic Persian ends in the pseudo-learned, feminine Arabic plural *āt* (Hedāyat sd:109):

arabic plural "Latinisms" "Latin"

لاتینیات ← لا تینی

t ā i n i t ā l   i n i t ā l ←

The politics of the alphabet will continue to divide Persian-users along generally predictable lines. Traditionalists will insist on preserving the Arabic spellings of Persian words. Reformers will advocate simplifying, phoneticizing, reversing the direction, even romanizing the traditional system. The resisters of change will invoke culture, religion, history, literacy, etc. to support their opposition, while the changers will appeal to science, modernism, programmability, ease of learning, etc. to justify their reforms. Of course, no one can win such battles. Natural systems of communication evolve by themselves. If linguistic engineers change them, they do not stay engineered forever. Alphabetic conflicts in Persian are interesting not so much for their combatants but for the topics that surface when they are joined.

Chapter IV

The Pleasures of the Alphabet

Literal Pictures

The alphabetic battle lines in modern Persian should be clear by now. On one side stand the dissatisfied, those eager to eliminate redundant letters, add short vowels, standardize spellings, and liberate Persian from 1400 years of Arabic orthographic oppression. On the other, are the content, those who oppose changing the writing system because it would disrupt cultural and religious continuity and rob the language of what makes it Persian. The clarity of the lines makes it easy to argue well for one position or the other. But in one important way, this debate is a false dichotomy. The stark question—To reform or not to reform?—excludes a vital feature of the Arabo-Persian writing system: its beauty.

Almost from the beginning of its literary use, the Persian alphabet was more than a set of symbols for meaningful sounds. The letters also had intriguing shapes, straight lines, curves, sweeps, slants, slopes, dots, tails, teeth, and eyelets. Poets turned these shapes into new images. For example, Maʿrufi of Balkh (fl. mid-tenth century) used two letters, *jim* and *ʿayn*, to spell out the look of his lover's hair (Lazard 1964:134):

گشت بر گشت سیه جعد چو عین اندر عین

تاب بر تاب سیه زلف چو جیم اندرجیم

Twist on black twist, tresses like *ʿayn* upon *ʿayn*,
Curl on black curl, locks like *jim* within *jim*

The nested ع ع ع reproduce the endless folds of hair with their tails, while the cascading ج ج ج provide dots that punctuate the cheeks with beauty marks. Letters can also symbolize religious ideas. For example, *alef* often represents the divine unity and eternal rectitude in mystical Persian poetry (Schimmel 1975:417-18). Hafez (1983:1:636) speaks of the *alef* of a love's (the object of his mystical desire) stature engraved on his heart:

نیست بر لوح دلم جز الف قامت دوست
چکنم حرف دگر یاد نداد استادم

Nothing is on the slate of my heart but the *alef* of my love's bearing,
What else can I write, my Master taught me no other letter.

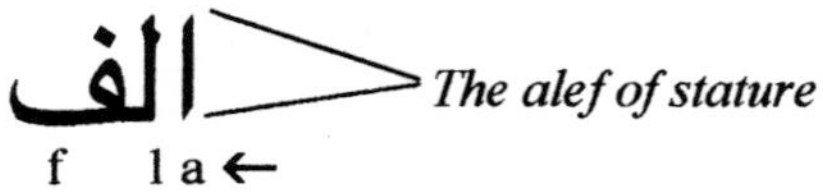

In erotic poetry, *alef* signifies the upright posture of the lover, while *dāl* is the emblem of the lover whose back is bowed by the weight of love:

Defeated lover, bent by unrequited love and other misery.
Proud alef-statured lover, unbowed by the miseries of love.

Another classical poet used the shapes of *alef*, *dāl*, *kāf*, and *nun* to allude to the promiscuity of a degenerate ruler:

چو دال و نون هم خم شد قد الف قدان

ز بس که کرد الف در شکاف کاف همه

Like *dāl* and *nun*, the *alef*-statured began to stoop,
So much has *alef* penetrated the crack of everyone's *kāf*. [Qazvini 1984:5:123]

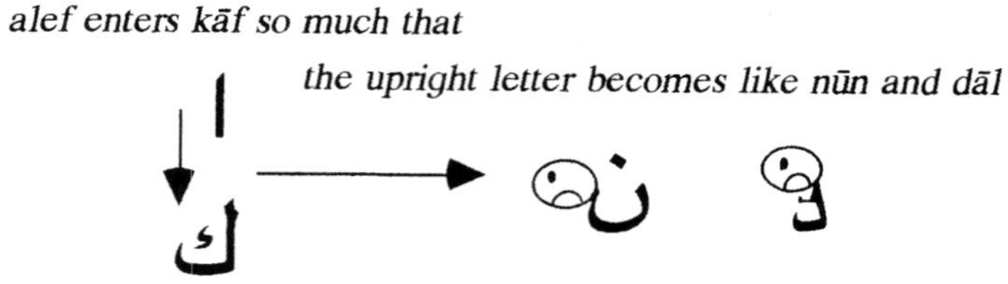
alef enters kāf so much that
the upright letter becomes like nūn and dāl

Rather than using figures of speech, classical Persian poets often relied on the visual aspects of Arabic writing system, figures of script, to express themselves. Audiences valued their poetry not so much for what it said (often pedestrian), but for how it exploited the connectivity or dottedness of the letters (often ingenious). To write *moqaṭṭaʕ* or "disjointed" poetry, for example, was to use only those letters that do not connect to the letters that come after them:

زار و زردم ز درد دوری او

u ir ud drd z mdr z u r ā z ←

I am weak and pale from the pain of separation from her/him [Browne 1969:2:67]

The opposite of disjointed poetry, *movaṣṣal* or "joined," employs words composed only of letters that connect to the letters before and after them. Another form of writing called "speckled" (*raqṭa'*), required that the poet alternate dotted and undotted letters:

غمزه شوخ آن صنم بگشاد اشك خونم

mnukh k sha dā shgb mn ṣ nā khu sh hezmgh ←

The wanton glances of that idol have loosed my blood-stained tears...[Browne 1969:2:67].

Until recently good penmanship was highly prized in Persian culture, as essential to a proper education in the language as grammar and composition. An Arabic proverb attributed to Imam ʿAli (d. 661), one of the most revered figures in Islam, says: "hand writing is half of learning" (Qommi 1980:13): *al-khaṭṭ neṣf al-ʿelm*:

الخط نصف العلم

m l ʕ l a f ṣ n ṭṭ kh l a ←

ʿAli's dictum held true for more than 1300 years, but with the advent first of typesetting and, later, of computer-generated, scalable fonts (like those used in this book), the importance of this art has diminished considerably among Persian-users.

Writing as Refuge: Sohrāb Sepehri

Because it was integral to traditional education, calligraphy often appears in memoirs. In an autobiographical essay, the poet and painter Sohrāb Sepehri (d. 1981) recalls how he used the alphabet to avoid the boredom of primary school. Though his grades put him at the top of his class, his teacher prevented him from doodling. In his school, drawing was a fault not something to be nurtured. The school had no art classes, only reading and writing

It was hard to read what the teacher wrote on the blackboard from the long benches that lined the walls of the schoolroom. Sepehri writes that one of his classmates mistakenly subtracted a dot from the word *barg* "leaf" and got *marg* "death" (1998:30):

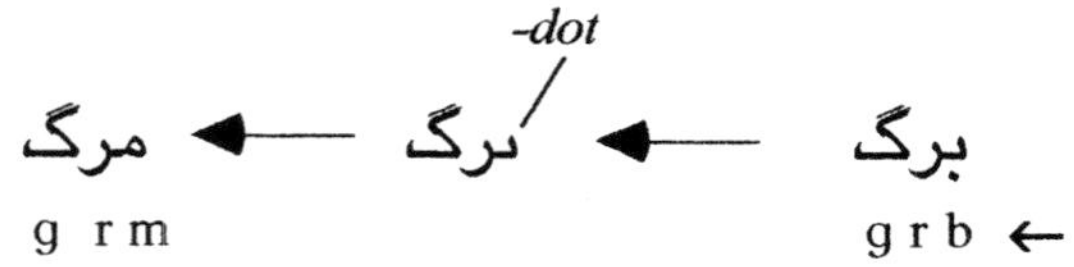

Another student misread three dots where there was only one, and put them below the verbal skeleton ـحـ , which turned the word *khub* "good" into *chub* "cane":

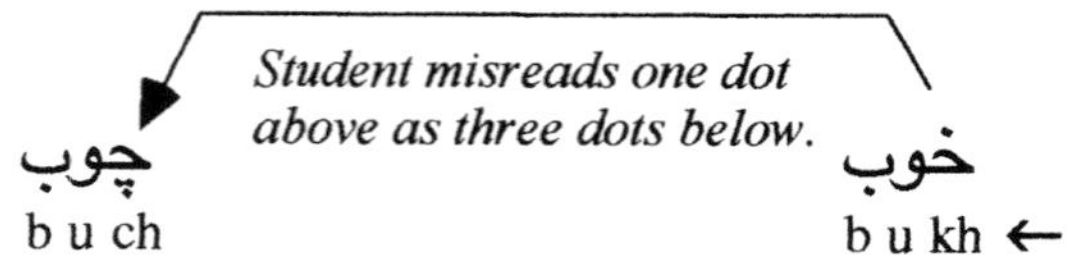

For his misdotting he received *chub-e khubi*, "a good beating," which is a pun on the fact that the two words share the basic shape حوب:

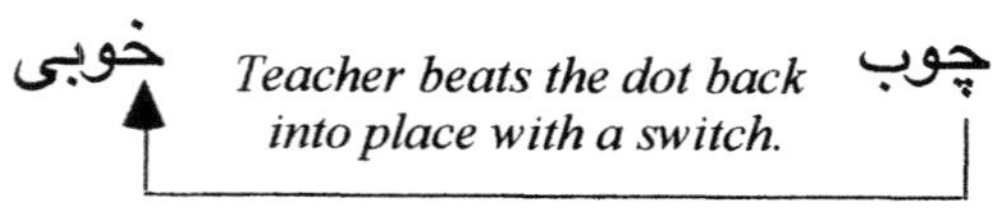

The novice spellers quickly learned the pain of a misplaced dot. Caning with a pomegranate switch was a regular part of the curriculum. Moreover, reports Sepehri (1998:30), the teacher welcomed the students' "laziness and dim-wittedness" because they gave " his schoolroom sadism free reign."

Sepehri could not oppose the rote learning of primary school overtly. On the surface he was a good student, but under it the sound of the school bell "severed his imagination" (1998:33). The only bell that awakened his interest was the one that sounded penmanship class. This class channeled Sepehri's rebellion into the dots, curves, loops, descenders and risers of Persian calligraphy. He won prizes for his penmanship. Here was an art that religion and society sanctioned; whereas drawing figures, people and animals, was doodling, or something immoral: iconophilia.

The samples the students copied were from Saʕdi's *Golestān* (see Chapter II), a model of Persian classical prose. Many phrases that originate in the *Golestān* have become the aphorisms of calligraphic exercises. One of the most famous of these justifies the corporal punishment Sepehri saw in school:

جور استاد به ز مهر پدر

r dp r h m z hb dāt s o r u j ←

"The teacher's cruelty is better than the father's caring" (Saʕdi 1984:155)

Sepehri's fine rendering of the phrase caught the attention of his teacher who brought it to the principal. With the students assembled in the school courtyard, the principal praised Sepehri's scholarship, discipline, even his character—judgments based on the form rather than the content of his writing.

To the students and many of their teachers great literature was a collection of phrases and lines of poetry to be copied into notebooks and memorized. In elementary and even well into secondary school, words were iconic rather than meaningful. The better one made them look on the page, the better one's grades. Discussing intent and context was not part of the curriculum. Of course, mediocre pupils, the majority, were content with parroting the classics. If their work saved them from a caning, it was adequate. But a few students, the good ones, went beneath the calligraphic surfaces and got to the meaning of the words. Even fewer, artists like Sepehri, used their love of words to defy the teachers' facile equation of form and content.

One day he turned the alphabetic tables on his teacher. The rebelliousness that Sepehri had kept bottled up as a model student finally emerged when the class was studying

> a piece from Moḥmmad ˤAwfi against treachery. We had our heads in our books, as the teacher read aloud. When he reached the part that said, 'The written skeleton of the word "treachery" is the same as the skeleton of "crime" to show the wise that they are both one,' I got up and asked permission to speak. I said, '"Plane tree" and "cucumber" have the same skeleton, so they must be one also.' With this the teacher suddenly rose from his seat and ran me from the room [Sepehri 1998:40-41].

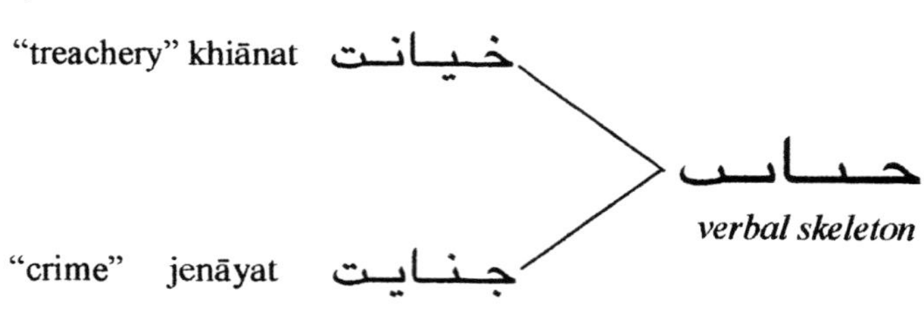

In reaction to the selection, Sepehri applied the principle that form is meaning to two other words that share a verbal skeleton. Though not as intimate as "treachery" and "crime," "plane tree" and "cucumber" are close enough to deflate ˤAwfi's pedantry. In addition, the phallic undertones of "cucumber" in Persian deepened the wound to the teacher's dignity. No wonder he threw Sepehri out of class:

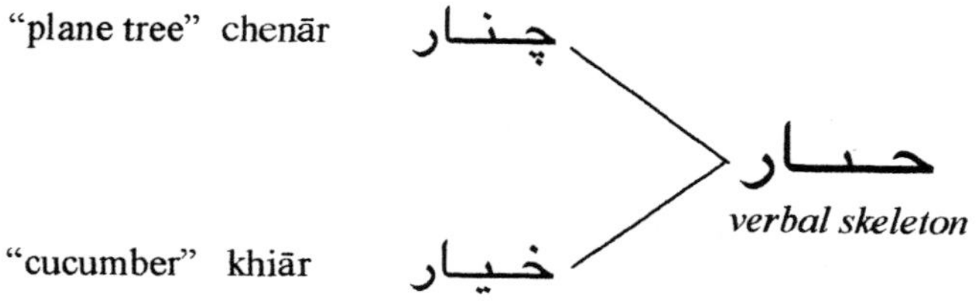

Other Figures of Script and Speech

Sepehri was not the only modern author to mine the humor in figures of Persian script and speech. The journalist Abu al-Qāsem Ḥālat, who often lamented the decline in Persian literacy in his columns (see Chapter III), also built anecdotes around words that accidently share verbal skeletons or pronunciations. One of his writings describes a vacation in Europe. Like many middle class Iranians of the time (mid 1970s), Ḥālat was part of a package tour of Rome, Paris, and London. He says that the tour leader

> spoke constantly of the educational aspects of travel in Europe, while I was thinking of recreation. While he had knowledge on his mind, mine was on dancing [Ḥālat 1997:1:25-6].

The pun needs to be spelled out: without dots the verbal skeleton دانس reads *dāns* or “dance,” but with dots it becomes *dānesh* or “knowledge.”

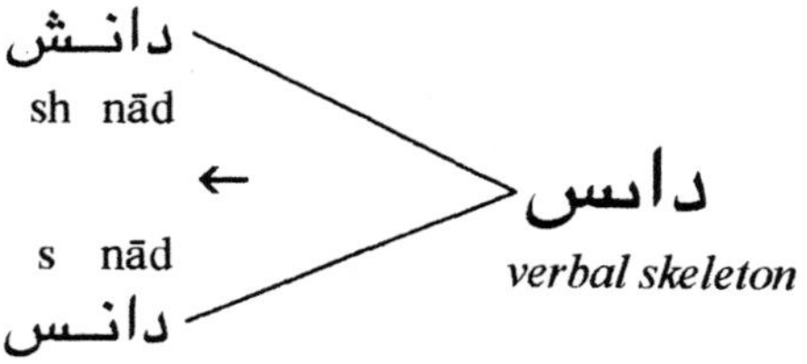

In this case, Ḥālat exploits on the chance similarity between a "pure" Persian word and one borrowed from Europe.

As long as Persian remains permeable to "foreign" words, the number of دانس/دانش type of figures of script will increase. But most of the punning in modern Persian draws on its extensive Arabic vocabulary. As explained in Chapter II, Persian speakers nativized the pronunciation of the Arabic consonants that entered the language beginning in the seventh century. Because as many as four letters can represent one sound, the number of Arabo-Persian homophones is quite large. One of these puns is the centerpiece of another column by Ḥālat about a party he attended. To open a conversation with one of the guests, he asked her about her daughter:

> She said, 'You mean Sandra?... Sandra wants to study nutrition, because it's something that really interests her.' At this point another guest said, 'But, madam, at least as far as I know, hasn't Sandra always expressed an interest in law?' The woman became flustered, not knowing how to respond. Her husband came to her rescue saying, 'No, no, there must be some misunderstanding. Sandra's major has always been nutrition (with غ and ذ) not law (with ق and ض)' [Ḥālat 1997:1:108].

The pun is impossible to translate because it depends on phonology. The two words *ghaḏā'i* "nutrition" and *qaḍā'i* "law," are pronounced the same in Persian.

قضائی = غذائی

i ' ḍ q   i ' āḏ gh ←

In modern Persian poetry, one also finds puns based on chance similarities between word skeletons. This type of punning is not as overt or conditioned by convention (see Kadkani 1971:326) as the medieval examples that appear at the beginning of the chapter. Modern readers have to be especially vigilant when looking for figures of script. But if they are anagrammatically inclined, they can find many puns. An obvious example comes in "The Iranian Spring," a poem by Esmāʿil Nuri ʿAlā' (1969:68) that catalogs fragrances. The skeleton سسر (see Chapter I) recurs in consecutive lines of the poem:

"The aroma of garlic" ʿaṭr-e sir عطر سیر
سسر
"The green aroma" ʿaṭr-e sabz عطر سبز

Less obvious is the figure of script in Nāder Nāderpur's poem (1969:18) "The Antimony of the Sun," because were it not for the first-person pronominal suffix م the pun would not work:

می سوختم چو هیزم تر در خویش
هسرم
دود به چشم بی هنرم می رفت

"As I burned like wet wood from within
The smoke would go into my artless eyes"

This line pairs the single word *hizom* ("wood") with the compound *honar-am* ("my art").

To Connect or not to Connect

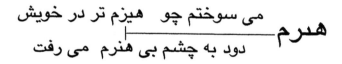

The strings of consonants and long vowels of Persian words often reach such lengths that they break under their own weight. While many conventions and rules govern these breaks, when to separate them is often a matter of taste. Some words look good broken, while others do not. By examining specific examples of these preferences, one can deduce an "aesthetics of connectivity."

Length seems to be decisive in determining whether or not to break. Most writers write the word *dāneshju* (literally "knowledge-seeker" or " college student"), for example, together and the word *dāneshpezhu* (literally "knowledge-delver" or "scholar") separately. Both words are composed of a noun and a verbal suffix, but one, written connected, is overly long and therefore breaks at the suffix, while the other, with noun and suffix connected, is the right size (Aḥmadi Givi 1994:72):

	less elegant	*elegant*
"student"	دانش جو	دانشجو
"scholar"	دانشپژوه	دانش پژوه

Another word that breaks at its suffix because it looks better is *tasalli bakhsh*, literally "solace-giving" (Aḥmadi Givi 1994:74):

less elegant	*elegant*
تسلیبخش	تسلی بخش

Related to length is the "tooth" factor. When the number of consecutive teeth, wave-like projections from the baseline, is five or more, according to one author (Neysāri1995:51), it is time to break. An "unbreakable" word is *naˤlband* (literally "shoe setter" or "horseshoer"):

	only two teeth
نعل بند	نعلبند

A word with the same suffix as *naˤlband* that because of its toothiness has to break in the middle is *ā'in bandi* (literally "decoration setting" or "adorning"):

too many teeth	*middle break*
آئیبندی	آئین بندی

A notable exception to this rule is the hyper-toothy, present subjunctive of the verb "to see" (infinitive = *didan* دیدن; non-past stem = *bin* بین), whose prefixes and suffixes are inseparable:

bebinand = "they may see"	*nabinand* = "they may not see"
ببینند	نبینند

unavoidable ugliness: too many unbreakable teeth

In Afghan and Iranian schools where dictation or *emlā* is "one of the most important and established" (Dāvodi 1997:5) parts of the Persian curriculum, students have to know when to break and when to join. Any juncture (*etteṣāl*) or break (*enfeṣāl*) that is "wrong" lowers a writer's grade by half a point (maximum number of points = 20). The criteria used to judge dictation are not aesthetic but grammatical. For example, the object marker *rā* is always to be written apart from the noun it marks no matter how short (Dāvodi 1997:52):

correct	*incorrect*
کتاب را ketāb-rā	کتابرا ketāb-rā
break	*no break*

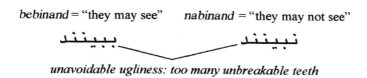

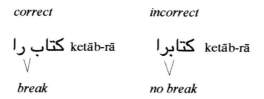

Rules governing how to write other elements are more complicated. The prefix *ham*, analogous to English "co-", is joined sometimes to the noun that follows it and separated from it at other times. When the prefix fronts a noun that maintains its original meaning in the new term, هم is written separately. For example, in *ham manzel* ("housemate") *manzel* "house" retains its lexical meaning in the هم phrase.

correct	*incorrect*
هم منزل	همنزل
V	V
break	*no break*

But when the noun does not maintain its identity in the new phrase, هم must be joined to it. For example, in *hamsāyeh* (literally "co-shadow" or "neighbor"), the dictionary meaning of *sāyeh* "shade, shadow" disappears in the compound word.

incorrect	*correct*
هم سایه	همسایه
V	V
break	*no break*

Not all هم phrases follow this rule, however. *Hamˁaqideh* is literally "co-opinion" or "in agreement." One can argue that the noun is both subsumed and not subsumed in the new phrase. For this reason a standard dictionary of Persian (Moˁin 1976) admits both the joined and the unjoined forms and modern Persian prose works use the joined form (e.g., Begdelu 2001:143).

correct	*correct*
هم عقیده	همعقیده
V	V
break	*no break*

This ambivalence about joining leads to unintended messages when هم phrases are transliterated into English. *Ham safar* or *hamsafar* literally "co-trip" or "travel companion" is the name of a bus company in Iran. The company has chosen to write the two elements separately in large letters on the sides of its buses:

break
/\
HAM SAFAR

a form that might lead some English readers to assume that pork is involved.

Romancing Writing

One can trace the magic in good penmanship to at least as far back as the second half of the thirteenth century when the collection of tales known as *The Arabian Nights* achieved written form. On the forty-eighth night (168-70; translation 105-06), Shahrzad is in the middle of narrating the story of the second dervish, whom a demon has turned into an ape. The demon deserts the ape on an island, but a merchant ship comes to its rescue. The merchants try to kill the ape but recognizing something human about it, the captain stops them. The ship reaches a great city where by chance the royal calligrapher has just died. Looking for a replacement, the king's herald asks the merchants on the ship to give samples of their writing on a long scroll. Before they can, the ape snatches the paper from the captain and produces excellent specimens of six basic Arabic hands. Judging merely on the evidence of his (at this point the ape becomes human so "its" no longer applies) calligraphy, the king awards a robe of honor to the primate and appoints him his scribe. In Arabic literature, a good hand reverses a demon's black magic, transforming an ape into a vizier.

To Persian-users, by contrast, the growth and development of calligraphy is an example of how native genius bloomed in Arabic dress. An Abbasid vizier associated with the codification with the six basic Arabic hands mentioned above was Abu ʿAli

Moḥammad b. Moqlah (d. 940). Ebn Moqlah, as he is commonly transliterated from Persian to English, is reported to be the first to standardize the shapes and sizes of Arabic letters with geometrical precision. He made the diamond-shaped dot ♦ formed by the tip of a beveled reed pen on paper the basic unit of penmanship. In Ebn Moqlah's system, the stature of *alef* is seven dots and the base of *ˁayn* is five dots wide, while its curved head is two dots high (Safadi 1987:17).

The early sources say Ebn Moqlah was born in Baghdad and give his full name as Abu ˁAli Moḥammad b. Ḥosayn b. ˁAbdallāh Baghdādi (quoted in LN). But later sources assert Ebn Moqlah's Persian roots by tracing his family to Beyḍā, a town in Fars province (Moṣāḥeb 1966), though this is not absolutely certain (*Dā'erat al-Maˁāref*). A book recently published in a series of works that make complicated subjects accessible to young readers Persianizes Ebn Moqlah even more. In *Khiālhā-ye Khaṭṭ Khaṭṭi* ("Illegible Dreams") not only does Ḥaqiqat (1999:86) say uneqivocally that he came from Iran, she replaces the al-Baghdādi ("the Baghdadian") element in the traditional form of Ebn Moqlah's name with al-Fāresi ("the Persian").

Chauvinists like Ḥaqiqat are proud to claim that the man reputed to be the founder of Arabic calligraphy was originally Iranian. The point also serves a larger thesis that many Persian writers support. They argue that the Arabs may have conquered Iran, changed its history, writing system and religion, but Iranians unlike the Syrians, Egyptians, Libyans, etc. did not succumb to Arabization, did not lose their heritage. Rather, not only did they

Persianize their Arab conquerors, they were among the principal architects of Islamic civilization (*The Persian Presence*). Holders of the essentialist view consider many of the major achievements of that civilization in art, music, literature, historiography, even religion, manifestations of an eternal Persian genius.

Romantic notions about calligraphy often appear in modern fiction about the Middle East. Authors that want to paint "authentic" pictures of traditional areas and cultures using local color embellish their stories with the Arabic alphabet. Ahdaf Soueif, an Egyptian novelist who writes in English, does this in *The Map of Love.* The novel is a family saga that alternates between colonial (1900-14) and contemporary (1997) Egypt. It begins when Amal al-Ghamrawi (1952-) discovers papers belonging to her grandmother, Anna al-Ghamrawi (neé Winterbourne, 1872-1933), in an old trunk (Soueif 1999:5). Among the papers are samples of Anna's *ruq'a* calligraphy, which is immediately recognizable because of the characteristic "'ya' tucked under its body."

normal yā	*tucked under yā*
ي	

Later in the novel readers look over Anna's shoulder as she practices her calligraphy, tracing "the cunning, curving letters: gliding with the stem of an 'alef' bursting into flower, following the tail of a 'ya' as it erupts into a spray of fireworks that scatter the text with diacritics" (Soueif 1999:80-1).

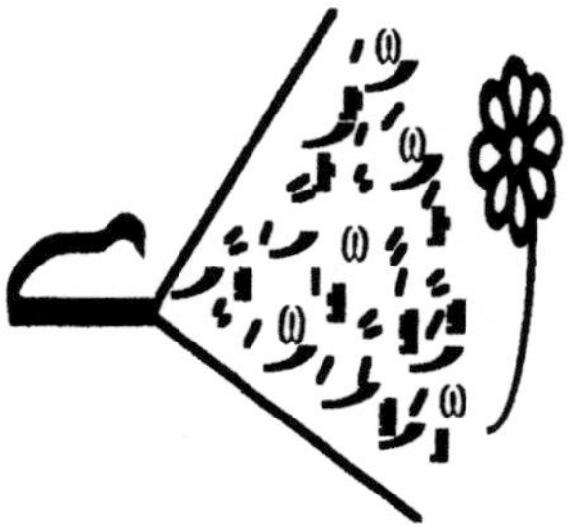

flowering alef with yā as vowel marks and other diacritics burst from its tail

In Soueif's novel Arabic letters assume magical properties. Calligraphy has the power to beautify the ugly. Through the alchemy of Arabic literacy an Englishwoman, the embodiment of colonial power, transforms into a proper spouse for the scion of an aristocratic Egyptian family. As her command of various words for "love" in Arabic grows, so does her affection for her husband and his affection for her (Soueif 1999:386-87). Like the ape in *The Arabian Nights*, Anna evolves from a repulsive figure into a human by learning to write Arabic.

Sohrāb Sepehri's experience as an aspiring calligrapher also speaks of the iconic nature of letters in the Persian tradition. Elegant writing is decorative, not meant to be read and processed like ordinary written communication. Rather than conveying messages, calligraphy acts like a painting or, as a sample of fine Persian handwriting in an ornate frame is called, a "tableau." Like the poetic figures of script mentioned at the outset of this chapter, these tableaus are appreciated not for what they say (often well-known sayings taken from the Qoran or the works of classical Persian poets or "mere" letters and ligatures) but for the artistry of their expression. The exclamations of the master calligrapher in "Illegible Dreams" are typical of reactions to fine pieces of calligraphy displayed in a museum: "Notice...the proportionality of these letters, the uniform loops, the clarity of the extenders, the control of the hand—how could someone actually write like that!" (Ḥaqiqat 1999:21). Never does it occur to the calligrapher to read the literal meaning of the pieces at the exhibition. Nor does he dream of exchanging the Arabic letters for European ones.

Chapter V

Naming and Interrogation

Persian *Yous*

Like French, German, and Spanish, Persian is a "double-you" language. *Shomā* شما is the formal, distancing, polite, and plural *you.* The familiar, endearing, and singular *you* used to address intimates, children, servants, pets, political prisoners, other inferiors is *to* (تو ; although this word appears to be voweled long u, as if it were تُو , it is the consonant with a short vowel تُ). Under normal circumstances people who are not acquainted use *shomā* until their relationships become less formal. However, children may call their elders *shomā* out of respect no matter how close they are; likewise, elders can use *to* no matter how old their "juniors" become.

The brutality of a deliberate تو in place of a polite شما is clear from the prison memoirs of Shahrnush Pārsipur. The writer first went to prison during the Pahlavi era in 1974, and was also a prisoner under the Islamic Republic for four years in the mid-1980s (*Stories* 1991:483). In this work, Pārsipur recalls her interrogation by the Pahlavi state security apparatus known as SAVAK (*sāzmān-e eṭṭelāʕāt va amniat-e keshvar*):

سـازمـان اطـلاعـات و امـنـيـت كـشـور

r v sh **K** t i n m **A V** t ā ʕ ā l ṭṭ **A** nā mz ā **S** ←

Pārsipur had just finished her first novel, in which she tried to address the problem of the Left in Iran and, at the same time, avoid government censorship. Since her arrest coincided with the finishing of the manuscript, she thought that the book was the cause. But this was not the case; Pārsipur went to jail for her political views. She also imagined SAVAK agents to be human, though her boss, managing director of National Iranian Television Reẓā Qoṭbi, tried to disabuse her of the idea. In any case, she soon learned that the etiquette of interrogation was not customary Persian politeness (*taʿārof,* see Chapter II).

While she resented her arrest, what galled Pārsipur most was the interrogator's use of the intimate *you*. Since they had just met, *taʿārof* required a formal شما. The bald تو shocked her. This breach of politeness opened the gate to another indignity: the insinuation of intimacy with a noted dissident. An unjust arrest paled in contrast to the deliberate use of the wrong pronoun.

The following excerpt from Pārsipur's prison memoirs (1996:21-22) illustrates the use of most Persian pronouns. It also shows how speakers can use the pronominal system to express respect or disdain for those whom they address. Illustrative pronouns and pronominal suffixes are outlined the first time they appear in the passage, glossed in the margins, and italicized in the translation.

کتاب در آخر تابستان به پایان رسید. با یك ماشین
تحریر کوچك دستی آن را در پنج نسخه ماشین کردم. دو
نسخهٔ آن را برای مطالعه به دو نفر از دوستان دادم. بعد
یك روز در مهر ماه ۱۳۵۳ (۱۹۷٤) سه نفر از اعضای
ساواك ... به خانهٔ ما آمدند. به خاطر می آوردم که در — our
هنگام گفتنگو با مهندس قطبی، هنگامی که ایشان گفته — they meaning he
بود مرا بازداشت خواهند کرد، گفته بودم «اشکالی ندارد — me
و من بسیار خوشحال خواهم شد تا با اعضای ساواك — I
حرف بزنم. باید با آن ها بحث کرد و اشتباهاتشان — their

متذکر شد.» مهندس قطبی پاسخ داده بود که در اشتباه هستم و اعضای این سازمان به طور کلی حالت آدمیزاد را ندارند تا بشود با آن ها حرف زد...

صبح بود و صبحانه می خوردم تا بعد به کلاس فرانسه
بروم. خودم دررا گشودم. مردان به داخل آمدند و یکی my
از آن ها کارتی به من نشان داد و سپس سلاح و
دستبندش را نیز به نمایش گذاشت و گفت اگر مقاومت his
کنم وضع بدی پیش خواهم آمد. با او دست دادم و مرد him
به شدت یکّه خورد. گفت باید خانه را بگردند. آن هارا راهنمایی کردم و خانه مورد بازدید قرار گرفت. نسخه های ماشین شدهٔ «سگ و زمستان بلند» توقیف شد و من دیگر هرگز آن هارا ندیدم. چیز دیگری در خانه نبود که
جلب توجه آن ها را بکند و ما به سوی اتومبیل..راه their
افتادیم.

مرا پیاده کردند و به یك ساختمان یك طبقه بردند. در اتاقی را گشودند و وارد شدم. دو یا سه مرد در اتاق بودند. یکی از آن ها که احتمالاً پرویزی نام داشت با
حالتی خشن و به تندی از من پرسید، «ما برای چه ترا we
دستگیر کردیم؟ یاالله! زود بگو!»

از لحن او یکّه خورده بودم. به ویژه که بدون دلیل مرا
«تو» خطاب می کرد. گفتم، «فکر می کنم به این دلیل که you fam.
از محل کارم استعفا داده ام.»

با خشونت پرسید، «برای چه استعفا دادی؟»

گفتم، «به اعدام خسرو گلسرخی و کرامت الله دانشیان

اعتراض دارم.»

گفت، «عجب! عاشق گلسرخی هستی؟ می خواهی ترا you fam. obj.

در همان سلولی بیندازم که او در آنجا بود؟» he

گفتم، «من عاشق هیچکس نیستم و کمونیست هم نیستم. فقط اینطور به نظرم می رسد که این اعدام ها ظالمانه بوده اند.»

اکنون مرا روی یك صندلی نشانده بودند و او در آنسوی میز، پشت میز قرار داشت. دستش را به صورت مشت کرده به طرف من آورد و آن را روی بینی ام قرار داد. گفت، «ببین! داری عصبانیم می کنی. یك

کاری نکن که دماغت را لِه کنم.» به شدت یکّه خورده your fam.

بودم. تمام مدت مؤدّب صحبت می کردم و به هیچ عنوان حالت ستیزه جویی نداشتم. با این حال مرد در هر پاسخ و پرسشی می کوشید یا مرا تحقیر کند یا بترساند. ...

پرسیدم، «ببخشید، من که مؤدّب هستم، چرا مرا "تو" خطاب می کنید؟»

گفت، « من به خدا هم "تو" می گویم.»

The book was finished by the end of summer. I typed it in five copies on a small portable. I gave two copies of it to friends to read. Later, one day in the fall of 1974, three SAVAK agents came to *our* house. I remembered that during a conversation I had had with Mohandes [engineer] Qoṭbi, when *he* said they were going to arrest *me*, I answered, 'It makes no difference; *I* will be very happy to speak with members of SAVAK. One must debate them and point out their mistakes.' Qoṭbi then said that I was mistaken, for members of SAVAK are generally not human enough to hold a conversation....

It was morning and I was having breakfast before going to French class. I opened the door *my*self. The men came into the room and one of them showed me a card and then put *his* weapon and handcuffs on display and told me that if I resisted, there would be trouble. I gave *him* my hands, which startled the man. He told me that he had to search the house. I showed them around, and the house was subjected to scrutiny. The typescripts of 'The Dog and the Long Winter' were confiscated, and I never saw them again. Nothing else in the house attracted *their* attention, so we went to the car. ...

They dropped me off and brought me to a one-story building. They opened the door to a room and I entered. There were two or three men in the room. One of them, whose name may have been Parvizi, seemed fierce and asked me sharply, 'Why have *we* arrested you?' Come on! Out with it, quickly!'

I was startled by his tone, especially since for no reason he was addressing me as '*you*' [fam.]. I said, 'I think it was because I resigned from my job.'

Savagely he asked, 'Why did you resign?'

I said, 'I object to the executions of Khosrow Golsorkhi and Karāmatallāh Dāneshiān.'

He said, 'Is that so! Are you Golsorkhi's lover? Do *you* want me to put you in the cell that *he* was in?'

I said, 'I am nobody's lover, nor am I a Communist. It is just that these executions seemed despotic in *my* view.'

Now they sat me in a chair, and he was on other side of the table. He made a fist and held it over my nose, saying, 'Look! You are starting to get on my nerves. Don't do anything that'll make me smash *your* face in.' I was floored; the whole time I spoke politely and never became confrontational. Despite that, with each answer and question the man was trying either to demean or terrify me....I asked, 'I beg your pardon. I have always been

polite, so why are you calling me "you [fam.]"?'
He said, 'I also use "you" when I talk to God.'

The passage shows that pronouns can either stand alone or attach to other words. It also shows that Persian, like English, has three "persons" and both singular and plural forms of pronouns.

plural	*singular*	
mā ما *we*	man من *I*	1
shomā شما *you*	to تو *you*	2
ānhā ishān ایشان/ آن ها *they*	u او *he, she, it*	3

For reasons explained in the next chapter, Pārsipur rarely uses the first person singular *man* explicitly. Most of the time readers know the subject of verbs from the way they end, but at one point she writes (completely transliterated and literally translated):

من بسیار خوشحال خواهم شد

dosh mahā ^{v}kh l ā ḥ sh o kh rā y s eb nam ←
become will happy very I

Here she uses the pronoun to emphasize her willingness to speak to SAVAK: meaning, "*I, for one, shall* be very happy..." Pārsipur's writing uses familiar *you* often, as it is the focus of the passage, but there is only one example of the third person singular in it. When the interrogator suggests that Pārsipur occupy the same cell that her "lover" did, the pronoun *u* insinuates intimacy:

که او در آنجا بود

d ub ā j nā rad u hek

was there in he that ←

The interrogator's use of the first person plural pronoun *mā* is very instructive. Trying to get his prisoner to incriminate herself, he asks:

ما برای چه ترا دستگیر کردیم

m idrak r i g t sad ārot hech eyārab ām

arrested you what for we ←

Presumably the SAVAK agents knew why they took Pārsipur, but the question with familiar *you* as the object of "arrested" throws Pārsipur off guard and she opens roads to further interrogation. The sentence also shows how pronouns become direct objects in Persian. The basic rule is to add the object marker *rā* to the independent pronoun:

plural	*singular*	
mā-rā مارا *us*	man-rā ma-rā من را/مرا *me*	1
shomā-rā شمار *you*	to-rā تو را/ترا *you*	2
ānhā-rā آن هارا *them*	u-rā اورا *him, her, it*	3

As the chart shows, there are two ways of writing *me* and *you* (familiar) in Persian; مرا and ترا take up less space than من را and تورا respectively.

The passage also contains pronouns that fasten to other words to express personal possession. In the phrase "our house," ***khāneh*** and *mā* are joined with a universal connector (*-e*/*-eh*) called in Persian *eḍāfeh*. Though raised *hamzeh* ء marks the juncture in this case, in most cases it is not indicated:

juncture

به خا نـــهٔ مـا آ مـدنـد

dnadam ā ām ey-he n ā kh heb ←

they came our house to

Another way to indicate possession in Persian is to use six pronominal suffixes that correspond to the six independent pronouns:

plural	*singular*	
-im ـمان— *our*	-am ـم— *my*	1
-etān ـتان— *your*	-at ـت— *your*	2
-eshān ـشان— *their*	-ash ـش— *his, her, its*	3

Two examples. Referring to past wrongs committed by SAVAK, Pārsipur joins the suffix meaning "their" to "errors":

their *errors*

ا شـتـبـا هـا تـشـا ن

n ā sh et ā h ā b et sh e ←

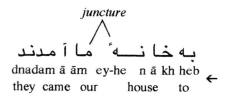

When the SAVAK interrogator menaces Pārsipur's face with his fist, he suffixes the insulting singular *-at* to the dehumanizing "snout":

your *snout*

دماغت

t a gh ā ma d←

We have seen how the interrogator tries to degrade Pārsipur with an improper *to*. The passage also contains examples of how the right pronoun can do the opposite: elevate or esteem the person addressed. At one point Pārsipur refers to her boss with a plural pronoun "they," *ishān*, when logic demands the use of the singular. Reporting how he warned of her impending arrest, she writes:

ایشان گفته بود

d u b het f og n ā sh i
had said (he) they ←

The plural pronoun comes in deference to her boss, while the verb agrees with its singular, logical subject.

God as تو

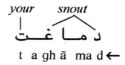

At the end of the passage, as if to excuse his calculated insults, Pārsipur's interrogator explains that he addresses God as *to*. Heartfelt or not, the statement reveals how intimate the pronoun can be in Persian. A celebrated example of this use of *to* comes in the first grade Persian textbook used in Iran (*Fārsi-e Avval-e Dabestān* 2001:88). Immediately after mastering the alphabet, the children meet a reading that also speaks to God in the second person singular (the text is partially voweled for the benefit of young readers):

ای خدای مهربان که برای ما همه چیز آفریده ای؛
i he d i rafā z i chhemah ām eyārab hek n ābar hem eyādokh ye ←
created thing all us for who kind God O

ما همیشه تو را می پرستیم
m i t s arap i m ār ot he sh i mah ā m ←
worship you always we

Or: "O benevolent God, [*you* fam.] who have created all things for us, we [will] always worship you [fam.]."

Vital Statistics, *Politely*

Maḥmud E^ʕtemādzādeh (1914?-2002), pen-named Behāḏin, was an author who also went to jail for his politics both before the Islamic Revolution and after it. Before the Revolution, SAVAK arrested him for signing a petition protesting the arrest of a fellow writer. The following excerpt from his prison memoirs (Behāḏin 1970:31), "The Guest of these Men," describes his first interrogation. We see from it that Behāḏin fared better than Pārsipur, as the interrogator consistently uses respectful *shomā* instead of intimidating *to* throughout his interrogation. Besides showing that SAVAK agents were capable of civility, the passage is instructive because the interrogator asks about Behāḏin and his family in a very direct way. In the following, polite pronominal and verb forms are outlined, glossed in the margins, and italicized in translation.

اسم؟ پدر، مادر، برادر، خواهر؟ زن دارید؟ (2nd plural verb)

فرزند؟ پسر، دختر؟ کجا هستند، چه کار می کنند؟

(2nd plural suffix) پسرتان گفتید دانشجوی پزشکی است؟ کجا، تهران؟ –

نه، مسکو. لابد دانشگاه لومومبا؟ – بله. شما (you formal)

فرستادیدش؟ – من فرستادمش آلمان، پس از چند ماهی

خودش اقدام کرد و توانست برود. شغلتان؟ (2nd plural suffix)

Name? Father, mother, brother, sister? Are *you* married? Children? Son, daughter? Where are they, what do they do? *Your* son, you said, is a medical student? Where, Tehran?—No, Moscow. Lumumba University, no doubt?— Yes. Did *you* send him?—I sent him to Germany; several months later he acted on his own and was able to go. *Your* profession?

The interrogator's abrupt questions use the basic vocabulary of family relationships. From some of these terms, one can immediately see that Persian and English are also related. "Father" is *pedar*, "mother" *mādar*, "brother" *barādar*, and "daughter" *dokhtar*. Two relative words mentioned in the passage do not seem to have English cognates: *pesar* "son" and *farzand* "child." The following diagrams the words in the passage to show family relationships in Persian; in the diagram, political prisoner Behāḏin occupies a double rectangle in the center and his close relatives radiate from it.

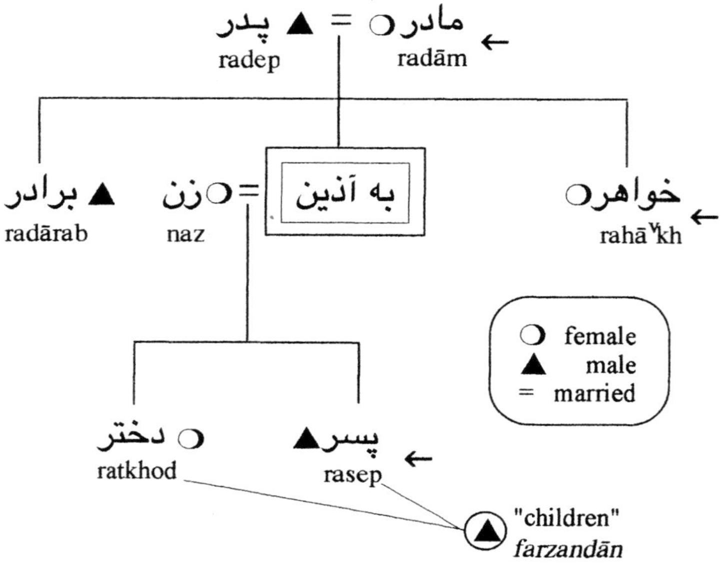

The nouns and pronouns introduced in this chapter—some under duress—tell only part of the story of naming in Persian. Even so, certain patterns, which the next chapter explores in greater detail, are clear. Using singular forms when etiquette calls for plurals insults, and, conversely, using plurals when logic demands the singular esteems. The reason for this is that Persian like German, French, Spanish, etc. has several ways of identifying others. Another feature of the language found in the passages is that Persian, unlike English, prefers to omit subject pronouns—especially the first person singular. This is both because verb endings reveal who does what in sentences and because humility discourages the use of "I."

Chapter VI

Humility

Avoiding من and شما

Chapter II used the word *qorbān* (literally "sacrifice") and the phrase *qorbān-e shomā* ("your sacrifice") to introduce the complex system of politeness in Persian called *taʿārof*. This system is comparable to modes of expression in other languages that mark levels of formality. When translated literally into English, these expressions often seem archaic or servile, but they are sometimes necessary for using Persian adroitly. Practitioners of *taʿārof* generally avoid referring to themselves as *man* or "I." They likewise refrain from referring to those whom they are addressing as *shomā*, merely "you." Instead, they use certain words and phrases as pronouns that are politely self-effacing (similar to archaic the English "your humble servant" for "me" and "your honor" or "your excellency" for "you"). Three first-person self-effacers are:

بنده　　　　نوکر　　　　چاکر

Bandeh is literally "one who is bound" or "slave"; *nowkar* and *chāker* mean roughly the same thing: "servant." Speakers use these nouns-turned-pronouns when they choose to humble themselves and thereby esteem those with whom they converse. In doing so, they enter a verbal servitude that characterizes humility in Persian.

In addition to *qorbān*, the terms most commonly used to esteem or elevate those one addresses are:

جنابعالی   حضرتعالی

Virtually synonyms, *ḥaḍrat-e ˁāli* and *janābˁāli* convey the English honorifics "your excellency" or "respected sir." Some users eschew the self-effacers and the honorifics, though they certainly hear them in polite conversation and encounter them in writing. In fact, in modern Persian, speakers often introduce candid statements with *bedun-e taˁārof*:

politeness without

← بدون تعارف

Or: "All *taˁārof* aside." Be that as it may, to understand Persian well one needs to know how and when to be polite.

The following excerpt from Esmāˁil Faṣiḥ's novel "Soraya in a Coma" (1983:3) contains many of the *taˁārof* nouns introduced above as well as a verb that goes with them. It is a conversation between the narrator and an older man named Soheyli. The two are on a bus from Tehran to Istanbul towards the end of fall 1980, when Iran and Iraq were at war. Soheyli begins the conversation by mentioning the possibility of an Iraqi air raid. All polite expressions are outlined in the Persian excerpt and italicized in translation.

«وضعیت قرمز!»

«بله»

3 «فکر نکنم برنند، جناب؟ نظر حضرتعالی چیه؟»

«من که چیزی روی آسمان صاف نمی بینم.»

«حتماً چیزی روی رادارهاشون دیدند؟»

«لابد.»

«یا شاید یك شیء مشکوك گزارش شده.»

می پرسم: «بار و بندیلتان تمام شد؟»

9 «بله. جنابعالی هم با "بی بی تی" به اروپا تشریف

10 می برید؟»

«با اتوبوس تا استانبول.»

"Red Alert!"

"Yes."

"Don't think they'll strike, *excellency*? What is *your honor's* view?"

"Me, I don't see a thing in the clear sky."

"Must be something they saw on their radar?"

"No doubt."

"Or, maybe, something suspicious was reported."

I ask, "They finish loading your things?"

"Yes. Is *your excellency* also *traveling* TBT [bus company] to Europe?"

"By bus to Istanbul."

Soheyli begins the conversation politely, using *ḥaḍrat-e ʿāli* (line 3) and *janābʿāli* (line 9) to address his traveling companion. He also uses an polite way to express "to go" or "to travel": *tashrif bordan.* This expression is a compound verb that literally means "to carry that which honors by its presence (i.e. the being of the person one addresses)":

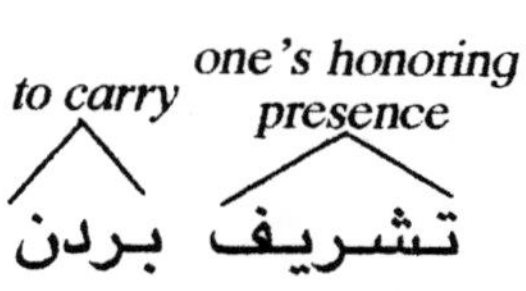

This phrase entered English recently when the Anglo-Indian writer Vikram Seth has one of his characters speak in courtly Urdu: "you have just brought your presence" (1993:120).

The verb *tashrif bordan* is usually found in the second (lines 9-10) and third person plural:

2 تشریف می برید

3 تشریف می برند

Meaning respectfully, "You (plural or polite) are going" and "they (plural or he, she polite) are going." To be ironically self-esteeming, one could use the first-person singular, saying *tashrif mi-baram* or "I am bearing my esteemed presence."

Two other important parts of the *taʕārof* system are the verbs *ʕarḍ kardan* and *farmudan*. Both convey "to utter," but *ʕarḍ kardan* humbles what is said, while *farmudan* ennobles it. The two verbs appear (in past tense) contrastively in the following excerpt from the memoirs of Ayatollah Khalkhāli (2001:291). Khalkhāli, the cleric Ayatollah (Imam) Khomeini put in charge of judging the previous regime's political figures, sentenced many to death during the early days of the Revolution. According to this part of his memoirs, Khalkhāli was not sure he was the man for the job. As in the case of the previous excerpt, polite forms are outlined in Persian and italicized in translation.

1 عرض کردم : متشکرم؛ اما این کار خون دارد و بسیار
سنگین است.
3 حضرت امام فرمود : برای شما سنگین نیست، من
4 حامی شما هستم.

[Khalkhāli]: I *submitted*, "I am grateful, but this job will involve blood and is very burdensome."

His Excellency the Imam *opined*, "For you it is not

burdensome; I am behind you."

By using *ˁarḍ kardam* (line 1), Khalkhāli makes his misgivings about taking on the role of judge a "submission," which in turn dignifies Khomeini's reassuring "opining." The Imam's words are not merely "said" but *farmud* (line 3), literally "decreed." Because of the humble role it plays in politeness, *ˁarḍ kardan* is rarely used in the second person plural; likewise *farmudan* is almost never encountered in the first person singular. In fact, it was not uncommon in Iran for people to joke that only the Emperor himself could say من می فرمایم *man mi-farmāyam* ≈ "I *firman*."

Pronouns also show the lines and direction of politeness in the passage. Khalkhāli addresses Khomeini as *ḥaḍrat*, (line 3), while the Imam simply calls him *shomā* (line 4). The honor flows toward Khomeini. Based on the polite usage introduced in this chapter, one can rewrite the pronoun chart found in the last:

3 او	2 شما	1 من
ایشان *ishān*	قربان *qorbān*	بنده *bandeh*
	حضرت *ḥaḏrat*	نوکر *nowkar*
	حضرتعالی *ḥaḏratˁāli*	چاکر *chāker*
	جنابعالی *janābˁāli*	

Grammaticalization

Of course the polite words in the chart are not, technically speaking, pronouns. They are nouns that became pronouns because social convention required it. The pronominalization of nouns also happens in other languages for the same sociolinguistic reasons it occurs in Persian. Linguists call when one grammatical category becomes another "grammaticalization." In a work on the subject, Heine (1991:35) writes

> the Chinese loanword *boku* 'slave' is said to have developed into a first-person pronoun 'I'; and, in a similar way, the Indonesian pronoun *saya* 'I' derives from a literate noun *sahaya* 'servant.' Furthermore, Old Japanese *kimi* 'lord' has been grammaticalized to a second-person pronoun, 'you' (hon.), and finally to 'thou.'

When one compares the Japanese words Heine mentions to polite Persian pronouns, the similarity between the two languages becomes apparent. Japanese *boku* is analogous to Persian بنده, while Japanese *kimi* is analogous to Persian حضرتعالی. All four terms survived as pronouns long after the ancient societies that gave birth to them as nouns had vanished.

grammaticalization

بنده ≈ 僕 *boku*: "slave," "servant" ⟶ "I"

حضرتعالی ≈ 貴君 *kimi*: "master," "lord" ⟶ "you"

One can take the parallels between Persian and Japanese to mean that they preserve ancient speech traditions. English, a relatively new language, sheds archaisms more readily. When teaching Persian to English-language students one needs to make them aware of the antiquity and durability of the culture they enter through language.

Humility that Insults

The passages in this chapter suggest that *taʿārof* lies along a graded scale. On one end is an informality that can be impolite; on the other is a humility that is required when speaking to elders or those in positions of authority. In between is polite neutrality.

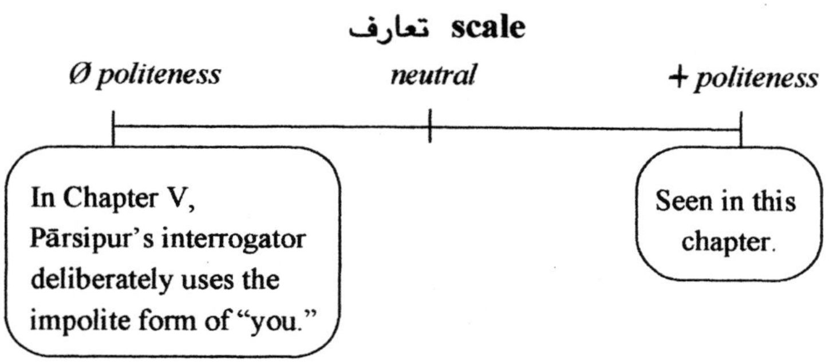
تعارف scale
Ø politeness
neutral
+ politeness
In Chapter V, Pārsipur's interrogator deliberately uses the impolite form of "you."
Seen in this chapter.

The impoliteness that Pārsipur's interrogator used to throw her off guard (Chapter V) is not the only way to wound in Persian. Speakers can also extend the genteel end of the *taʿārof* scale so far that they insult by being excessively humble. The third passage in this chapter sits on the fawning extremity of the scale. It is from Ebrāhim Golestān's "The Secrets of the Treasure of the Hexed Valley" (1994: 278), a lampoon of life in late Pahlavi Iran. In the novel, a poor farmer accidentally finds a vast burial chamber filled with precious objects from an ancient civilization. He hacks off bits of gold and silver from the mother trove and sells them to become wealthy and powerful. Naturally, the farmer assumes he can buy everyone and everything.

In the excerpt, the farmer addresses an artist he has hired to paint his wedding portrait. The artist, resentful of the farmer's sudden wealth and power, decides to caricature him. Accordingly, he pushes conversational تعارف so far in the direction of servility that he is actually insulting; but his patron, blinded by rusticity and immeasurable wealth, sees only the artist's abject humility.

مرد اکنون به قهقهه میخندید. ازاینکه روی پرده نقش خانه نوساز و کوه و دشت تمام است و هیکل و لباس نوعروس و خودش هم درست کشیده ست اما در روی گردی صورت ها از چشم و از دهان و ابرو و بینی اثر به کلی نیست میخندید. از نقاش پرسید «یعنی این منم؟ پس کو چشام؟ دهن ندارم؟»

نقاش به تواضع گفت «اختیار دارین. حضرت عالی تمام دهنین.»

The man was laughing hard now, laughing because on the canvas the newly-built home, the mountain, the plain were all complete, and his new bride's form and his own, their clothes, were all drawn correctly; but in the roundness of the faces there was not the slightest trace of eye, mouth, eyebrow, nose. He asked the painter, "You mean, this is me? So where're my eyes? I got no mouth?"

The painter *humbly* said, "*You are entitled to your opinion, your excellency* is all mouth."

In this passage, the painter does not merely answer the man's question, he responds *be tavāḍo*ˁ (line 7):

humility *with*

← به تواضع

Likewise, he does not meet the patron's objection to the faceless portraits he has drawn directly. Instead, he demurs with a civil expression that literally means "you have the preference" (*ekhtiār dārid*, line 7):

you have preference
اختیار دارید ←

Later in the novel, Golestān (1994:287) identifies three basic elements in the painter's false humility: *ḥojb* "modesty," *ḥormat* "face," and *adab* "manners." The three words neatly circumscribe *ta*ˁ*ārof*.

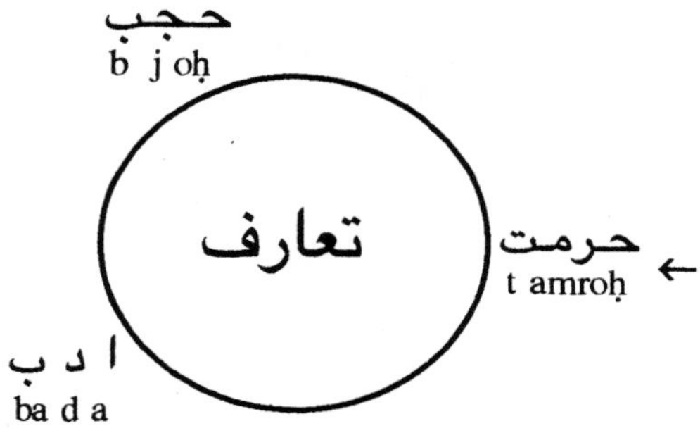

The painter's insulting humility takes the elements to their socially proscribed extremes. Modesty becomes "groveling," face "vanity," and manners "insufferable civility."

Persian learners often find themselves in the same position as the farmer, unable to tell when to take humility seriously or when to dismiss it simply as good manners or when to react to it as pointed irony. They do not know, for example, when to accept a dinner invitation as genuine or when to politely decline what is actually an expression of *ta*ˁ*ārof*. This is the mark of a very rich point in any language.

Chapter VII

Marriage and Mating

Prenuptial and Verbal Agreement

Chapter II introduced *ṣigheh* as a word that uses the letters ص and غ and as a way of broaching the topic of temporary marriage. Needless to say, صیغه گیری (*ṣigheh-giri*, literally "taking a *ṣigheh*") is not the most customary form of mating in Persian. This chapter is about a far more common union that joins a man and a woman in permanent matrimony called *ezdevāj* ازدواج (generally) or *nekāḥ* نکاح (in legal parlance). Like the temporary union, *ezdevāj* involves a ceremony of some kind and a dowry. Marriageable people are desirable because of family wealth and/or social, political and religious status. Highly desirable females choose among many suitors, called *kh*[v]*āstgārān* (outlined on line 3 of the first passage in this chapter). Go-betweens (usually relatives) approach prospective brides and grooms to arrange meetings.

The first excerpt in this chapter presents a picture of courtship (*kh*[v]*āstgāri*) in Persian. It is from the prose of the poet Simin Behbahāni (b. 1927) and may reflect her own marital experiences. In 1944, when she first came on the market, Behbahāni's value as a bride was high. Her father, Abbas Khalili, was a noted author and translator, and her mother, Fakhri Arghun, came from a privileged family that gave their daughter a broad education, including instruction in French from a Swiss governess (Behbahāni 1999:xviii-xix). After her association with the Iranian Communist (Tudeh) Party cut Behbahāni's early academic career short, she became resigned to marriage, and, as soon as she became available, many suitors appeared. This excerpt from Behbahāni's fiction (1996:27-28) shows the role of.the paternal side of the family in instigating marriage.

من هم بزرگ شده ام، شکفته ام. زن عمو خریدارانه نگاهم می کند. خان عمو می گوید عقد دختر عمو و پسر عمو در آسمان بسته شده....من خواستگاران فراوان دارم. همین دو ماه پیش چندتا خانم شیک پوش آمدند و رفتند و خبر دادند که پسندیده اند. پدرم می گوید: این یکی هفتاد پارچه آبادی در اطراف شیراز دارد، ثروتش حساب ندارد، ماشینش را هر سال عوض می کند، راننده اش لباس مخصوص می پوشد و خانهٔ تهرانش به قصر شبیه است و خانهٔ شیرازش به موزه.

> I have also grown up, have blossomed. Auntie looks at me like a buyer. My worthy uncle says that the match of a niece and her first cousin is made in heaven...I have a bunch of *suitors*. Just these past two months, several well-dressed women came, went, and indicated that they have approved. My father says: This one has seventy developed tracts of land around Shiraz; his wealth has no limit. He replaces his automobile every year, his driver wears special clothes, and his Tehran residence is like a palace, while the one in Shiraz is like a museum.

In this passage, the father's side of the family begins the prenuptials. The wife (*zan,* line 1) of the narrator's paternal uncle (*ˁamu*, line 2) appraises her newly ripened niece as though she were fruit about to go to market, while the uncle repeats standard wisdom about first-cousin marriage. The narrator's father offers more practical advice. The lady emissaries from the *kh*^{v}*āstgār*'s side are fashionably dressed (*shikpush*, line 4: French *chic* mated to Persian پوش "dress").

Behbahāni's prose is also instructive because it shows how a variety of tenses coexist in one Persian paragraph. The writing begins in the present perfect (often called *māḍi naqli* in Persian grammars): *man ham bozorg shodeh-am*

have become big also I ←
من هم بزرگ شده ام

As in English, this indicates something that *has happened* recently. The next verb, *shekofteh-am* ("I have blossomed"), is also present perfect for the same reason. With subsequent verbs, the passage leaves the perfect and enters the present, or, more accurately, the non-past (*moḍāre*ˤ مضارع in Persian terminology). The non-past indicates a habitual, on-going, or future action. The aunt *looks* or *is looking* at the narrator (*zan-e* ˤ*amu kharidārāneh negāh-am mi-konad*, lines 1-2):

is looking — at me — like a buyer — uncle wife ←
زن عمو خریدارانه نگاهم می کند

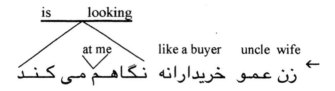

Here the object of the verb, "me," has been suffixed to the non-conjugated element of the compound verb *negāh kardan*. Other non-past forms include: *mi-guyad* ("he says," lines 2, 5); *dāram* ("I have," line 3); ˤ*avaḍ mi-konad* ("he replaces," line 7); *mi-pushad* ("he wears," line 8). Finally, the well-dressed emissaries from the groom's side operate first in the simple past (*goḏashteh* in grammatical terms): they *āmadand* ("came," line 4) , *raftand* ("went," line 4), *khabar dādand* ("informed, indicated" line 5), and, second, when they give their collective opinion of the prospective bride, in the present perfect: *pasandideh-and* ("they have approved," line 5).

The verbs in the passage suggest certain patterns. First, most of the non-past verbs share the prefix *mi-*, which marks an on-going action. Second, regardless of tense, the verbs often end in predictable ways: *-am, -d, -and*. With this information and what was said about the verbs already introduced in the book, one can write out paradigms for the past, present perfect, and non-past. Each Persian verb has two stems that are conjugated: the infinitive (the form listed in dictionaries) and the non-past stem. Infinitives and non-past stems usually differ to such an extent that learners must memorize them as separate entries in the lexicon. Take, for example, *kardan* ("do, make, perform"), the conjugated element in the compound *negāh kardan* (literally "to do looking"):

infinitive
کردن

No ن ↓

past		*non-past*
کرد kard		کن kon
کردم kard**am**	*I*	می کنم mi-kon**am**
کردی kard**i**	*you* (sing.)	می کنی mi-kon**i**
کرد kard	*he, she, it*	می کند mi-kon**ad**
کردیم kard**im**	*we*	می کنیم mi-kon**im**
کردید kard**id**	*you*	می کنید mi-kon**id**
کردند kard**and**	*they*	می کنند mi-kon**and**

Forming the past tense is quite simple: take the ن from any infinitive and apply the endings: *-am, -i, -Ø, -im, -id, -and.* The non-past is trickier because the stem is not predictable from the infinitive; but once known, one merely adds endings to it that, except for the third person singular, are identical to the past endings, namely: *-am, -i, -ad, -im, -id, -and.*

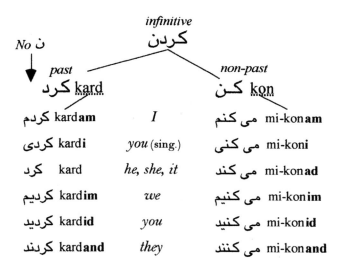

The present perfect ("have blossomed," "have done," etc.) is also easy in Persian. It follows the pattern of the past, starting with the ن-less infinitive. Suffixed to this form is *-eh*, ـه , which marks the past participle. To conjugate one adds a euphonious *alef* and all but one (again, 3rd sing. is exceptional) of the usual endings. For example, "to blossom" is *shekoftan*; "blossomed" is thus *shekofteh*. "I have blossomed" is *shekofteh* + *am*; "you [sing.] have blossomed" is *shekofteh* + *i*; "he, she, it has blossomed" is *shekofteh* + *ast*,; "we have blossomed" is *shekofteh* + *im;* "you [pl.] have blossomed" is *shekofteh* + *id*; and "they have blossomed" is *shekofteh* + *and*:

Present Perfect ماضی نقلی

past stem

past participle — *infinitive*

شکفته ← شکفت ← شکفتن

+ ه ن –

شکفته ام	شکفته ایم
شکفته ای	شکفته اید
شکفته است	شکفته اند

Marriage in Legal Persian

The Family Laws of Iran are good sources of Persian on mating and marriage. Couched in Arabic terminology, these laws exemplify the history in the alphabet introduced in Chapter II. Though they have changed somewhat since the Islamic Revolution, the laws articulate expectations that many users of the language bring to marriage. The first three reflect three important pre-marital considerations: 1) the age of the bride and groom, 2) their religion, and 3) the *mahr* or *mahrieh*, the "bride price." Important Arabic expressions in the laws are outlined.

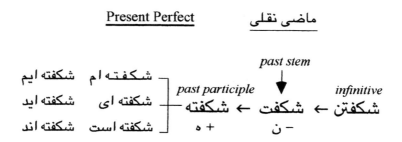

نکاحِ اناث قبل از ۱۵ سالِ تمام و نکاحِ ذکور قبل از
رسیدن به سنِّ ۱۸ سالِ تمام ممنوع است.

1. The *marriage of females* before completing 15 years of age and the *marriage of males* before completing 18 years of age is forbidden [Naqavi 1971:210].

The Arabic terms for females, *enāth* (Hebrew אנש, "to be weak" Klein 1987:42), and males, *ḏokur* (Hebrew זכור), tie these modern laws to their Semitic origins. To understand Law 1 one has to know the term for marriage mentioned at the beginning of this chapter: *nekāḥ*, which in Arabic is unidirectional, i.e. "to marry a woman," but in Persian goes both ways.

nekāḥ-e enāth ○ اناث

نکاح

nekāḥ-e ḏokur ▲ ذکور

Law 2 also uses *nekāḥ* and, at the same time, exemplifies how an Arabic borrowing equips Persian with something it normally does not have: gender marking (*nekāḥ-e moslemeh bā gheyr-e moslem jāyez nist*):

نکاحِ مسلمه (○) با غیر مسلم (▲) جایز نیست.

2. The *marriage of a female Muslim* with a *non-Muslim* is not permitted [Naqavi 1971:212].

Male *moslem* varies from female *moslemeh* by a final *-eh*. The law, which prohibits inter-faith marriage, promotes conversion to Islam. One of the excerpts in Chapter XIII illustrates the consequences of this statute in Persian.

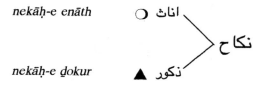

Law 3 mentions the bargaining that takes place before marriage. The ***mahr*** or ***mahrieh*** is actually a form of divorce insurance. If the couple separate, the bride walks out the door with her مهریه. Law 3 also shows how another borrowing from Arabic has supplied Persian with a suffix that expresses "couple of" or the "dual."

تعیینِ مقدارِ مهر منوط به تراضیِ طرفین است.

> 3. The determination of the amount of *bride price* (*mahr*) is contingent upon the mutual satisfaction of *both parties* [Naqavi 1971:214].

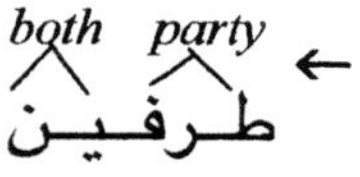

The dual noun in this phrase, *ṭarafeyn*, consists of *ṭaraf* (literally "direction") and the Arabic suffix *-eyn*. The dual form is particularly apt in Persian whose topic is marriage.

The next three statutes address the mutual satisfaction (*tarāḍi*) mentioned in Law 3. They also abound in Arabic borrowings. Law 4 legislates how the couple are meant to behave during the marriage (*zan va showhar mokallaf beh ḥosn-e moʕāsharat bā yakdigar-and*):

زن و شوهر مکلف به حسنِ معاشرت با یکدیگرند.

> 4. The wife and the husband are required to *behave decently* toward one another [Naqavi 1971:218].

The syntactic simplicity of Laws 1-4 contrasts sharply with their lexical intricacy. They are all statements that end in forms of the verb "to be": 1 and 3 end in *ast* ("is"); 2 ends in *ast*'s negative *nist* ("is not"). 4 ends in *-and* ("they are"). The dense Arabic falls into the basic Persian structure: Subject + Complement + Copula ("to be"):

to be	*complement*	*subject* ←
نیست.	جایز	نکاحِ مسلمه با غیر مسلم
است.	منوط به تراضیِ طرفین	تعیینِ مقدارِ مهر
ند.	مکلف به حسنِ معاشرت با یکدیگر	زن و شوهر

Law 5 spells out the *nafaqeh* or "what the husband gives his mate to maintain the household," which promotes the good relations specified in the previous statute (*nafaqeh-ye zan beh ʿohdeh-ye showhar ast. nafaqeh-ye zan ʿebārat ast az maskan va lebās va ghaḏā va athāth al-beyt*):

نفقهِ زن به عهدهٔ شوهر است. نفقهٔ زن عبارت است از
مسکن و لباس و غذا و اثاث البیت....

> 5. The wife's maintenance is the responsibility of the husband. The maintenance consists of housing and clothing and food and furnishings [Naqavi 1971:218].

This law also shows that using many *and*s (*va*) in Persian is not the stylistic fault it is in English.

Law 6 asserts the father's determinant role in child custody (*tefl-e motavalled dar zamān-e zowjiat molḥaq beh showhar ast*):

طفلِ متولد در زمانِ زوجیت ملحق به شوهر است...

> 6. [Any] child born during the time of marriage belongs to the husband [Naqavi 1971:222].

Here again the simplicity of the syntax clashes with density of the legalisms. “Child” here is not the perfectly acceptable Persian *farzand* introduced in the previous chapter, but Arabic *ṭefl* (Hebrew טפל, Klein 1987:248); “marriage” is not the colloquial *zan-o showhari* زن و شوهری nor the standard *zanāshuyi* زناشویی , but the contrived Arabic *zowjiat* (Hebrew זוגיות, Klein 1987: 195, literally “duality”).

طفل ◄——————— فرزند

Legalization

زوجیت ◄——————— زن و شوهری

Unromantic Unions

Not all marriages in Persian uphold the ideals legislated in the Family Laws. The following excerpt describes the *māh-e ʿasal* (line 2, literally “moon of honey”) in the story by Simin Behbahāni that opened this chapter. The couple spend their ماه عسل on the southern coast of the Caspian Sea, where, during the Pahlavi period, two casinos stood within commuting distance of one another. Important honeymoon vocabulary is outlined in Persian and italicized in translation.

کازینوی بابلسر، کازینوی رامسر، من و شوهرم ماه عسل را به تناوب در این دو کازینو سپری می کنیم. شوهرم هر شب کنار همپالکی ها می نشیند و من در اتاق هتل آن قدر تنها می مانم که خوابم می برد. نزدیك صبح که می آید اگر برده باشد حوصله دارد که نوازشم کند، و اگر باخته باشد بیدارم نمی کند. صبح که بر می خیزم پیکر خسته اش را در خواب بی هوشی

می بینم. بوی تنفسش فضارا ترشانده است. پنجره را
باز می کنم و به امواج خیره می شوم.

> Babolsar Casino, Ramsar Casino. I and my husband spend our *honeymoon* alternating between these two casinos. Every night my husband sits beside his buddies [gambling], and I am left so alone in the hotel room that I fall asleep. Near dawn when he comes, if he's won, he'll feel like *fondling me*; but if he's lost, he *won't wake me*. In the morning when I get up, I see his *tired form* in comatose sleep. The odor of his breath has soured the air. I open the window and stare at the waves [Behbahāni 1996:31].

This passage contains verbs like *negāh kardan*, a hybrid that the author used in the passage on prenuptials (line 2). Compound verbs consist of two elements: 1) either a noun or an adjective and 2) a conjugated element. Another example in the first passage (line 5) is *khabar dādand* "they informed," literally they "gave the news":

conjugated element		*noun adjective*
خبر دادند ◀——	دادن	خبر

In the sour honeymoon paragraph, we read: *ḥowṣaleh dārad* (line 5), literally, "he has the patience" or "he feels like":

حوصله دارد ◀——	داشتن	حوصله

The paragraph also contains three verbs with *kardan* as the conjugated element: *navāzesh-am konad* (line 6), literally, "he'll do fondling of me":

نوازش کردن ——◄ نوازشم کند؛

bidār-am nami-konad (line 6), literally, "he'll not make me awake":

بیدار کردن ——◄ بیدارم نمی کند؛

and *bāz mi-konam* (line 9), literally, "I make open":

باز کردن ——◄ باز می کنم.

The two phrases نوازشم کند and بیدارم کند are also like *negāh-am mi-konad*, because, as diagrammed above, the author has suffixed the object of the verb to the noun/adjective part of the compound.

Many Persian verbs are formed from the union of nouns/adjectives and conjugated elements like *kardan*, *dādan* ("to give), *dāshtan* ("to have"), and *shodan* ("to become"). The next chapter examines some of the many compounds formed when a noun, often inedible, joins *khordan* ("to eat, consume"; "suffer, take") .

past stem	*non-past stem*	*infinitive*
داد dād	ده deh	دادن "to give"
داشت dāsht	دار dār	داشتن "to have"
شد shod	شو shav	شدن "to become"

Based on the information in the chart, one can construct full paradigms for the three verbs. .

non-past			*past*			
شو	دار	ده	شد	داشت	داد	
می شوم	دارم	می دهم	شدم	داشتم	دادم	من
می شوی	داری	می دهی	شدی	داشتی	دادی	تو
می شود	دارد	می دهد	شد	داشت	داد	او
می شویم	داریم	می دهیم	شدیم	داشتیم	دادیم	ما
می شوید	دارید	می دهید	شدید	داشتید	دادید	شما
می شوند	دارند	می دهند	شدند	داشتند	دادند	آن ها

Rarely appears with the prefix mi- in the non-past.

Chapter VIII

Eating

Dialect and Diet

Persian becomes most local when the subject is eating. The all-purpose infinitive, *khordan* خوردن (non-past stem, *khor* خور), means "to consume." One can use it with solids as in *ghaḏā khordan* غذا خوردن "to eat food" and liquids as in *āb khordan* آب خوردن "to drink water" and *sharāb khordan* شراب خوردن "to drink wine." From خـــوردن grow two verbal nouns that are important parts of Iranian food: *khoresh* and *khorāk*.

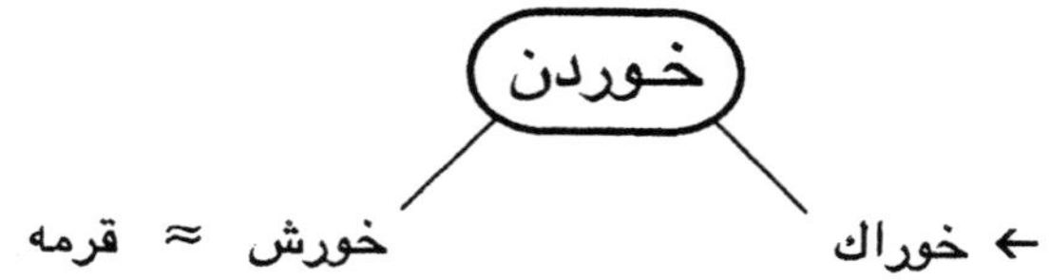

The term خوراك is "food, victuals" or a "meal in itself, served with bread and pickled vegetables or salad"; while خورش is a "stew served over rice" (Ghanoonparvar 1982:1:35). In Afghan Persian قرمه *qormeh*, a dish that the two dialects and diets share, often refers to what Iranian users of the language call *khoresh*. Eating in Persian is instructive about some of the important lexical differences between *fārsi* فارسی and *dari* دری.

Chelow Kabāb چـلـو كبـاب,"white rice kabāb," is the Iranian food most associated with a national identity. Because it is found everywhere, the dish can vary from place to place; however, one can construct a standard recipe from the many variants. The following list contrasts some of the Iranian ingredients and their Afghan analogs:

دری			فارسی	
chalaw	چلو	"white rice"	*chelow*	چلو
sikh kabāb	سیخ کباب	"lamb fillet"	*kabāb-e barg*	کباب برگ
bonjon-e rumi	بنجن رومی	"tomato"	*gujeh-ye farangi*	گوجهٔ فرنگی
morch	مرچ	"pepper"	*felfel*	فلفل

The last two items are indicative of a general dialectical tendency. "Tomato" was originally foreign to both cuisines. *Dari* uses Hindi *bainjan* बैंगन to nativize it; thus, an Afghan tomato is literally a "Roman eggplant." *Fārsi* finds a domestic equivalent and then looks westward for an adjective derived from the medieval term for European: "Frank"; an Iranian tomato, then, is a "Frankish plum." Afghan "pepper," is similarly related to the Hindi spice *mirch* मिर्च, while the Iranian is a homegrown variety, which entered Hebrew and Arabic through ancient "Persian mediation" (Klein 1987:512).

Qabili Pilaw قابلی پلو is particularly Afghan. It contains rice, vegetable oil, onions, carrots, black seedless raisins and a combination of spices called *chār* [*chahār*] *masala* or "four spices" (Saberi 2000:132, 27). *Masala* is Hindi मसाले. To *fārsi*-users the phrase sounds like *chahār mas'aleh*, four "propositions" or "questions," which has more to do with philosophy than food. A similar combination of spices used in Iranian food is called *advieh-ye khoresh* (Batmanglij 1992:377). The *fārsi* term derives from Arabic "medicines." The two types of spicing also seem to support the theory that دری vocabulary orients east, while the فارسی lexicon looks west.

دری		فارسی
چار مسأله	"composite spicing"	ادویهٔ خورش

Chelow Kabāb Dissident

Not all skilled Persian-users are as charmed by Chelow Kabāb as writers of Persian cookbooks N. Purjavādi (2000:2), editor of the scholarly quarterly *Nashr-e Dānesh*, reports unhappily that it has become the Persian national dish in a part of the Southern California diaspora known as Tehrānjeles تهران جلس or Irānjeles ایران جلس. This version of his remarks begins with a transliteration, followed by the Persian and an English translation (food vocabulary is outlined in the Persian and italicized in translation): ...*chelow kabāb ast keh emruzeh ham dar dākhel-e irān va ham dar khārej beh manzaleh-ye ghaḏā-ye melli irān shenākhteh mi-shavad. va in māyeh-ye ta'āsof ast ta'āsof az in keh mā ḥattā honar-e āshpazi-e khod-rā ham khub nami-dānim...*

..چلو کباب است که امروزه هم در داخل ایران و هم در
خارج به منزلهٔ غذای ملی ایران شناخته می شود. و این
مایهٔ تأسف است، تأسف از این که ما حتی هنر آشپزی
خودرا هم خوب نمی دانیم ...

> ...it is *Chelow Kabāb* that nowadays both in Iran and out is becoming known as the *national food* of Iran. And this is cause for regret, regret for the fact that we do not even know *the art of* our own *cooking* well...

Purjavādi's brief against چلو کباب is that its plainness belies the rich variety of Persian food. That this simple combination of meat and rice would come to epitomize a cuisine that is thousands of years old appalls him. For dissidents the Chelow Kabābization of the intricate world of Afghan, Iranian, and Tajik eating is tantamount identity-theft, deracination through emigration.

Purjavādi's writing portrays Iranians as victims of ignorance of their own cuisine. For this reason it contains examples of the passive (*majhul* مـجـهـول in Persian, because the subject is "unknown"), a grammatical construct that highlights the object of a verb and hides its subject. The basic sentence with a passive verb (extracted from lines 1-2) is:

passive

چلو کباب به منزلهٔ غذای ملی ایران شناخته می شود.

is becoming known of Iran national food as Chelow Kabāb

This statement does not reveal who has made Chelow Kabāb the national dish, only that is has regretfully become so. The sentence shows that the passive in Persian is the union of the past participle (in this case *shenākhteh* "to be known, recognized") and conjugated forms of the verb *shodan* (introduced in the previous chapter). The full, non-past paradigm is:

مجهول

shodan

شناخته می شوم
شناخته می شوی
شناخته می شود
شناخته می شویم
شناخته می شوید
شناخته می شوند

past participle شناخته ← شناختن *infinitive*

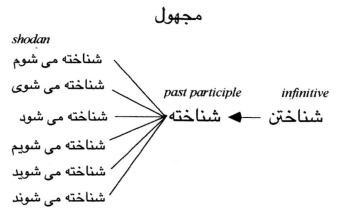

To put the passive into the past, one changes the non-past of *shodan* to its past form. "I became known" is thus *shenākhteh shodam*; "you [sing.] became known" *shenākhteh shodi*; "he, she, it became known" *shenākhteh shod*, etc.

	singular	*plural*
1	من شناخته شدم	ما شناخته شدیم
2	تو شناخته شدی	شما شناخته شدید
3	او شناخته شده است	آن ها شناخته اند

Symbolic Kabāb

Kabāb often appears in modern Persian literature. Though ordinarily a token of everyday life, at certain times it can transcend the mundane and become symbolic. Its celebrity as the national food, its basic definition (meat on a stick) and its various textures (ribbed, hard outside, moist inside), make *kabāb*'s association with of a body part and function that one dare not name in polite company inevitable.

One literary use of *kabāb* comes in the novel "The Patient Stone," by Ṣādeq Chubak, which is not about polite society. In it some of the most despairing characters from the Iranian underclass address readers directly. Non-standard language is the chief way Chubak underwrites the realism of his novel (Mir ʿĀbedini 1998:1:443). Instead of symbolism, "The Patient Stone," uses simile; *kabāb* is *kabāb* and its association with the male member is explicit. Belqis, a woman whose ugliness renders her insatiable, makes the association when complaining about the paltry fare served at a popular coffeehouse: *ham-ash yeh duneh sikh kabāb be-qadd-e yeh dul-e antar....*

همش یه دونه سیخ کباب، بقد یه دول انتر

> Alls it was was one stick of *kabāb*, the size of a baby monkey dick... [Chubak 1990:26]

The orthography of passage illustrates how authors represent dialectical Persian (*zabān-e goftār* زبان گفتار; see Najafi 1999:1:vi.) in writing. Rewritten in polite, standard language (*zabān-e me*ʕ*yār* زبان معيار), the passage might read:

همه اش يك دانه سيخ كباب، بقد يك ... انتر

To mimic colloquial Persian, Chubak has made two substitutions:

زبان گفتار			زبان معيار
yeh يه	"one"	*yek* يك	←
	dropped ک		
duneh دونه	"piece"	*dāneh* دانه	
	و ◄— آ		

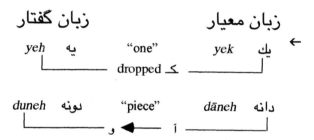

Fully symbolic *kabāb* comes in "The Secrets of the Treasure of the Hexed Valley," which Chapter VI uses to illustrate humility that insults. Originally the treatment for a film of the same name, the novel contains consecutive chapters that segue from one to the other cinematically. The following excerpt begins at the end of one chapter and ends at the beginning of the next. In the first part, there is a seduction that, though quite explicit, for reasons of propriety can only go so far. Next, the chapter (scene) ends and liver *kabāb* enters in full costume to perform a transitional role. In this version of the excerpt, terms related to sex and food are outlined in the Persian and italicized in translation. Transliteration: *zan dast-e mard-rā gereft va su-ye khod āvard bar ru-ye rān-e khod feshār-ash dād, dar lā-ye rān-e khod rahā-yash kard, abru-ash-rā larzānid, dast-ash-rā dar*

emtedād-e rān-e mard laghzānid vaqti rasid rāsteh-ash-rā navāzesh kard, garm-ash kard, gereft-ash, feshār-ash dād....khunābeh va namak keh at nuk-e sikh-e jegar miān-e doghāl gerefteh mi-oftād jezz mi-kard va mi-tarakid.

زن دست مردرا گرفت و سوی خود آورد، بر روی ران خود فشارش داد، در لای ران خود رهایش کرد، ابروش را لرزانید، دستش را در امتداد ران مرد لغزانید وقتی رسید راسته اش را نوازش کرد، گرمش کرد، گرفتش، فشارش داد.... خونابه و نمك كه از نوك سيخ جگر ميان ذغال گرفته میافتاد جزّ می کرد و میترکید.

> The woman took the man's hand and brought it toward her, pressed it against her *thigh*, let it go between her *thighs*, batted her eyelashes, slid her hand along the man's *thigh* and when it arrived, *stroked* his *upright*, *warmed* it, *took* it, *pressed* it....When the *bloodjuice and salt* that were dripping from the tip of the *liver stick* fell onto the burning *coals*, they would sizzle and burst [Golestān 1994:88-90].

In Hollywood, heated scenes such as this one traditionally segue to the Washington Monument, pounding surf, a long train going through a tunnel, etc. In Persian, a hot skewer of *kabāb* is the obvious metaphor.

The association of sex and cooking in this excerpt is not coincidental. Golestān exploits body-part words, *rān* ران (lines 1, 2, 3) and *rāsteh* راسته (line 4), that apply equally to *kabāb*-bearing animals—sheep, goats, etc.—and to human limbs. When the context involves animals, food comes to readers' minds; but, when the subject is people, ordinarily inedible, they infer intercourse:

body part	animal	human
ران	"leg, shank"	"thigh"
راسته	"*kabāb*-fillet, loin"	"erection"

The compound verbs used to describe the woman's foreplay are also used to prepare *kabāb*; one "strokes" *navāzesh kardan* نوازش کردن , "warms" *garm kardan* گرم کردن , "presses" *feshār dādan* فشار دادن it (literally, "give pressure," lines 4-5), etc.

The passages also teaches how Persian verbs express an action that is on-going in the past. After the seduction shifts to the *kabāb*stand, the writing (camera) focuses on the "dripping," "the hissing," and the "bursting" of the meat (lines 5-6)—all *continuous* in the past. To build the past continuous tense (*māḍi estemrāri* in Persian) one adds the marker *mi-* (used in the non-past in the previous chapter) to the past tense forms of the verb. "I was pressing/would press" is *feshār mi-dādam*, "you (sing.) were pressing/would press" is *feshār mi-dādi*, "he, she, it was pressing/would press" is *feshār mi-dād*, etc.

ماضی استمراری

	past stem	infinitive
فشار می دادم		
فشار می دادی		
فشار می داد	← فشار داد	← فشار دادن
فشار می دادیم		
فشار می دادید		
فشار می دادند		

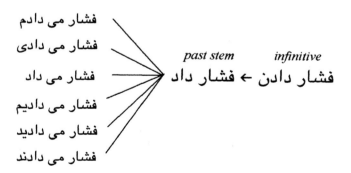

Consuming the Inedible

خوردن is also the conjugated element in numerous compound verbs. As a result, Persian-users "eat" many things that to others are inedible. A previous chapter (IV) describes how one of Sohrāb Sepehri's classmates received a beating for misdotting a word. The poor dyslexic literally "ate wood" *chub khord* چوب خورد. In a part of his memoir that discusses corporal punishment Sepehri (1998:31-32) mentions many other things students eat in Persian: *kotak* ("a beating"); *shallāq* ("whip"); *sili* ("slap, smack"); and *tarkeh* ("switch, thin branch used to beat"):

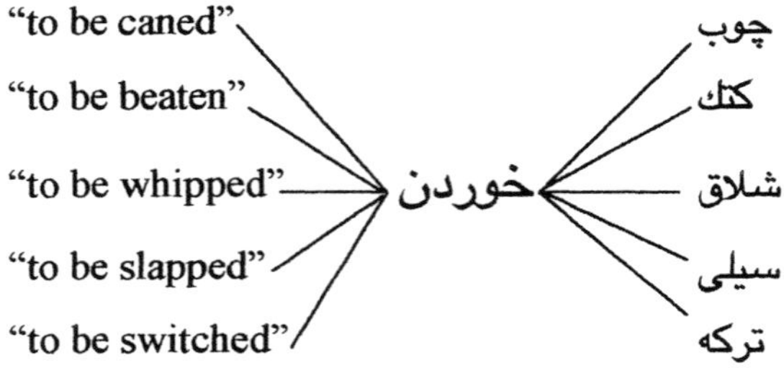

A general pattern emerges from these examples: when ordinarily active خوردن is paired with something inedible and unpleasant to form a compound verb, it becomes passive. It is similar to English "take" in "take a beating." Thus, instead of using the passive introduced in this chapter, one can use خوردن compounds to put the victim of an act at the beginning of a sentence and, at the same time avoid mentioning its perpetrator.

This list does not exhaust the class of Persian edible inedibles. The last excerpt in this chapter comes from the post-revolutionary diary of Mehrzād Farrokh. At one point in these notes, which begin with the first signs of the Islamic Revolution in 1978 and end in December 1993, Farrokh (1995:83) mentions خوردن's wide lexical range. Here the inedibles are outlined in Persian and italicized in translation Transliteration: *movarrekhi dar aḥvāl-e iraniān neveshteh … keh in mardom-e ˁajib hameh chiz-rā mi-khorand, ghoṣṣeh, zamin, māl, afsus, kotak, va haṭṭā goh. va bāyad eḍāfeh kard keh ḥālā hameh chiz mi-khorand, ḥaqq-o ḥoquq-e mardom, ḥaqq-e ḥajj, kupon, daftarcheh-ye sahmieh, ḥaqq-e ṭebābat…*

مورّخی در احوال ایرانیان نوشته که این مردم عجیب همه
چیزرا می خورند، غصه، زمین، مال، افسوس، کتك، و حتی
گُه. و باید اضافه کرد که حالا همه چیز می خورند، حق
و حقوق مردم، حقّ حج، کوپن، دفترچهٔ سهمیه، حق طبابت

> A historian has written the following on the nature of Iranians: these strange people eat everything: *worry, earth, property, regret, beating*, and even *shit*. But now one must add that they are eating even more: *the rights of the people, money for the Hajj, coupons, ration booklets, medical fees*…

Most of the new inedible nouns cited in line 2 are of the *kotak* variety, disagreeable experiences that the subjects of خوردن reluctantly undergo: *ghoṣṣeh, zamin, afsus*, even *goh*:

actual meaning	*literal meaning*	*inedible noun*	
"to worry"	"to eat worry"	غصه	
"to fall"	"to eat dirt"	زمین	خوردن
"to be sorry"	"to eat regret"	افسوس	
"to screw up"	"to eat shit"	گه	

But with the mention of *māl* ("property"), another, more sinister meaning of خـــوردن emerges. "To eat property" is to steal it. Inedibles like *ḥaqq* "right, expense, payment, fee" and its plural *ḥoquq* "rights, entitlements" restore خوردن to active status. The subject of the compound verbs حق خوردن and حق و حقوق خوردن are ravenous expropriators of the rights and property of the people, of deposits they make to book pilgrimages to Mecca and Medina, even of the ration booklets that enable them to buy food in times of war- and embargo-induced shortages.

Needless to say, this chapter is does not exhaust the subject of eating in Persian. The many gut feelings expressed with خـوردن are far too numerous to fit into such a short space. Chapter IX examines nostalgia, another aspect of culture evoked by food.

Chapter IX

Estrangement and Nostalgia

Questioning the Familiar

Because of historical, social, and economic circumstances, a lot of writing in contemporary Persian is about emigration. Students travel abroad to study and decide to settle in their new homes. Binational marriages necessarily involve long-term home-leaving of one kind or another. Refugees from deteriorating economic conditions, war, oppression, and revolution become émigrés. This dislocation, which is often unhappy, leads writers to remember what they left behind fondly. The writing of the diaspora (*mohājerat* مهاجرت; see Mir ʕAbedini 1998:3:936-43) contains many examples of Persian estrangement and nostalgia.

The first excerpt in this chapter is by Mahshid Amirshahi (1995:intro.), who has spent many years abroad, first as a student and, later, as a writer and teacher. She was in Tehran when the 1979 Iranian Revolution took place and went into exile, *tabʕid* تبعید , while it was still under way. The writing expresses feelings she had when the familiar suddenly became unfamiliar, when she became a stranger in her own home. It also contains or implies the desperate inquiry of pre-emigration: What happened?; Why did it happen?; Who *are* these people?; What am I doing here? In "On the Scene," a novel about life in Tehran during the Revolution, the narrator often speaks of her estrangement from the people, who, suddenly observant, had incorporated the Arabic jargon of Islamic Republicanism mentioned in Chapter II into their daily speech.

In the following version, question words are outlined in Persian and italicized in translation. Transliteration: *man in mardom-rā nami-shenāsam--mardumi keh dar chashm-hā-shān beh jā-ye ḥayā-ye āshnā, bi-sharmi-e bigāneh jā dārad. zabān-eshān-rā nami-fahmam -- zabāni keh dar ʿavaḍ-e sokhan-e shirin, bār-e talkh-e sheʿār gerefteh-ast...in mardomi keh dast-eshān chang va del-eshān sang, bā man nistand. man in mardomān-rā nami-shenāsam, zabān-eshān-rā nami-dānam. in ʿarbadeh-juyān az kojā āmadeh-and? beh kojā mi-ravand?*

من این مردم را نمی شناسم - مردمی که در چشم هاشان به جای حیای آشنا، بی شرمی بیگانه جا دارد. زبانشان را نمی فهمم - زبانی که در عوض سخن شیرین، بار تلخ شعار گرفته است....این مردمی که دستشان چنگ است و دلشان سنگ، با من نیستند. من این مردمان را نمی شناسم، زبانشان را نمی دانم. این عربده جویان از کجا آمده اند؟ به کجا می روند؟

I don't know these people—people in whose eyes an alien shamelessness has replaced the familiar modesty. I don't understand their language—a language that instead of sweet speech conveys a bitter load of slogans.... These people, whose hands are claws and whose hearts are stone, have nothing to do with me. I don't recognize these people, I don't know their language. *Where* have these thugs [brawl-seekers] come *from*? *Where* are they headed?

Amirshahi's alienation is plain here The modesty, *ḥojb* حجب (Chapter VI) or *ḥayā* حیا (line 2), that she had come to expect from people bound by common *taʿārof* disappeared suddenly. When the Revolution knocked the props of everyday life out from under her, she became *az khod bigāneh* از خود بیگانه,

literally "from herself alien." No wonder she asks (line 7):

این عربده جویان از کجا آمده اند؟

have come where from thugs these ←

After Amirshahi went into exile in Paris, she also questioned the familiar surroundings of the city she knew so well. Exile made it as alien as the revolutionary Tehran she had left behind. She had cut her ties with Iran in many ways. Moreover, a major newspaper falsely accused her of being a "dogged, anti-revolutionary monarchist" *ḍedd-e enqelāb-e salṭanat-ṭalab-e moʕāned* ضد انقلاب سلطنت طلب معاند (Ganji 2000:357). Despite this political and cultural estrangement, however, Amirshahi still missed Iran sorely. In fact, her hankering was so great that it evolved into a kind of false nostalgia. In the following excerpt from "On the Journey" (Amirshahi 1995a:151), a companion novel to "On the Scene," the narrator confesses that she misses cities that she never visited. In this version, question words are outlined in Persian and italicized in translation. Transliteration: *cherā man bā in shahr, keh kucheh-hā va khiābān-hā-yash-rā, kāfeh-hā va muzeh-hā-yash-rā, te'ātr-hā-yash va benā-hā-ye tārikhi-ash-rā mi-shenākhtam va beh abʕād-e zibāi-hā-yash āgāh budam, ānqadar eḥsās-e bigānegi mi-kardam? cherā pāris az kermān-e nā-shenākhteh, kāshān-e na-dideh, shirāz-e nayāzmudeh barā-yam gharibeh-tar bud?*

چرا من با این شهر، که کوچه ها و خیابان هایش را،
کافه ها و موزه هایش را، تئاترها و بناهای تاریخی اش را
می شناختم و به ابعاد زیبایی هایش آگاه بودم، آنقدر
احساس بیگانگی می کردم؟ چرا پاریس از کرمان
ناشناخته، کاشان ندیده، شیراز نیازموده برایم غریبه تر
بود؟

> *Why* was I feeling so alienated from this city, whose streets and avenues, cafés and museums, theatres and historic buildings I knew so well and whose aesthetic dimensions were so familiar? *Why* was Paris stranger to me than unfamiliar Kerman, unseen Kashan, and untried Shiraz?

An important part of Amirshahi's estrangement is expressed in questions. Some of the texts in previous chapters also include questions. For example, the rude interrogator's "What did we arrest you for?" (Chapter V):

ما برای چه ترا دستگیر کردیم؟
m i dr ak r i g t sad ārot hech ey-ār ab ā m ←

or the deferential " What is your honor's view?" (Chapter VI):

نظر حضرتعالی چیه؟
← hei ch i l ā ˁt ar ḍa ḥ e-raẓ a n

The first question uses a word equivalent to English "which" *cheh* چه, and the second "what" *chi* چی. In the first, چه follows a preposition برای چه: "for which [thing]." In the second question, چی comes at the end and is joined to a conversational form of "is": ه The formal "what is?" is *chist* :

formal	*informal*
چی + است = چیست	چی + ه = چیه

Thus, the formal "What is your name"? is *esm-e shomā chist* اسم شما چیست؟ (Faṣiḥ 1998:64). When Amirshahi (first excerpt, line 7) wonders about the origin and destination of the "thugs," she also joins a question word (*kojā*) to prepositions (*az* and *beh*):

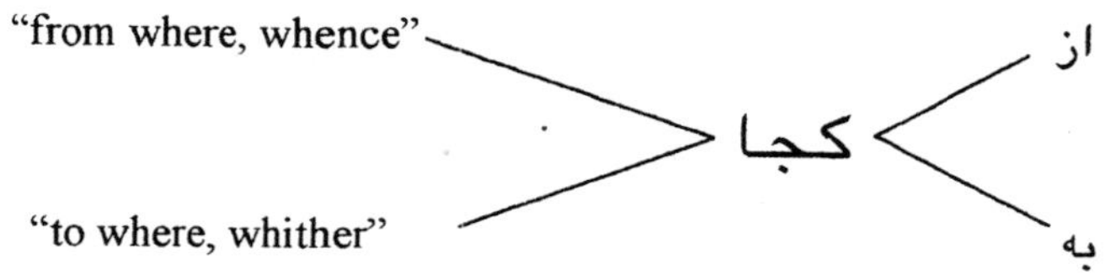

In the second excerpt, when she asks rhetorically about why Paris has become alien to her (lines 1 & 4), she begins the questions with "why" *cherā*, which is nearly synonymous with *barā-ye cheh*.

چرا ≈ برای چه

From this limited sample, a tentative inference emerges. Persian question words fall into two categories: those that begin with *ch* and those that begin with *k*. In this they appear to have the formal regularity of English questions words, which begin either with *wh* or *h*. The following list contrasts how question words start in the two languages:

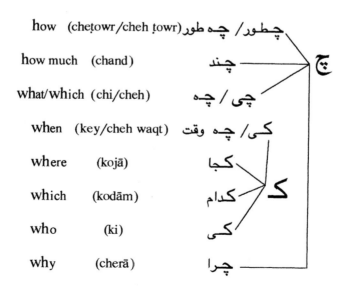

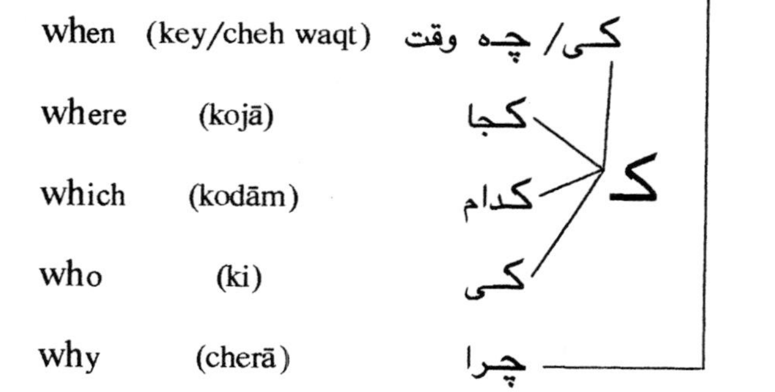

The following questions come from popular texts. They show how writers use the Persian question words listed above.

1. "How is father?"; *āqā ḥāl-ash cheh ṭowr ast* (Sanāpur 2000:6):

← آقا حالش چه طور است؟
is how his condition father

2. "How old was he?"; *chand sāl-ash bud* (Golshiri 1971: 21):

← چند سالش بود؟
was his year how much

3. "How much is his salary?"; *mozd-ash chand ast* (Behāḏin 1973:30):

← مزدش چند است؟
is how much his salary

4. "Who are you?"; *to ki hasti* (Dowlatābādi 1973a:58):

← تو کی هستی؟
are you who you

5. "Then when? When will the fate of this son of mine finally become clear?" *pas key? be-l-ākhareh taklif-e in pesar-e man key rowshan mi-shavad?* (Ḥājj Seyyed Javādi 1998:65):

←
پس کی؟ بالاخره تکلیف این پسر من کی روشن می شود؟
become clear when my son this fate finally when then

6. "What self-respect? ...I eat the leavings of foreigners..."; *kodām ghorur?...tah-māndeh-hā-ye bigānegān-rā mi-khoram* (Karimpur Shirāzi 1999:280):

← کـــدام غـرور؟ ...تـه مانده های بـیگانـگان را می خورم...

I eat foreigners of leavings self-respect what (which)

Like چیست, کجا and کدام have colloquial variants. When the illiterate farmer asks the painter, "Where're my eyes?" (Chapter VI), he shortens *kojā* to *ku*: پـس کـو چـشام؟ . Informal *kodām* is *kodum* in "What village do you (inf.) come from?": *az kodum deh mi-āi* (Dowlatābādi 1973b:95):

کدام
↓
← از کـدوم ده مـی آی؟

you come village which from

Holiday Nostalgia

Nostalgia is a longing for something remote in time or place. While in English nostalgia can be positive, in Persian it is usually painful. A classical Persian phrase used by the poet Nāṣer-e Khosrow (fl. 11th century, quoted in LN; satirized in Golestān 1994:101) is the alliterative *ghamm-e ghorbat* غـــم غربـــت "the sadness of estrangement." Another expression that approximates the English word is *deltangi* دلـتـنـگـی "heartache." "On the Journey" (Amirshahi 1995a:151) speaks of پــرده سـیــاه بی وطنی "the black curtain of being without country."

The next excerpt in this chapter is also from "On the Journey" (Amirshahi 1995a:8-9). The narrator longs for the activities, sights, and smells associated with Nowruz نـوروز (literally "new day") the New Year's celebration of spring's return. Yearning for this holiday perhaps exerts the strongest tug on the hearts of the Persian-users abroad. No matter how riven with social, ethnic, religious, and political faults, exile communities are able to unify around holiday celebrations that begin with the vernal equinox on March 21st and continue for thirteen days. The excerpt also invokes the places of Nowruz springtimes: Shemirān (also Shemrān; Golābdarreh'i 1985) is a scenic area in the mountains north of Tehran and Qazvin is a city in northwestern Iran famous for a kind of rice cookie that guests might bring to the Nowruz table. In the following version, the vocabulary of recall is outlined in Persian and italicized in translation. Transcription: *dar har nowruz dar tabʿid, beh yād-e ʿaṭr-e gol-hā-ye in faṣl...hastam, beh yād-e bu-ye pārcheh-ye novi-e lebās va charm-e tāzeh-ye kafsh, beh yād-e rāyeḥeh-ye khosh-e shirini-hā-ye khāneh-paz, beh yād shamim-e bahār-e shemirān keh majmuʿeh-'i bud az hameh-ye in ʿaṭr-hā. dar āghāz-e bahār va dar in shahr-e gharib, beh yād sonnat-hā-ye āshnā hastam, beh yād-e raft-o āmad-hā, ʿidi dādan-hā va gereftan-hā, chāi khordan-hā va ṣad sāl beh in sāl-hā goftan-hā. 'dar āghāz-e har sāl sorāgh-e* *nowruz-hā-ye kudaki-am-rā mi-giram. barā-ye did-o bāz did-hā-yi-e keh dar ān zamān deltangi mi-āvard deltang-am. havas-e nān-e berenji-e qazvin-rā dāram keh dar goḏashteh nami-khordam. mi-kh^{v}āham hamān kafshi-rā be-pusham keh mokhtaṣari pā-rā mi-zad va hamān lebās-e shaqq-o raqqi-rā keh yaqeh-ash gardan-rā mi-āzard. havā-ye sofreh-ye haft sini-rā dāram keh sib-e sorkh-ash, bar khelāf-e revāyat-e afsāneh-hā, dar laḥẓeh-ye taḥvil-e sāl dar ẓarf-e āb nami-charkhid...*

در هر نو روز در تبعید، به یاد عطر گلهای این فصل...
هستم، به یاد بوی پارچهٔ نوی لباس و چرم تازهٔ کفش، به
یاد رایحهٔ خوش شیرینی های خانه پز، به یاد شمیم بهار
شمیران که مجموعه ای بود از همهٔ این عطرها.
در آغاز بهار و در این شهر غریب، به یاد سنت های
آشنا هستم، به یاد رفت و آمدها، عیدی دادن ها و گرفتن
ها، چای خوردن ها و صد سال به این سال ها گفتن ها.
در آغاز هر سال سراغ نوروزهای کودکیم را می گیرم.
برای دید و باز دید هایی که در آن زمان دلتنگی می آورد
دلتنگم. هوس نان برنجی قزوین را دارم که در گذشته
نمی خوردم. می خواهم همان کفشی را بپوشم که
مختصری پارا می زد و همان لباس شق ورقی را که یقه
اش گردن را می آزرد. هوای سفرهٔ هفت سینی را دارم
که سیب سرخش، بر خلاف روایت افسانه ها، در لحظهٔ
تحویل سال در ظرف آب نمی چرخید...

At each New Year in exile *I remember* the fragrance of the season's flowers..., the smell of the fabric of new

> clothes and of the fresh leather of new shoes, of the aroma of home-cooked cakes, and the scent of spring in Shemiran, which was an amalgam of all these fragrances.
>
> At the beginning of spring and in this foreign city, familiar customs *come to mind*, and *I recollect* the comings and goings, the Nowruz gift-givings and receivings, the tea-drinkings, and the times we wished, 'May there be a hundred more years to this one.'
>
> At the outset of each year, *I track down* the Nowruzes of my childhood: *I grow homesick* for those visits and re-visits that at the time had made me plain sick. *I have a craving* for the rice cookies of Qazvin, which I had never eaten in the past. *I want* to wear the very shoes that chafed my feet a bit, and the same starched and stiff dress with the collar that hurt my neck. *I'm in the mood for* the table spread with seven things that begin with the letter *sin* with its red apple that, despite what the fairy tales say, would not revolve in the bowl of water at the very moment the year changed…

Exile sharpens Amirshahi's Nowruz longing so much that she is nostalgic for the disagreeable. It also fuels the same false nostalgia found in the previous passage. *Did-o bāz did-hā*, literally "to see and see agains" (line 9; in English through Tara Bahrampur's memoir [2000]) are part of the reciprocal hospitality that Nowruz celebrants practice. The exclamations of relatives and friends about how big she had grown or how cute she looked, which probably mortified the child Amirshahi during such visits, became grist for nostalgia in Paris.

The seven things beginning with *sin* refer to the traditional adornments of the Nowruz table. They are part of folk memory and tie the holiday to the remote Persian past. All related to food somehow, the seven سs are edibles in themselves (*sib*, *senjed*, *samanu*) or some form of flavoring (*sir*, *serkeh*, *somāq*) or garnish (*sabzi*):

"garlic"	*sir*	سیر
"vinegar"	*serkeh*	سرکه
"apple"	*sib*	سیب
"sumac"	*somāq*	سماق
"wheat -pudding"	*samanu*	سمنو
"Chinese date"	*senjed*	سنجد
"green sprouts"	*sabzi*	سبزی

7 س

Like Christmas lore about Santa Claus, Nowruz tradition can also be a starting point for childhood skepticism in Persian.

In a great deal of Amirshahi's prose, the syntax of nostalgia is both simple and elegant. The narrator repeats the phrase *beh yād*-e *X budan* or "to be in mind of *X*" or "to recall *X*." For example, lines 1-2 read:

← به یاد عطر گلهای این فصل ... هستم،
I am season this of flowers of the fragrance memory in

She does not simply "remember" her childhood Nowruzes, she "tracks them down" (line 8), literally:

← سراغ نوروزهای کودکیم را می گیرم.
I take of my childhood Nowruzes the trail of

Her nostalgia also involves the two principle types of Persian hankering. First, *havas* (line 10), the kind of random craving some associate with pregnancy:

← هوس نان برنجی قزوین را دارم
I have of Qazvin rice bread craving of

Second, *havā* (line 13), literally "air, weather," figuratively, a "mood":

← هوای سفره ٔ هفت سینی را دارم

I have *sin* the seven the spread of the mood for

Both *havas dāshtan* and *havā dāshtan* are compound verbs that behave like *ḥowṣaleh dāshtan* ("to have the patience for"; see Chapter VII). The objects of the verbs are bound to the noun elements of the compounds by the universal linker *eḍāfeh*:

translation	*verb*	*object*	*noun element*
"to have a craving for X"	داشتن	X	هوسِ
		eḍāfeh	←
"to be in the mood for X"	داشتن	X	هوایِ

Amirshahi's nostalgia is also grammatically complex. The passage is useful to students because it illustrates how the verb *khᵛāstan* خواستن "to want, wish" functions in Persian. It requires the subjunctive (*eltezāmi* التزامی). So when Amirshahi *wants to wear* something, "wear" (*pushidan* پوشیدن) is in the non-past subjunctive:

← می خواهم همان کفشی را بپوشم

I wear the shoes very I want

The non-past subjunctive is exactly like the non-past except the prefix *mi* می becomes *be(o)* بـ . The full paradigm "want to wear" is:

	singular	*plural*
1	من می خواهم بپوشم	ما می خواهیم بپوشیم
2	تو می خواهی بپوشی	شما می خواهید بپوشید
3	او می خواهد بپوشد	آن ها می خواهند بپوشند

Estrangement and the West

Chapter II introduced the terms *sharq* and *gharb* as the opposite ends of a range that encompasses all location. At one extreme, lies the familiar East and at the other the alien West. The literal relationship between *gharb* and Persian terms for "stranger," "strangeness," and "feeling foreign" is obvious. As the following tree shows the three Arabic letters غ , ر , and ب that form "west" are very productive in the vocabulary of oddity:

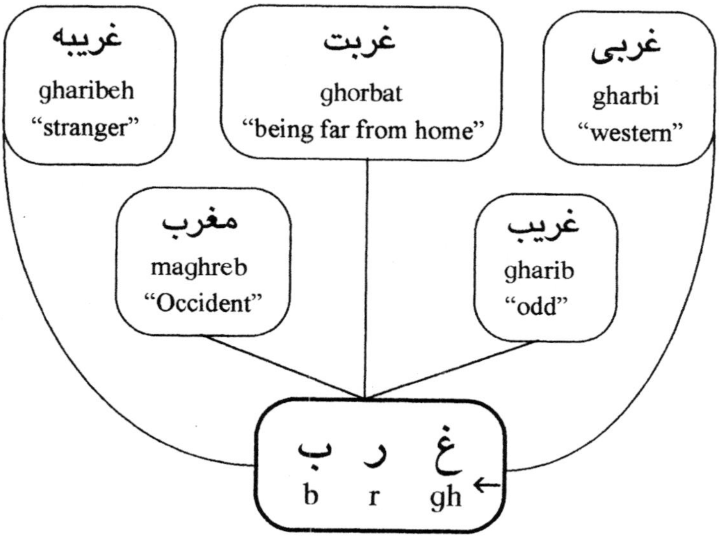

In the second excerpt of this chapter (line 5), *gharibeh* becomes the comparative adjective *gharibeh-tar*, when the narrator of Amirshahi's novel wonders why she feels "more like a stranger" in familiar Paris than in Iranian cities she has never visited:

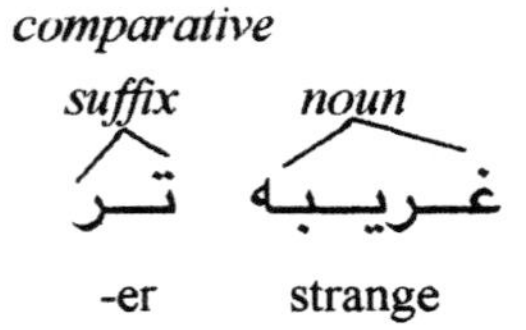

Another fruit from this tree is the title of a work on the alienation of the west, *ghorbat-e gharb* ("The Feeling of Being Far from Home in the West," Narāqi 1976b). Both the ancient *ghamm-e ghorbat* mentioned at the outset of this chapter and the book title exploit the alliterating *gheyn*s of estrangement:

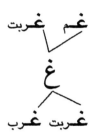

These expressions are a linguistic record of the long history in Persian of associating the unfamiliar, the novel, even the hostile with the West. In the minds of many Persian-users, the world has been and to some extent is still divided into two mutually exclusive realms: "east-land" *mashreq-zamin* and "west-land" *maghreb-zamin* (Ha'eri, ʕA. 1988:406). East-lander reaction to the obvious west-lander technological and scientific superiority is of two kinds, both of which are expressed in Persian with *gharb* and various suffixes. On one hand, Persian-users can display a "gravitation to the west" *gharb-garāyi* or *gharbi-gari* a natural, inevitable and, to some, positive reaction (Zarrinkub

1974:33). On the other, they are prone to Westitis *gharbzadegi* (see Chapter II) and "anti-Westernism" *gharb-setizi*, which some see as nothing more than the blind denial of modernity (Zibākalām 1998:28):

غرب گرایی		غربزدگی
+	————————	–
غربیگری		غرب ستیزی

For many Persian-users living in exile, the West is not only *gharb* but also *gharib* and *ghorbat* (Nāderpur 1992). Because they cannot return to their homes in *mashreq-zamin*, they remain eternally *gharibeh*. With the rise of a second generation of users living abroad, the situation has changed. The exile Persian of these people, who are more at home in the cultures of *maghreb-zamin*, rarely associates being alien with the West. To many in the second generation *gharb* is home.

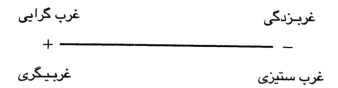

Chapter X

Coming of Age

Motherly Advice

Chapter V is about how Persian expresses personal identity in the impersonal terms of interrogation: name, father, mother, children, etc. This chapter presents how two young women—one in a novel, the other in a poem—define themselves as individuals. The first excerpt is from a spectacularly popular novel called *Bāmdād-e Khomār* "The Morning's Hangover" (Ḥājj Seyyed Javādi 1998:1-2). The title is part of Saʿdi's aphorism "one night's drinking is not worth the morning's hangover" (Haim 1956:274). The novel has been reprinted in runs of 10,000 to 20,000 and even 30,000 at least twenty times (Ferdowsi 1998:676), making it a best-selling phenomenon in Persian. It opens with an argument between Sudābeh and her mother. Sudābeh asserts the right to choose her own marriage partner. Her mother, however, reminds her that passion is momentary, while background and education are more lasting. Their argument shows where the responsibilities of adulthood and the demands of class intersect in Persian. It also adds detail to the picture of finding suitors and courting drawn in Chapter VII.

Like many inter-generational conversations, this one is full of advice. English-speaking elders often express such advice with modals: "can," "should," "ought," and "must." Like Sudābeh in the novel, offspring often counter with the plaintive "But why can't I…?" The excerpt from *Bāmdād-e Khomār* that begins this chapter often uses the advice modal "should" in Persian: *bāyad* باید; negative "shouldn't" = *nabāyad* نباید. In this version of the excerpt motherly advice and daughterly protest are outlined in Persian and italicized in translation.

Transcription: *ākher cherā? man keh nami-fahmam. kheyli ˤajib ast hā! yak dokhtar-e taḥṣil-kardeh beh senn-o sāl-e man hanuz nami-tavānad barā-ye zandegi-e khod-ash taṣmim be-girad? nabāyad khod-ash mard-e zandegi-e khod-ash entekhāb konad?*

cherā, mi-tavānad. yak dokhtar-e taḥṣil-kardeh-ye emruzi mi-tavānad khod-ash entekhāb konad. bāyad khod-ash entekhāb konad. vali nabāyad bā pesari ezdevāj konad keh kheyli rāḥat dāneshkadeh-rā vel mi-konad va mi-ravad donbāl-e kār-e pedar-ash. nabāyad zan-e pesar-e mardi shavad bā in tharvat va emkānāti keh dārad, keh mi-tavānad pesar-ash-rā beh behtarin-e dāneshgāh-hā be-ferestad, beh u mi-guyad biā bā khod-am kār kon, pul tu-ye gach-o simān ast. nabāyad zan mardi be-shavad keh pedar-ash esm-e khod-ash-rā ham balad nist emḍāʿ konad. sudābeh, dar zendagi faqaṭ chashm-o abru keh sharṭ nist. pedar-e to shab-hā tā yaki do sāˤat moṭālaˤeh nakonad kh^{v}āb-ash nami-barad. to cheh ṭowr mi-tavāni bā in khānavādeh zendagi koni? bā pesari keh tanhā honar-e mādar-ash in ast keh gheybat-e in-o ān-rā be-konad...

sudābeh az jā-ye khod boland shod. māmān, man beh pedar-o mādar-ash cheh kār dāram?

eshtebāh mi-koni. bāyad kār dāshteh bāshi. in pesar-rā ān mādar bozorg kardeh. sar-e sofreh-ye ān pedar nān khordeh. farhang-eshān bā farhang-e mā zamin tā āsmān farq dārad....

pas faqaṭ mā khub hastim? mā aṣālat dārim? farhang dārim, ostokh^{v}ān dārim, vali ān-hā nadārand?....

«آخر چرا؟ من که نمی فهمم. خیلی عجیب است ها!
یك دختر تحصیلکرده به سنّ و سال من هنوز نمی تواند
برای زندگی خودش تصمیم بگیرد؟ نباید خودش مرد
زندگی خودش را انتخاب کند؟»

«چرا، می تواند. یك دختر تحصیلکرده ٔ امروزی می تواند خودش انتخاب کند. باید خودش انتخاب کند. ولی نباید با پسری ازدواج کند که خیلی راحت دانشکده را ول می کند و می رود دنبال کار پدرش. نباید زن پسر مردی شود که با این ثروت و امکاناتی که دارد، که می تواند پسرش را به بهترین دانشگاه ها بفرستد، به او می گوید بیا با خودم کار کن، پول توی گچ و سیمان است. نباید زن مردی بشود که پدرش اسم خودش را هم بلد نیست امضاء کند. سودابه، در زندگی فقط چشم و ابرو که شرط نیست. پدر تو شبها تا یکی دو ساعت مطالعه نکند خوابش نمی برد. تو چه طور می توانی با این خانواده زندگی کنی؟ با پسری که تنها هنر مادرش این است که غیبت این و آن را بکند....

سودابه از جای خود بلند شد. «مامان، من به پدر و مادرش چه کار دارم؟»

«اشتباه می کنی. باید کار داشته باشی. این پسررا آن مادر بزرگ کرده. سر سفره ٔ آن پدر نان خورده. فرهنگشان با فرهنگ ما زمین تا آسمان فرق دارد.»...

«پس فقط ما خوب هستیم؟ ما اصالت داریم؟ فرهنگ داریم، استخوان داریم،...؟»

"*Why not, after all*? I myself can't understand it. It's so strange, you know! An educated girl my age still can't make decisions about her own life? *Shouldn't* she *choose* the man of her own life herself?"

"Of course, *she can*. A modern, educated girl *can make* her own decisions. She *should make* her own decisions. But she *shouldn't marry* a boy that abandons college so easily and goes into his father's business. She *shouldn't become* the wife of a boy whose father with all his wealth and possibilities can send his son to the best universities, but says to him instead, 'Come work with me, there's money in plaster and cement.' She *shouldn't become* the wife a man whose father doesn't even know how to sign his own name. Sudābeh, good looks aren't the only important things in life. Your father, if he doesn't read for a couple of hours a night, can't fall asleep. How *will you be able to live* with this family? With a boy whose mother's only talent is to say bad things behind people's backs..."

Sudābeh rose from her seat, "Mama, *what do I have to do* with his father and mother?"

"You're making a mistake. You *have to have* something to do with them. That mother raised the boy. He ate at that father's table. Their culture is as different from ours as night from day."...

Then we're the only ones who are good? Only we *have a pedigree, have culture, have a bloodline*...?

One of the reasons for the popularity of this novel is that it raises the eternal question of who is a suitable marriage partner in very Persian ways. At the heart of suitability are notions of *farhang* "culture" (lines 22, 23) and *aṣālat* "pedigree, breeding" (line 23). It appears that culture implies education, while pedigree draws the familiar boundary between old and new money:

فرهنگ اصالت

←

✓ دانشکده را ول می کند (7-8)

he abandons college

✓ پول توی گچ و سیمان است (11-12)

is cement and plaster in money

✓ اسم خودرا هم بلد نیست امضاء کند (12-13)

to sign he doesn't know even own name

Farhang and *aṣālat* are not only germane in discussions of suitable boys, they also apply to understandings of Persian-using society as a whole. According to Jamshid Arjomand (Kimiāyi 2001:18), possessing culture and breeding distinguishes one type of bourgeois family (desirable, avant-gard) from another (undesirable, reactionary).

اشراف نیست، اما ثروتمند است، البته ثروت مبتنی و متکی بر ملك، منتها فـئـودال هم نیست. صاحب فرهنگ و اصالت است...

> [The family] is not aristocratic, but it is wealthy; of course it's wealth is based on property, although it is not feudal either. It possesses *culture* and *breeding*...

A good bourgeois family, then, must be wealthy *tharvatmand* ثروتمند but not aristocratic *ashrāf* اشـراف ; its wealth shall derive from property *molk* مـلـك but not feudal فـئـودال holdings. Finally, its respectability derives from possessing *farhang* and *aṣālat*.

As the conversation between Sudābeh and her mother goes on, modals proliferate. In addition to *bāyad*, they often use *tavānestan* (non-past = *tavān*) or "can." In line 3, we see how Persian expresses "can't"

یک دختر... نمی تواند ... تصمیم بگیرد؟

to take decision can not girl one

In the next sentence (lines 3-4), Sudābeh uses negative *nabāyad* to buttress her rhetorical argument. The two sentences are structurally similar:

نباید ... انتخاب کند؟

make choice should not

These examples indicate that like *kh*^{v}*āstan* (see Chapter IX) *tavānestan* and *bāyad* are followed by the subjunctive. In this coming-of-age conversation, the subjunctive verb is often *entekhāb kardan* "to choose" (literally, "to make choice"). The full paradigms "can choose" and "must choose" are:

should, must	*can*	
باید انتخاب کنم	می توانم انتخاب کنم	*I*
باید انتخاب کنی	می توانی انتخاب کنی	*you*
باید انتخاب کند	می تواند انتخاب کند	*he, she, it*
باید انتخاب کنیم	می توانیم انتخاب کنیم	*we*
باید انتخاب کنید	می توانید انتخاب کنید	*you*
باید انتخاب کنند	می توانند انتخاب کنند	*they*

Often the subjunctive verb, in this case *kardan*, lacks the prefix *be-* بـ (see Chapter IX). In fact in this passage, the author decides to use it in one place and not in another, which is almost identical to the first. In advising whom to marry, Sudābeh's mother repeats the verb *shodan* "become" in the subjunctive, once without the prefix (line 9) and once with it (line 12):

no prefix

9 نباید زن پسر مردی شود

become a man son of wife of should not

prefix

12 نباید زن مردی بشود

become a man wife of should not

The Semantics of Bāyad

The inter-generational conversation that begins "The Morning's Hangover" does not exploit باید's full range. Mother and daughter merely trade *should*s, the proprietary sense of the word. Bāṭeni (1975:193-99) divides the modalities of *bāyad* three ways: *eḥtemāl* "possibility"; *shāyestegi* "propriety"; and *ejbāri* "necessity":

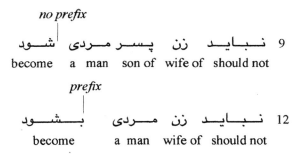

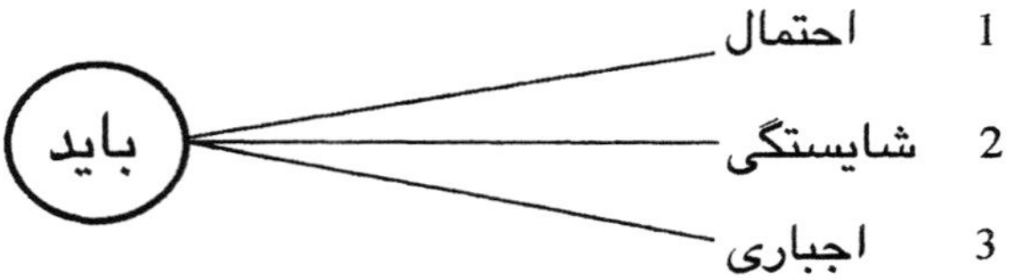

Among Bāṭeni 's examples are:

1. Possibility: "Aḥmad must be here because I saw his wife and child"; *aḥmad bāyad injā bāshad chun zan-o bachcheh-ash-rā man didam*:

احمد باید اینجا باشد چون زن و بچه اش را من دیدم

saw I his child and wife because be here must Aḥmad

2. Propriety: "I should tell him because it's not fair for him to wait for us until evening"; *bāyad beh u khabar be-deham chun bi-enṣāfi ast keh tā shab montaẓer-e mā bāshad*:

باید به او خبر بدهم چون بی انصافی است که تا شب منتظر ما باشد

be for us waiting night to is unfair because I inform him should

3. Necessity: "He has to sell his house, because he is very much in debt"; *u bāyad khāneh-ash-rā beforushad chun kheyli bedehkār ast*:

او باید خانه اش را بفروشد چون خیلی بدهکار است

is indebted very because sell his house has to he

Coming of Age on Paper

Another important marker of maturity is the *shenāsnāmeh* or "identity card." It is the state's recognition of official existence *vojud-e rasmi* وجود رسمی . The *shenāsnāmeh* defines identity in the stark terms of Behādin's interrogator (see Chapter V):

name	*nām* ______	نام
family name	*nām-e khānavādegi* ______	نام خانوادگی
father's name	*nām-e pedar* ______	نام پدر
mother's name	*nām-e mādar* ______	نام مادر
birth place	*maḥal-e tavallod* ______	محل تولد
spouse and children	*hamsar va farzandān* ___	همسر و فرزندان

The second reading in this chapter is part of a poem by Forugh Farrokhzād (1935-1967), in which the poet reacts sharply to the bare facts of bureaucratic identity. Farrokhzād was a poet, artist, director, and film maker. Like Simin Behbahāni (Chapter VII), she married young (16), became a mother, and soon divorced (at 19; see *Persian Literature* 1988:367). Farrokhzād's poetry was startlingly frank about matters that most Persian-using women did and do not discuss in public: rebellion, love, sex (see the next chapter), etc. Though her outspokenness and unconventional pursuits distanced her from both polite and impolite society, her sense of both everyday and official language remained acute throughout her short artistic life.

The poem *ey marz-e por gohar* ("O Realm full of Jewels"; Farrokhzād 1967:96-7) is about the impersonal nature of official identity. The title alludes to the Iranian national anthem at the time (for a spirited version, listen to Marzieh 199-). Farrokhzād resented becoming a number in the eyes of the state. She wanted her coming of age to be more than mere enumeration. Her poem plays on the contrast between the idealized land of the anthem and the ugly reality she knew in Tehran. In this excerpt from the poem, the elevated register of official discourse is outlined in Persian and italicized in translation. The sounds of the poem appear in transliteration near the Persian.

ای مرز پر گهر

فاتح شدم *fāteḥ shodam*

خودرا به ثبت رساندم *khod-rā beh thabt rasāndam*

خود را به نامی، در يك شناسنامه، مزین کردم

khod-rā beh nāmi, dar yak shenāsnāmeh mozayyan kardam

و هستیم به يك شماره مشخص شد

va hasti-am beh yak shomārah moshakhkhaṣ shod

پس زنده باد ٦٧٨ صادره از بخش ٥ ساکن تهران

pas zendeh bād 678 ṣādereh az bakhsh-e 5 sāken-e tehrān

دیگر خیالم از همه سو راحتست

digar khiāl-am az hameh su rāḥatast

āghush-e mehrabān-e mām-e vaṭan آغوش مهربان مام وطن

پستانك سوابق پر افتخار تاریخی

pestānak-e savābeq-e por eftekhār-e tārikhi

lālā' i-e tamaddon-o farhang لالائی تمدن و فرهنگ

jaqq-o joq-e jeqjeqeh-' i qānun و جق و جق جقجقهٔ قانون

āh آه

دیگر خیالم از همه سو راحتست

digar khiāl-am az hameh su rāḥatast

az farṭ-e shādmāni از فرط شادمانی

رفتم کنار پنجره، با اشتیاق، ششصدو هفتاد و هشت بار هوارا که از غبار پهن

raftam kenār-e panjareh, bā eshtiāq, sheshṣad-o haftād bār havā-rā keh az ghobār-e pehen

و بوی خاکروبه و ادرار منقبض شده بود

o bu-ye khākrubeh va edrār monqabeḍ shodeh bud

darun-e sineh foru dādam درون سینه فرو دادم

O Realm full of Jewels

I became *conqueror*
I *registered* myself
I *graced* myself with a name, on an *identity card*
And my being became *distinguished by a number*
So, long live 678 *issued from district 5 residing in Tehran*
Now my mind is at ease on all fronts
The loving embrace of the *motherland*
The pacifier of *the illustrious historical past*
The lullaby of *civilization and culture*
And the clatter of the rattle of the *law*

Ah
Now my mind is at ease on all fronts
From a surfeit of joy
I went to the window and eagerly downed six hundred
  and seventy-eight gulps of air dense with the dust of
  dung and the smell of street-sweepings and urine

The bite of this part of the poem comes from the coupling with *eḍāfeh* of two types of Persian that are rarely on speaking terms. Farrokhzād juxtaposes noun phrases composed of words associated with babyhood and phrases made of the elevated vocabulary of formal speech. This conjunction suggests that instead of marking the bearer's adulthood, the *shenāsnāmeh* infantilizes her.

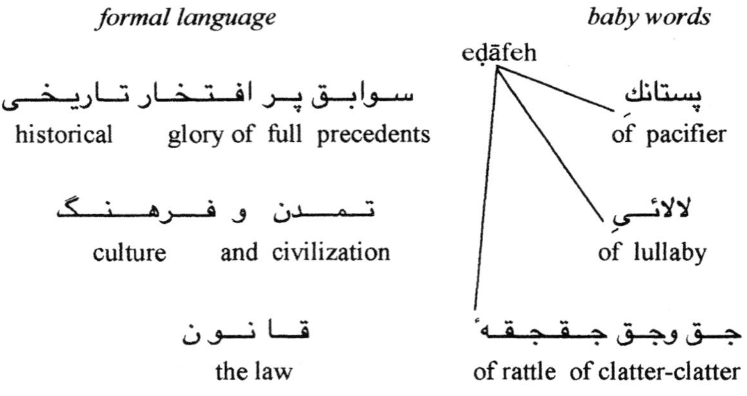

The Shape of Autonomy

"O Realm full of Jewels" opens with the term *fāteḥ*, which is formed according to the Arabic paradigm consonant$_1$ + ā + consonant$_2$ + consonant$_3$:

C_3	C_2 ā	C_1	
ح	تـــــــ	فـــا	←
ḥ	t	f	

The paradigm is associated with independence of action. One of the traditional terms for an actor with free will is *fāˁel-e mokhtār* فـاعـل مـخـتـار (Dashti 1983:36). Because of these associations, the paradigm is perfectly suited to express coming of age; in fact, a common Persian expression for "adult," ***bālegh*** بـالغ, conforms to it. Words formed this way convey the basic meaning of "performer of" or "being" that which the three root letters imply. Thus, because the basic meaning of the letters *f, t,* and *ḥ* is "to open, conquer," *fāteḥ* can mean "conqueror." By terming the mere act of receiving an I. D. card a "conquest" (a term usually followed by the name of a country or a region, even entire populations), Farrokhzād makes the first line of the poem hyper-ironic. The contrast is unmistakable; potent *fāteḥ* clashes with the trivial *shenāsnāmeh.*

C_1 ā C_2 C_3 words make up a significant part of the modern Persian lexicon. Chapter II introduces the following examples:

meaning	C_3	C_2	C_1	
"being inside"	ن	ط	ب	باطن
"being outside"	ر	ه	ظ	ظاهر
"preserver"	ظ	ف	ح	حافظ

Every term formed this way also has the short vowel e between its second and third root consonants. The silhouette they all share is:

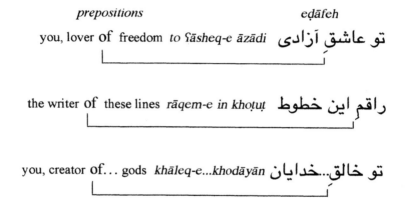

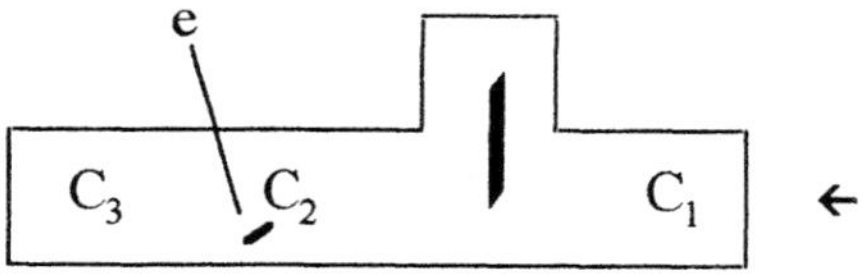

C_1 ā C_2 C_3 expressions are joined to words that follow them by means of *eḍāfeh*. English often marks this relationship with prepositions. The following examples come from the first three paragraphs of "Moments," Maḥmud Golābdarreh'i's account of the Islamic Revolution's bracing first days (1986:11):

prepositions		*eḍāfeh*
you, lover of freedom	*to ʕāsheq-e āzādi*	تو عاشقِ آزادی
the writer of these lines	*rāqem-e in khoṭuṭ*	راقمِ این خطوط
you, creator of… gods	*khāleq-e...khodāyān*	تو خالقِ...خدایان

Golābdarreh'i begins his memoir with three C_1 ā C_2 C_3 words. The first and third examples address the "rising masses" *tudeh-ye tapandeh.* The second phrase is common authorial conceit. Avoiding "I," the writer modestly refers to himself in the third person. On one hand, the repetition of the form in "Moments" suggests a popular uprising, spontaneous activity, people coming of political age. On the other, Farrokhzād's opening C_1 ā C_2 C_3 word has the opposite effect; ironic "conqueror" conveys the very absence of autonomy.

Chapter XI

Love and Eroticism

Breaching Verbal Decorum

Explicit descriptions of love making are uncommon in polite Persian today. Writers rarely mention parts of the body that verbal and written decorum *ˁeffat-e kalām va qalam* عفت کلام و قلم keep covered. Persian was not always this way. Medieval users of the language were very blunt about all forms of erotic love or *ˁeshqbāzi* عشقبازی, also *tan-kāmegi* تن کامگی (Khaleghi Motlagh 1996). Two of the greatest authors of classical literature, ˁObeyd-e Zākāni (d. ca. 1372) and Saˁdi, for example, used indecent expressions, *kāf* کاف-words (so-called because the three obscene terms for genitalia in bowdlerized texts begin with *kāf* followed by an ellipsis ...ک), in their ribald tales of homo- and heterosexual lust. These works were primarily meant for their wealthy male patrons. Few women could or would admit to knowing such things much less express their own desires openly.

The situation changed abruptly early in the 1950s, when Forugh Farrokhzād (1968: 295) published the poem "Sin" *gonāh* گناه (also, *gonah* گنه), which broke the male monopoly on writing about sexual desire in Persian. "Sin" caused many of Farrokhzād's contemporaries to brand her "reckless," "rebellious," and "hedonistic" (Langaroodi 1998:2:193). Farrokhzād later regretted writing the poem on artistic grounds.

After reading "Sin," those familiar with Western erotic writing might wonder what the fuss was about. Tame by Western standards, the poem elicits an instructive difference between modern Persian and English. Persian today is the medium of largely homosocial societies in which any discussion of sex in "mixed company" is taboo. By confessing her sins in public, Farrokhzād crossed a line that continues to divide users of the language. Similar poems in English, however, appear neither revolutionary nor transgressive.

In the following version of the poem, terms difficult to utter in mixed company are outlined in Persian and italicized in translation. The transliterations appear as close to the Persian as possible.

گناه

1

gonah kardam gonāhi por ze leḏḏat	گنه کردم گناهی پر ز لذت
dar āghushi keh garm-o ātashin bud	در آغوشی که گرم و آتشین بود
gonah kardam miān-e bāzuāni	گنه کردم میان بازوانی
keh dāgh-o kineh-jui-o āhanin bud	که داغ و کینه جوی و آهنین بود

2

dar ān khalvatgah-e tārik-o khāmush	در آن خلوتگه تاریك و خاموش
negah kardam beh chashm-e por ze rāz-ash	نگه کردم به چشم پر ز رازش
del-am dar sineh bi-tābāneh larzid	دلم در سینه بی تابانه لرزید
ze kh^{v}*āhesh-hā-ye chesm-e por niāz-ash*	ز خواهش های چشم پر نیازش

3

dar ān khalvatgah-e tārik-o khāmush	در آن خلوتگه تاریك و خاموش
parishān dar kenār-i u neshastam	پریشان در کنار او نشستم
lab-ash ru-ye lab-hā-yam havas rikht	لبش بر روی لبهایم هوس ریخت
ze anduh-e del-e divāneh rastam	ز اندوه دل دیوانه رستم.

4

foru kh^{v}āndam beh gush-ash qeṣṣeh-ye ʿeshq	فرو خواندم به گوشش قصه ی عشق
to-rā mi-kh^{v}āham ey jānāneh-ye man	ترا می خواهم ای جانانه ی من
to-rā mi-kh^{v}āham ey āghush-e jānbakhsh	ترا می خواهم ای آغوش جانبخش
to-rā ey ʿāsheq-e divāneh-ye man	ترا ای عاشق دینوانه ی من

5

havas dar didegān-ash shoʿleh afrukht	هوس در دیدگانش شعله افروخت
sharāb-e sorkh dar peymāneh raqṣid	شراب سرخ در پیمانه رقصید
tan-e man dar miān-e bestar-e narm	تن من در میان بستر نرم
be-ru-ye sineh-ash mastāneh larzid	بروی سینه اش مستانه لرزید

6

gonah kardam gonāhi por ze leḏḏat	گنه کردم گناهی پر ز لذت
kenār-e peykari larzān-o madhush	کنار پیکری لرزان و مدهوش
khodāvandā cheh mi-dānam cheh kardam	خداوندا چه می دانم چه کردم
dar ān khalvatgah-e tārik-o khāmush	در آن خلوتگه تاریك و خاموش

Sin

I sinned a *sin full of pleasure*
In *an embrace* that was *warm and fiery*
I sinned *between arms*
That were ablaze and avenging and ironlike.

In that private place dark and silent
I looked into his eyes full-of-confidences
My heart in my breast trembled impatient
From the *yearnings of his eyes full-of-desire.*

In that private place dark and silent
Agitated I sat beside him
His lips poured passion onto mine
I escaped the grief of the insane heart.

Down into his ear I recited the story of love
I want you, O beloved of mine
I want you, O *animating embrace*
You, O insane lover of mine.

Passion ignited the flame in his eyes
Red wine danced in the goblet
My body in the midst of the soft bed
Shuddered drunkenly upon his chest.

I sinned a *sin full of pleasure*
Beside a form trembling and senseless
O God, what do I know what I did
In that private place dark and silent.

Though "Sin" does not reach the rotisserie temperatures of Golestān's *kabāb* lust (Chapter VIII), it is enlightening about the traditional vocabulary of passion. The second line contains two important constituents of eroticism: *āghush* "embrace" and *ātashin* " fiery." The prefix *ham-* "co-" (see Chapter IV) and the noun-forming suffix *-i* often join *āghush* to form *ham-āghushi*, literally "co-embrace-ness," or "love-making" (Khaleghi Motlagh 1996:20):

هم + آغوش + ی = هم آغوشی

love-making ness embrace co ←

The adjective *ātashin* is formed from *ātash* "fire" and the suffix *-in*, which is also comes at the end of *āhanin* "ironlike" in the same stanza:

آهن + ین = آهنین				آتش + ین = آتشین			←
ironlike	-y	iron		*fiery*	-y	fire	

The poem also contains *jānbakhsh* (stanza 4) and *kineh-ju* (stanza 1), words formed with two common agentive suffixes: *-bakhsh* "giving" and *-ju* "seeking," both of which figure in the discussion of connectivity (Chapter IV):

←

کینه + جو = کینه جو				جان + بخش = جانبخش		
avenging	seeking	vengeance		*animating*	giving	soul

Jān ranges over a broad semantic field: "soul," "life," "love," etc. In stanza 4, it bears the suffix *-āneh* آنه "like, in the manner of," which extends *jān*'s meaning to "like a soul" or "beloved." The same suffix is found in two other words in the poem: *divāneh* (stanzas 3 and 4) and *mastāneh* (stanza 5) :

←

مست + آنه = مستانه				دیو + آنه = دیوانه				جان + آنه = جانانه		
drunkenly	-like	drunk		*insane*	-like	devil		*beloved*	-like	soul

Locating Love-making

What pushes "Sin" far beyond the bounds of verbal decorum is its realistic depiction of an act of love. This realism comes about partly through the use of prepositions. The account of foreplay, sex, and post-coital shudder and stupor contains nearly all the important ways of indicating position in Persian. The poet is held *between* her lover's arms; her heart beats *in* her breast out of patience *from* (because of) the lust of her lover's eyes; his lips pour passion *onto* hers; she tells a story *down into* his ear; she lies *upon* him, *in the midst of* a soft bed, *beside* some wine dancing *in* a cup as a spark ignites *in* his eyes.

As the poem shows, prepositions can appear both by themselves as single-word expressions and in combination, as phrases, with other prepositions. *Dar* is the most frequently used single-word preposition in the poem:

Locations in three-dimension-al spaces; in, inside, within.	"in an embrace"	آغوشی	
	"in his eyes"	دیدگانش	→ در
	"in the cup"	پیمانه	

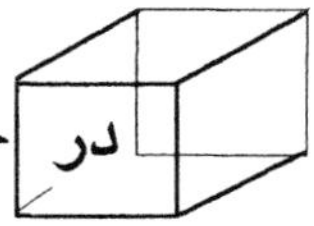

Dar can also join other prepositions. In "Sin," it combines with *miān* (by itself—as in stanza 1—meaning "between") to indicate "among," "enveloped by," or "in the midst of." *Miān* attaches to its object by means of *eḍāfeh*:

"in the midst of the bed" در میانِ بستر

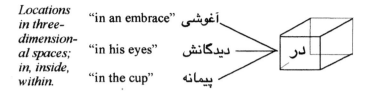

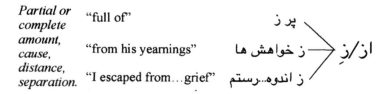

The poem also contains three senses of *az* (poetically *ze*) "of, from." In the first and last stanzas, ز combines with *por* "full"; in other instances (stanzas 2 and 3), it appears independently:

Partial or complete amount, cause, distance, separation.	"full of"	پر ز	
	"from his yearnings"	ز خواهش ها	→ از/زِ
	"I escaped from…grief"	ز اندوه...رستم	

Beh "at, to, in, into, with," perhaps the most frequently used preposition in Persian, is found alone (stanza 2) and with other prepositions, *foru* "down" (stanza 4) and *ru* "on" (stanza 5):

"into the eye...I looked" به چشم...نگه کردم  به

به گوش فرو

"down into the ear" *beh gush foru* 

بروی سینه اش

"upon his chest" *be ru-ye sineh-ash* 

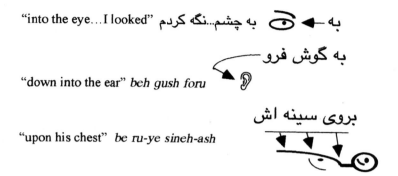

As the last example shows, the form به is often abbreviated as بـ, which always joins the element that follows it. The Introduction of this book contains the most frequent use of attached *be-*: بنام خدا *be-nām-e khodā* "in the name of God."

Expatriate Erotica

Direct references to body parts and functions also distinguish the expatriate Persian of Europe and the United States Asia from the forms of the language used in the Middle East and Asia. The heterosocial environments of the West have broader notions of what is permissible Persian in mixed company than the gender-segregated societies of the East. In the nineteenth century, Mirzā Ḥabib Eṣfahāni (d. ca. 1894), an Iranian scholar living in exile in Istanbul, edited and published unexpurgated versions of several works that could only circulate in manuscript form in Iran (Afshār 1965:161). Readers today can find Persian erotica in *Shahrzād*, a expatriate journal of original poetry and prose, and translations that touch taboo topics like clitoridectomy, homosexuality, and pre- and extra-marital love.

The second excerpt in this chapter comes from *Seven Sketches and Two Poems*, a pamphlet-size collection published in Germany by a skilled writer called Bijan Gheybi. Gheybi seems to have made a study of the conventions of medieval Persian erotica and translated them into modern language. The sketch "Return" (Gheybi 1997:14-16) describes the narrator's encounter with a dancer at a topless bar. The writing is instructive here because it broadens the compass of the prepositions introduced in the first part of this chapter. It also introduces other function words that are vital to an understanding of Persian. Finally, "Return" revisits *aṣālat* (the suitor's sine qua non in Chapter X), in its American form. In the following version of the excerpt, important relational expressions are outlined in Persian and italicized in translation.

Transcription: *sā^{ʕ}at az yāzdeh-ye shab goḏashteh, yaki az shahr-hā-ye gharb-e āmrikā, dar yak bār. dokhtari raqqāṣ, nimeh berehneh, nimeh hushyār. mi-guyad nasl-ash az yak ṭaraf mi-rasad beh sorkhpostān va beh hamin khāṭer beh aṣālat-e āmrikāi-ash mi-bālad. ṣurat-ash javān va lāghar ast va bā heykal-e khiki-ash aṣlan jur dar nami-āyad. yak māyu-ye yak-tekkeh-ye bedun-e rekāb beh tan dārad keh ru-ye ān naqsheh-ye jahān-namā kashideh-and. oqyānus-e hind ru-ye shekam va lā-ye pā-hā-yash-rā mi-pushānad va āmrikā-ye shemāli kun-e u-rā dar khod mi-girad. gāhi yak kolāh-e kābui-ye siāh va bozorg-rā keh goft dusti az montānā beh u dādeh az jā-rakhti bar mi-dārad va ru-ye pestān-hā-yash keh aknun ān-hā-rā berehneh sākhteh mi-goḏārad va dar ān ḥāl mi-raqṣad va khom-o rāst mi-shavad bedun-e inkeh kolāh be-oftad. sar-e miz barā-ye khoshāyand-ash bā ta^{ʕ}ajjobi-e sākhtegi porsidam keh cheṭowr in kār-rā mi-konad. u barā-yam ta^{ʕ}rif kard va bā dast neshān dād keh pestān-hā-rā keh beh ṭaraf-e ham be-feshārad va darun-e kolāh foru konad ba^{ʕ}d keh ān-hā-rā rahā konad beh do ṭaraf feshār mi-āvarand va nami-goḏārad keh kolāh be-oftad.*

ساعت از یازده شب گذشته، یکی از شهرهای غرب

آمریکا، در یك بار. دختری رقاص، نیمه برهنه، نیمه

هوشیار. می گوید نسلش از یك طرف می رسد به

سرخپستان و به همین خاطر به اصالت آمریکایی اش می

5   بالد. صورتش جوان و لاغر است و با هیكل خیكی اش

اصلاً جور در نمی آید. یك مایوی یك تكهٔ بدونِ ركاب به

تن دارد كه رویِ آن نقشهٔ جهان نما كشیده اند، اقیانوس

هند روی شکم و لایِ پاهایش را می پوشاند و آمریكای

شمالی كون اورا در خود می گیرد. گاهی یك كلاه كابویی

10 سیاه و بزرگ را كه گفت دوستی از مونتانا به او داده از

جا رختی بر می دارد و رویِ پستانهایش كه اكنون آنهارا

برهنه ساخته می گذارد و در آن حال می رقصد و خم و

راست می شود بدونِ اینكه كلاه بیفتد. سر میز برایِ

خوشایندش با تعجبی ساختگی پرسیدم كه چطور این

15 كاررا می كند. او برایم تعریف كرد و با دست نشان داد

كه پستانهارا كه به طرف هم بفشارد و درونِ كلاه فرو كند

بعد كه آنهارا رها كند به دو طرف فشار می آورند و نمی

گذارند كه كلاه بیفتد.

Past 11:00 at night, one of the towns of the American west, in a bar. A girl dancer, half naked, half conscious. She says her family on one side goes back *to* the Indians, and *for* this reason she brags *about* her American origins. Her face is young and thin, and doesn't go at all *with* her tubby figure. She is wearing a strapless, one-piece bathing suit, which has a map-of-the-world pattern *on* it; the Indian ocean covers her belly and *between* her legs, and North

> America takes up her ass. Sometimes she removes *from* a rack a large black cowboy hat that, she said, a friend from Montana had given her, and places it *over* her breasts—now bared—and dancing this way, she bends over and straightens up *without* letting the hat fall off. At the table, *in order to* make her happy I asked *with* feigned amazement how she did it. She explained it *to* me, and *with* her hand demonstrated how she squeezed her breasts *together* and stuffed them *down into* the hat, and then released them so that they pushed *in* two directions keeping the hat from falling.

As in classical writing of this type, the object of erotic attention here is only skin-deep; however, for reasons explained above, expatriate Persian erotica can be more explicit. While the poets of the medieval period alluded to physical charm with conventional images like the beloved's moon-bright face and jet-black mole that sets it off (see Chapter IV), Gheyby's dancer stands out as an individual. Unlike the symmetrical beauties of the past, the part-Native American's face does not match the rest of her body, and her breasts are not twin pomegranates but actual projections bulky enough to hold a ten-gallon hat in place.

Like "Sin," the excerpt from "Return" achieves a kind of realism with a thicket of prepositional phrases. Gheyby's prose, gives a more complete view of the semantics of *beh* than Farrokhzād's poem. When the dancer asserts that her line goes back *to*... (lines 3-4), the "up to a certain point" sense of *beh*, which is present in "Sin," emerged. When she boasts of her authentic American roots (lines 4-5), "about" *beh* emerges to complete the sense of the verb *bālidan*:

به اصالت آمریکایی اش می بالد

(she) boasts her American origin of/about

Finally, when Gheyby describes how the dancer's breasts compress and then hang free to keep the hat in place, he uses *beh* followed by the noun *ṭaraf* to describe both cases (lines 16-17):

→ ←	←——→
بـه طـرفِ هم	بـه دو طـرف
same direction in	direction two in

The passage also contains common prepositions, *bā* "with," *bedun* "without," and *barāi* "for," which do not appear in the poem. Both *barāi* and *bedun* connect to the elements that follow them (whether single words or entire clauses) by means of *eḍāfeh*, while *bā* does not.

	following element		*preposition*
	هـیـکـل خـیـکـی		با
(line 5)	tubby figure		with
	تـعـجـبی ساختگی	*no eḍāfeh*	با
(line 14)	feigned amazement		with
	دست		با
(line 15)	hand		with

	رکاب		بدونِ
(line 6)	strap		without
	اینـکـه کـلاه بـیـفـتـد	*eḍāfeh*	بدونِ
(line 13)	falls the hat that		without
	خوشایندش		برایِ
(line 13-14)	her pleasing		for

As *barā-yam* "for me" (line 15) shows, بـــــــــرای also admits the pronominal suffixes listed in Chapter V:

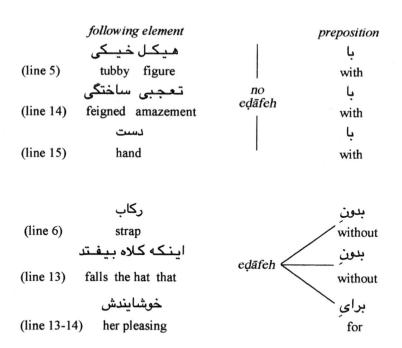

"for us"	برایمان	"for me"	برایم
"for you"	برایتان	"for you"	برایت
"for them"	برایشان	"for him, her, it"	برایش

The Direct Object: Where Sex and Grammar Meet

Mapping the dancer's bathing-suit print onto the dancer's ample figure, Gheyby (lines 8-9) writes:

object marker

آمریکای شمالی کون اورا در خود می گیرد

takes itself in her ass North America

In this sentence, *rā* indicates that *kun-e u* is the direct object of the verb *dar gereftan*. Other examples of the use of *rā* in this book include (the object marker is outlined in the examples):

1. *ramaḍān-rā maraḍān kh*^{v}*ānad ḥakimi-e dānā* (Chapter II):

رمضان را مرضان خواند حکیمی دانا

wise doctor reads [as] " patients" Ramadan

2. *ḥarf-e qorān-rā bedān ẓāherist* (Chapter II):

حرف قرآن را بدان که ظاهر یست

is an exterior that know Qoran word of

3. *kāri na-kon keh damāgh-at-rā leh konam* (Chapter V):

کاری نکن که دماغت را له کنم

I smash in your snout that don't do anything

4. *māshin-ash-rā har sāl ʕavaḍ mi-konad* (Chapter VI):

ماسینش را هر سال عوض می کند

he changes year every his car

5. *man in mardom-rā nami-shenāsam* (Chapter IX):

من این مردم را نمی شناسم

know not people these I

From these examples one can conclude that *rā* can mark both inanimate (1, 2, 3, 4), animate (5) objects.

The marking of an object is one of the most complex features of Persian grammar (Saʕādat 1999). Sometimes even skilled users of the language violate prescribed *rā* usage (Dabir-Moghaddam 1992). Indeed, as the next excerpt explains, one of the most important prose writers of modern Persian prose, Ṣādeq Chubak, faced criticism for not using the marker in his writing.

Before readers can understand the grammatical outrage and Chubak's prickly response to it, they must know about the private lives of Persian grammatical terms. The standard grammatical terms for active participle or "subject" of a verb is *fāʕel*, which obviously conforms to the C_1 ā C_2 C_3 paradigm described in the previous chapter. In addition to its grammatical significance, *fāʕel* bears a sexual meaning: the "doer" or active partner in intercourse. The corresponding term for "direct object" is *mafʕul-e mostaqim*. *Mafʕul* also has a sexual undertone in Arabic and Persian: the "done" or "pathic," the one who "receives" during intercourse. Both *fāʕel* and *mafʕul* stem from the same three-letter Arabic root:

Because of *maf*ˁ*ul*'s association with sexual passivity, traditionally the woman's role, the term is considered insulting when applied to men.

The following excerpt is part of an interview (Elahi 1993:249), in which the interviewer reports what happened when the noted scholar and critic Parviz Nātel Khānlari invited Chubak to a gathering of literary figures at his home in a posh, north Tehran district. In this version, direct objects are outlined in Persian and italicized in English. Transcription: *khānlari bedun-e moqaddemeh va bar sabil-e enteqād u-rā mokhāṭeb qarār mi-dehad va mi-guyad: āqā-ye chubak cherā shomā dar kār-hā-ye-tān rā'-ye maf*ˁ*uli-rā kheyli kam este*ˁ*māl mi-konid? cubak emruz mi-guyad: nami-dānam cherā khānlari in ḥarf-rā zad. agar dar khalvat dotā-yi bud eshkāli nadāsht amā dar ḥoḍur-e jam*ˁ*. va u az jā bar mi-khizad va* ˁ*aṣā va kolāh-ash-rā bar mi-dārad va javāb mi-dehad: barā-ye in keh man bā maf*ˁ*ul-hā kāri nadāram...va az khāneh-ye khānlari birun mi-āyad va bā otubus beh shahr bar mi-gardad.*

خانلری بدون مقدمه و بر سبیل انتقاد اورا مخاطب قرار می دهد و می گوید: «آقای چوبك چرا شما در کارهایتان راء مفعولی را خیلی کم استعمال می کنید؟» چوبك امروز می گوید: «نمی دانم چرا خانلری این حرف را زد. اگر در خلوت دوتایی بود اشکالی نداشت اما در حضور جمع.» و او از جا بر می خیزد و عصا و کلاهش را بر می دارد و جواب می دهد «برای این که من با مفعول ها کاری

ندارم.» و...از خانهٔ خانلری بیرون می آید و با اتوبوس به شهر بر می گردد.

> Without preamble and by way of criticism, Khānlari addressed *him*, saying, "Mr. Chubak, why do you use *the object marker* so little in your works?" Chubak says today, "I don't know why Khānlari said this. If it had been just the two of us in private, there would have been no problem, but in the presence of that gathering." He rose from his seat, picked up *his stick and hat* and responded, "Because I don't have anything to do with those who are done."...He then left Khānlari's home and returned to the city by bus.

There are four objects in the passage, both animate and inanimate, each marked properly with *rā*. First (line 1), Chubak himself by way of pronoun اورا; second (line 3), the object marker itself راء مفعولی را by way of criticism; third (line 4), Khānlari's words این حرف را by way of insult; and fourth (line 6), Chubak's walking-stick and hat عصا و کلاهش را by way of departure. Finally the sexual objects in the passage are not marked because they are involved in the prepositional phrase با مفعول ها.

Chubak's account does not mention any women at Khānlari's gathering. If the company had been mixed, the sexual connotations of the grammatical terminology would not have emerged. No matter how humiliated he was by Khānlari's rebuke, Chubak would not have breached verbal decorum. In the homosocial societies of Iran, Afghanistan, and Tajikistan, grammar is largely a male preserve. Men lay down the laws of syntax, prescribing what is correct and incorrect. But in the heterosocial arena of expatriate Persian, the sexual banter leaves the locker room and becomes part of public discourse. Chubak's retort could appear uncensored in a journal published in Rockville, Maryland.

Chapter XII

Death at Karbala

Prince of Martyrs, Paradigm of Martyrdoms

Fred Halliday, a writer on modern Middle Eastern politics, remembers a "former member of the Iranian left" who, after becoming a staunch Islamic Republican after the Revolution, said, "You must understand the culture of martyrdom in our country" (Halliday 2000:167) Many authors find that one cannot discuss contemporary history in Persian without referring to an event that took place late in the seventh century at Karbala, a date grove on the west bank of the Euphrates in modern Iraq. This event, the martyrdom or *shahādat* of Hoseyn, the second son of ˁAli and the Prophet Mohammad's daughter Fāṭimeh, continues to shape political discourse in Persian.

Hoseyn died because his refusal to swear allegiance to Yazid (sixth Caliph, 680-83) made him a threat to the recently established Omayyad dynasty (r. 661-750). After they came to power, the Omayyads were determined to crush any opposition to their legitimacy. Yazid's father, Moˁāwiya (Caliph 661-680) did not even accept ˁAli's succession to the Caliphate. Thus the claims made on behalf of direct descendants of the Prophet, the so-called Shi'i (Shiites) or "partisans of ˁAli," on behalf of his sons were especially troubling. Fortunately for the Omayyads, Hoseyn's older brother, Hasan, had forsaken his right to the caliphate some twenty years before Karbala. This made the sole politically active grandson of the Prophet an even sharper thorn in the their sides. The hereditary feuding between the two factions climaxed during the first ten days of October 680 (1-10 Moḥarram, 61 in the lunar, Islamic year), when thousands of Omayyad troops surrounded Hoseyn and a small band composed of his relatives and followers.

Because of their role in slaughtering the innocents at Karbala, the Omayyads are paragons of tyranny in Persian. The names of several members of the clan and the instruments of their anti-Shi'i policies are defamatory in colloquial language (Najafi 1999). For example, a *moʿāvieh* (as he is Persianized) is an "evil and corrupt man." Moʿāwiya's mother, Hend, is known as *jegar-khor* or "liver-eater" for chewing the heart of her enemy Hamza, uncle of the Prophet Mohammad. Finally, a *shemr* (the name of the man that tried but did not dare deliver the *coup de grâce* to Hoseyn [Jafri 1976:191]) is a "very brutal and wicked" individual.

The first two excerpts in this chapter are from a very popular retelling of the passion of Hoseyn. The author, Z. A. Rahnamā, turns the tragedy that comes down to us in dry and often incomplete and contradictory Arabic sources into a historical novel in Persian. His prose is simple but mannered like English translations of the Bible that try to convey the "timeless" antiquity of the original. Since the story it tells is "for the ages," the writing contains examples of *bāyad* (see the previous chapter) in its predictive, foreboding sense, as in "It *must* rain some time." For the same reason, the passage also shows how Persian expresses the future with a helping verb.

In the following version (Rahnamā 1970:2:655, 656), predictive *bāyad* and the future are outlined in Persian and italicized in English. Transcription: *tārikh-nevisān negāshtand keh asb-e zibā-ye ḥoseyn keh pishāpish-e qāfeleh rāh mi-raft hamin keh beh sar zamin-e karbalā rasid va nakhlestān-e anbuh-e ānjā-rā did az ḥarakat bāz istād. imām beh asb nahib zad va feshār āvard. asb az jā-ye khod ḥarakat nakard...imām az yaki az hamrāhān porsid: nām-e in ābādi chist?. ghāḍeria....āyā nām-e digari ham dārad?....cherā, karbalā. imām goft hamin ast. haminjāst. sarzamin-e anduh-o balā....injāst keh khun-hā-ye mā bāyad rikhteh shavad. sarāpardeh va ḥarim-e mā beh ghārat be-ravad. aṭfāl-e mā koshteh shavand va injāst keh...ārāmgāh-e abadi-e man kh^{v}āhad shod va ziāratgāh-e shiʿiān-e man.*

تاریخ نویسان نگاشتند که اسب زیبای حسین که پیشاپیش قافله راه می رفت همین که به سر زمین کربلا رسید و نخلستان انبوه آنجارا دید از حرکت باز ایستاد. امام به اسب نهیب زد و فشار آورد. اسب از جای خود حرکت نکرد .... امام از یکی از همراهان پرسید: «نام این آبادی چیست؟»...

«غاضریه.»

«آیا نام دیگری هم دارد؟»...

«چرا، کربلا.»

امام گفت، «همین است. همینجاست. سرزمین اندوه و بلا.» ...«اینجاست که خون های ما باید ریخته شود. سراپرده و حریم ما به غارت برود. اطفال ما کشته شوند و اینجاست که ... آرامگاه ابدی من خواهد شد و زیارتگاه شیعیان من.

Historians have written that when Hoseyn's beautiful horse, which was leading the caravan, reached the land of Karbala and saw the dense palm grove there, it stopped. The Imam shouted at the horse and prodded, but it would not budge.... The Imam asked one of the companions, "What is the name of this place?"

"Ghāḍeria."

"Does it have another name?"...

"Why yes, Karbala."

The Imam said, "This is it. This is the very place. The land of 'grief and affliction.'"...Here is where our blood *must be shed*; our camp and women's enclosure *must be pillaged*; our children *killed*. And it is here that...*shall become* my eternal resting place and the pilgrimage place of my partisans.

Nature is sympathetic to the plight of Hoseyn in popular accounts of Karbala. Here the horse makes out the killing ground among the palms before the Imam does. The name Karbala, which can be a Perso-Arabic pun, confirms the horse's intuition. The word *karbala* breaks into two words: *karb* "grief" and *balā* "affliction," which explains what Hoseyn says after he hears the name. Writers rarely tire of this pun. It appears in a slogan that salutes the martyrs of the Islamic Revolution (Golābdarreh'i 1986:68), "greetings to all the martyrs of grief and affliction" *dorud bar tamām-e shahidān-e karb-o balā*:

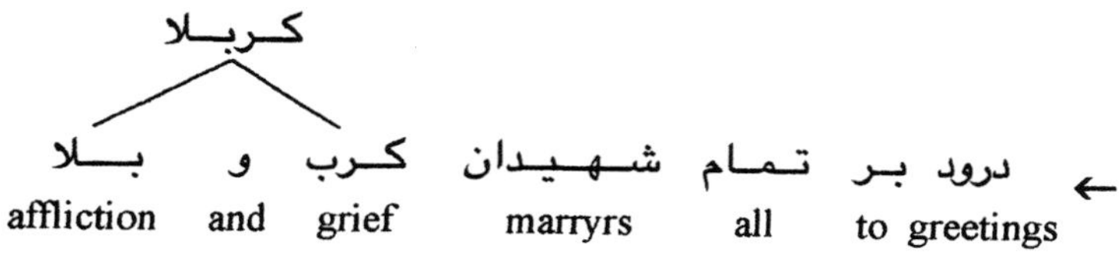

After he realizes where he is, Hoseyn uses the Persian of foreboding. Nature and language conspire in "telling" him that something bad *must* happen at Karbala. *Bāyad* governs the three consecutive subjunctives that come near the end of the passage (lines 11-12):

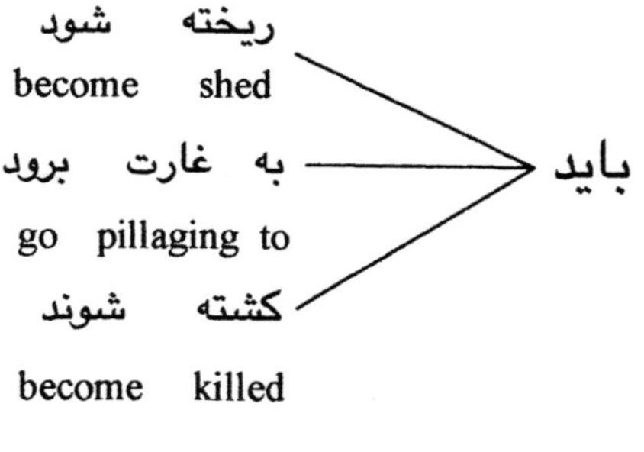

Hoseyn is just as certain when he predicts that Shiites *shall* make pilgrimages to Karbala (line 13). Here he uses a future form, *āyandeh*, composed of the helping verb *kh^{v}āh-*, which is conjugated, and the infinitive without final *n*:

short infinitive	*helping verb*				
شد	خواهد	من	ابدی	آرامگاه	←
become	shall	my	eternal	resting place	

The full paradigm of "shall/will become" is:

ما خواهیم شد	1	من خواهم شد
شما خواهید شد	2	تو خواهی شد
آن ها خواهند شد	3	او خواهد شد

Most solemn predictions conform to this pattern. For example, "Blessed are the meek, for they shall inherit the earth" (Matthew 5:5; *Enjil* 10) is ***khoshā be-ḥāl-e forutanān, zirā ishān mālek tamām-e jahān kh^{v}āhand gasht***: خوشا بحال فروتنان، زیرا ایشان مالک تمام جهان خواهند گشت . Ṭāhereh Ṣaffārzādeh (*Ṣedā-ye Sheʕr-e Emruz* 196) translates the Civil Rights anthem "We Shall Overcome" as *mā piruz kh^{v}āhim shod*: ما پیروز خواهیم شد.

More than any other event, the incident at Karbala confirms the Shi'i world view. Hoseyn is Seyyed al-Shohadā' or the Prince of Martyrs, and his martyrdom is the injustice of injustices. To many historians, however, the dispute between the Shi'i and the Omayyads was also the continuation of a pre-Islamic rivalry between two clans of the Qoreysh (the main tribal confederation in Arabia). On one side stood Hāshem, eponymous founder of the Prophet Mohammad's line, on the other ʕAbd al-Shams, whose son Omayya had the upper hand during the Prophet's lifetime. What had been intra-tribal feuding in pre-Islamic times when the caravan routes and pilgrimage sites of Arabia were at stake, became a series of civil wars for dynastic ascendancy when the Islamic empire contained large parts of North Africa and Central Asia. Shiites are convinced that justice was entirely on the side of the

Hashemites; they remained pious and brave, while the descendants of Omayya continued to do the very things that the Prophet had forbidden: drinking wine, womanizing, gambling, etc. In the Shi'i view, then, Karbala was a battle between Right and Wrong. One Persian writer (Amirshahi 1999:83) reduces the passion of Hoseyn to the "recital of Omayyad injustices against the Hashemites" *sharḥ-e maẓālem-e bani omayya beh bani hāshem*:

شرح مظالم بنی امیه به بنی هاشم ←

Hashem clan to Omayya clan injustices description

Over the centuries, the image of the army of a corrupt usurper, surrounding a small band of innocents, denying them water, dismembering some, slaughtering others in battle, has become indelible.

In the next excerpt, Rahnamā (1970:2:700) describes how the events at Karbala have grown in significance over the centuries. He mentions ways Shiites commiserate every Moḥarram. The last line, a prediction, contains an example of the helping verb future. Transcription: *emruz yak hezār-o si-ṣad-o bist-o chahār sāl az ān vāqeʕeh-ye nomuneh...mi-goḏarad va az ān chandin hezār tan va az yazid va moʕāwiya va az dastgāh-e por zarq-o barq-e chand ruzeh-eshān joz lanʕat...chizi bāqi namāndeh ast. amā az ān haftād-o do tan, milyun-hā peyravān be-nām-e shiʕiān-e ʕali bāqi-māndeh-and keh hamegi-e ānhā ʕazādāri va majāles-e sugvāri-rā...bar pā mi-sāzad va hanuz ham dar ketābkhāneh-ye maʕrefat va vejdān-e bashari faṣl-e zendagi-e ḥosehn... va vāqeʕeh-ye karbalā-ye u ḥassāstarin va setāyesh-āvartarin-e faṣl-hā-rā az jehat imān...tashkil dideh ast keh mānand-e ān neh dar goḏashteh bud va neh dar āyandeh kh^{v}āhad bud.*

امروز یك هزار و سیصد و بیست و چهار سال از آن واقعهٔ نمونه... می گذرد و از آن چندین هزار تن و از یزید و معاویه و از دستگاه پر زرق و برق چند روزه شان جز لعنت ... چیزی باقی نمانده است. اما از آن هفتاد و دو تن، میلیون ها پیروان بنام شیعیان علی باقیمانده اند که همگی آنها عزاداری و مجالس سوگواری را... بر پا می سازند و هنوز هم در کتابخانهٔ معرفت و وجدان بشری فصل زندگی حسین ... و واقعهٔ کربلای او حساسترین و ستایش آورترین فصل هارا از جهت ایمان ... تشکیل داده است که مانند آن نه در گذشته بود و نه در آینده *خواهد بود*.

Today marks the passing of one thousand and three hundred and twenty-four years since that exemplary event...and nothing remains of those several thousand [troops], of Yazid and Moʿāwiya and their short-lived machine—full of flash and glitter—but cursing. But from those seventy-two individuals, there are now millions of followers known as the partisans of ʿAli, all of whom observe the rites of mourning and hold commiseration meetings. And still in the library of human learning and conscience, the chapter of Imam Hoseyn's life...and his Karbala passion have formed the most emotional and praiseworthy chapters on faith...There has never been anything like them in the past nor *will there be* in the future.

The Arts of Karbala

Karbala remains current in the Persian world through a variety of Moḥarram mourning rituals that often involve the arts: literature, music, painting. Professional dirge-reciters, *rowḍeh-khᵛān* or *nowḥeh-khᵛān*, bring their audiences to tears with their enactments of the Shiite martyrologies. In Iran, amateurs and professionals act in passion plays called *taˤzieh*. Another common Persian expression of Karbala misery is the elegy or *marthieh*. The next reading is an excerpt from a *marthieh* by Qā'āni (d.1853), one of the "greatest and least moral" of poets (Browne 1969:4:177). Structurally Qā'āni's elegy is similar to Bach's "St. Matthew's Passion." The lyrics of both are in question-response form. Here is Bach (Canterbury 1977:2):

Come, ye daughters, share my mourning;
See Him! Whom? The Bridegroom Christ.
She Him! How? A spotless Lamb.
See it! What? His patient love.
Look! Look where? On our offence.

The similarities between the two passions are not merely structural. According to the first excerpt, Hoseyn, like Christ, knew he was to be martyred. Also like Christ he welcomed death because it would bring his followers an intercessor or *shafiˤ*. Finally, Qā'āni's Hoseyn shares Christ's lamb-like innocence.

Qā'āni's poem is instructive because it rehearses and builds upon the question words presented in Chapter IX. Prosody requires that both questions and answers be simple and succinct. The *marthieh* also traces the lineages of the two feuding families of early Islam. In the following version (Browne 1969:4:178), famous names are outlined in Persian and italicized in translation.

بارد چه؟ خون! که؟ دیده. چسان؟ روز و شب، چرا؟
bārad cheh? khun! keh? dideh. chesān? ruz-o shab, cherā?
از غم، کدام غم؟ غم سلطان کربلا،
az gham, kodām gham? gham-e soltān-e karbalā

نامش چه بود؟ حسین، ز نژاد که؟ از علی،
nām-ash cheh bud? hoseyn. ze nezhād-e keh? az ʕali,
مامش که بود؟ فاطمه. جدش که؟ مصطفی،
mām-ash keh bud? fātemeh. jadd-ash keh? mostafā
چون شد؟ شهید شد، بکجا؟ دشت ماریه،
chun shod? shahid shod. be-kojā? dasht-e māriya
کی؟ عاشر محرم. پنهان؟ نه بر ملا،
key? ʕāsher-e moharram. panhān? neh bar malā
شب کشته شد؟ نه روز. چه هنگام؟ وقت ظهر،
shab koshteh shod? neh ruz. cheh hangām? vaqt-e zohr,
شد از گلو بریده سرش؟ نی نی از قفا،
shod az golu borideh sar-ash? ney ney az qafā
سیراب کشته شد؟ نه. کس آبش نداد؟ داد،
sirāb koshteh shod? neh. kas āb-ash nadād? dād
که؟ شمر. از چه چشمه؟ ز سرچشمهٔ فنا
keh? shemr. az cheh chashmeh? ze sar-chashmeh-ye fanā
مظلوم شد شهید؟ بلی. جرم داشت؟ نه،
mazlum shod shahid? bali. jerm dāsht? neh,
کارش چه بُد؟ هدایه. و یارش که بُد؟ خدا،
kār-ash cheh bod? hedāyeh. va yār-ash keh bod? khodā,
این ظلم را که کرد؟ یزید. این یزید کیست؟
in zolm-rā keh kard? yazid. in yazid kist?
ز اولاد هند. از چه کس؟ از نطفهٔ زنا...
ze owlād-e hind. az cheh kas? az notfeh-ye zenā

Raining what? Blood! From? Eyes. How? Day and night. Why?
From grief. Which grief? Grief for the Sultan of Karbala.
What was his name? *Hoseyn*. From whose line? *ʿAli*'s.
His mother? *Fāṭimeh*. Who was his grandfather? *Moṣṭafā*.
What happened? He was martyred. Where? Māriyeh plain.
When? Tenth of Moḥarram. In secret? No, in plain sight.
Was he killed at night? No, day. What time? Noon.
Was his head cut off at the throat? No, no, from behind.
Was he killed with his fill of water? No. No one gave him some?
    They did.
Who? *Shemr*. From what source? The wellspring of annihilation.
Was he martyred an innocent? Yes. Was he at fault? No.
What was his work? Guidance. Who was his friend? God.
Who did this injustice? *Yazid*. Who is this Yazid?
One of *Hend*'s children. His father? Adultery....

When Shi'i artists paint the scene at Karbala, it invariably has two family trees, one fruit-bearing, the other poisonous.

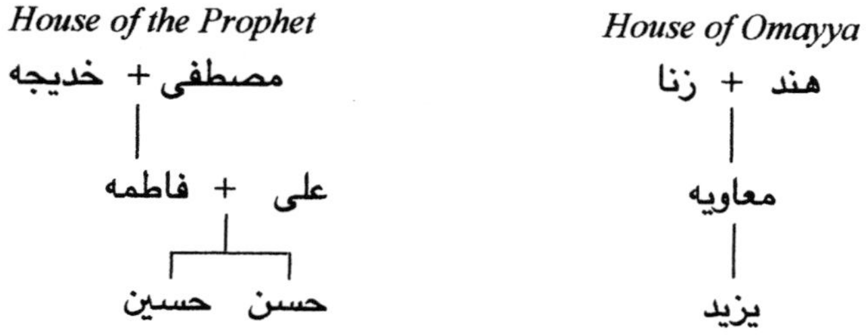

Fāṭimeh was the daughter of Mohammad (called Moṣṭafā for the rhyme; see Chapter III) and his first wife Khadijeh. The poem traces Yazid's paternal line back to *zenā* or "fornication" (his biological father was Abu Sofyān).

Karbala Today

The Karbala martyrology is also never far from modern politics. In the popular view, there are no doubts about the morality of Hoseyn's passion. This universal certainty makes it the ideal tool for the political orientation of Shiites. They know that the Prince of Martyrs is both their advocate in heaven and the consummate freedom fighter against earthly oppression. Hoseyn's resistance to the Omayyads and his martyrdom inform nearly all Shiite struggles against tyranny (Hegland 1983:221). During their war with Iraq, Iranian media identified Saddam Hussein as the Yazid of the age. The martyrdom narrative was also instrumental in marshaling anti-royalist factions at the outset of the Islamic Revolution (Momen 1985:288-89).

Leaders of countries with large Shi'i populations also make political use of Karbala. To Saddam Hussein the martyrdom represents two things: 1) a paradigm for resistance to his regime and 2) the political culture of his enemy. In the Persian Gulf War (winter 1990-91), Iraqi troops desecrated the shrines at Karbala to show their contempt for Iran and for any Hoseyn-like rebellion (Cockburn 1999:145).

The next reading in this chapter depicts the culture of martyrdom that Halliday's informant (quoted at the beginning of this chapter) mentioned. The excerpt is from a novel that takes place at the outset of the Iran-Iraq War (Faṣiḥ 1983:257-58). While in Paris visiting his hospitalized niece, the narrator goes to the embassy of the Islamic Republic to see about extending her residence permit. In the waiting room, he leafs through a magazine absentmindedly until one story catches his eye. The title, "A Day in the life of Fāṭimeh," signals modern martyrology. This excerpt from the story shows the extent to which the incident at Karbala lives on in modern society. It also adds to the stock of revolutionary Persian introduced in Chapter II.

In the following version of the story, the rhetoric of martyrology and Islamic Republican terms are outlined in Persian and italicized in translation. Transcription: *bist-o chahār sāˤat dar zendagi-e fāṭemeh khānom. fāṭemeh khānom, mādari keh chahārdeh tā bachcheh dārad ruz-hā mi-ravad rakhtshuyi va jozv-e kādr-e mostakhdemin-e hotel-e enqelāb....khod-ash majbur ast kār konad chun showhar-o pesar-e avval-ash shahid shodeh-and. khāneh-eshān dar janub-e shahr, do tā otāq kerāyeh-i...ast. mādar ṣobḥ...hameh-rā boland mi-konad. hameh voḍu mi-girand va pas az shenidan-e aḏān az boland-gui-e masjed namāz mi-khᵛānand. baˤd beh bakhsh-e barnāmeh-hā-ye razmandegān dar jebheh keh qabl az akhbār-e ṣobḥ pakhsh mi-shavad gush mi-konand. do tā az pesar-hā dar jebheh-and. pesar-e digari ham keh davāzdeh sāl dārad emruz bā basij ˤāzem-e jebheh ast. mādar qabl az inkeh beh sar-e kār beravad u-rā az zir-e qorān rad mi-konad va doˤā mi-konad keh shahid shavad, va beh behesht beravad. do-tā az dokhtar-hā-ye sizdeh va chahārdeh sāleh ham madraseh-rā tark kardeh-and dar kelās-hā-ye basij va tajvid-e qorān nāmnevisi kardeh-and. ānhā emruz hamchonin mi-khᵛāhand dar yak komiteh-ye masjed-e maḥal thabt-e nām konand keh nām-eshān jozv-e dāvṭalabān barā-ye ezdevāj bā maˤlulin-e bonyād-e shahid manẓur shavad va...in kār ham ajr-ash agar bishtar az shahādat nabāshad kamtar nist. vasaṭ-e ruz fāṭemeh khānom mashghul-e malāfeh-shuyi ast keh nāmeh-i az jebheh barā-yash mi-āyad. az khoshḥāli band-e del-ash pāreh mi-shavad. dar nāmeh beh u bā tabrik va tasliat mozhdeh mi-dehand keh yak pesar-e digar-ash dar jebheh shahid shodeh ast.*

بیست و چهار ساعت در زندگی فاطمه خانم

فاطمه خانم، مادری که چهارده تا بچه دارد روزها می رود رختشویی و جزو کادر مستخدمین هتل انقلاب .... خودش مجبور است کار کند چون شوهر و پسر اولش شهید شده اند. خانه شان در جنوب شهر، دو تا اتاق کرایه ای ... است. مادر صبح ... همه را بلند می کند.

همه وضو می گیرند و پس از شنیدن اذان از بلندگوی مسجد نماز می خوانند. بعد...به بخش برنامه های رزمندگان در جبهه که قبل از اخبار صبح پخش می شود گوش می کنند. دو تا از پسرها در جبهه اند. پسر دیگری هم که دوازده سال دارد امروز با بسیج عازم جبهه است. مادر قبل از اینکه به سر کار برود اورا از زیر قرآن رد می کند و دعا می کند که شهید شود، و به بهشت برود. دو تا از دختر های سیزده و چهارده ساله هم که مدرسه را ترک کرده اند در کلاس های بسیج و تجوید قرآن نامنویسی کرده اند. آنها امروز همچنین می خواهند در یك کمیتهٔ مسجد محل ثبت نام کنند که نامشان جزو داوطلبان برای ازدواج با معلولین بنیاد شهید منظور شود و ... این کار هم اجرش اگر بیشتر از شهادت نباشد کمتر نیست. وسط روز فاطمه خانم مشغول ملافه شویی است که نامه ای از جبهه برایش می آید. از خوشحالی بند دلش پاره می شود. در نامه به او با تبريك و تسلیت مژده می دهند که یك پسر دیگرش در جبهه شهید شده است.

Twenty-Four Hours in the Life of Mrs. Fāṭimeh

Mrs. Fāṭimeh, the mother of fourteen, spends her days at the laundry as a member of the cadre of employees at *Hotel Revolution*.... She herself has to work because her husband and oldest son were *martyred*. Their house in the southern part of the city is two rented rooms.... In the morning the mother...wakes everyone. They all do their ablutions, and, after hearing the call to prayer from

> the mosque loudspeaker, their prayers. Then...they listen to the *Warriors at the Frontline* programs that are broadcast before the news. Two of her sons are at the front. Another son, twelve years old, today is on his way there with the *Basij*. Before she goes to work, his mother has him pass under the Qoran, praying that he will become a *martyr* and go to *heaven*. Two of her daughters, thirteen and fourteen, have also left school and enrolled in *Basij* and Qoran recitation classes. Today they likewise want to register with the *Committee* at the local mosque so that their names will be in the pool of volunteer brides for the *war-wounded* at the *Martyr Foundation*. Though the reward for this act is no more than *martyrdom* it is also no less. In the middle of the day, Fāṭimeh is busy washing bedding when a letter addressed to her arrives from the front. Her heart bursts with joy. In the letter, they *congratulate and console* her with the tidings that another son of hers has been *martyred* at the front.

"A Day in the Life" recalls basic elements of the Karbala narrative. Fāṭimeh, true to her namesake, is a model martyr-mother. Her husband and sons fall victim to a later-day Yazid. Her daughters practice their own form of self-sacrifice by forgoing whole suitors for ones maimed in war. Islamic Republican Persian terms like those in Chapter III bring the old story up do date:

meaning	*line*	*term*
Paramilitary shock troops composed of dispossessed youth and tribal elements; instrumental in "militarizing" the masses (*Taʿlimāt* 44).	(11, 15)	بسيج
Committee, neighborhood associations set up to thwart counter-revolutionaries (Mohajeri 1982:79).	(17)	كميته

At the death of a martyr it is (23) تبريك و تسليت customary to offer one's congratulations (the martyr in the Hoseyni cause goes to heaven) as well as consolation.

The Shape of Victimization

The previous chapter introduced direct object *mafʿul*. This word conforms to the paradigm maC_1 C_2 u C_3 which appears in profile:

C_3 و C_2 C_1 am ←

The basic meaning of words built on this pattern is "acted upon," "receiver of the action implied by the root letters," which makes them ideal modifiers of nouns with little or no volition. MaC_1 C_2 u C_3 expressions that help establish the tone of undeserved torment in "A Day in the Life" are:

	line	$C_3C_2C_1$	*term*
Fāṭimeh is "forced" to work as a victim of circumstances.	(4)	ج ب ر	مجبور
The "sickened" or "wounded" at the front. The suffix *-in* is an Arabic plural.	(18)	ع ل ل	معلول
Fāṭimeh is "engaged" in washing the sheets and pillow cases of Hotel Revolution.	(20)	ش غ ل	مشغول

Another term, *maẓlum* or "tyrannized," is a maC_1 C_2 u C_3 expression that martyrologists often apply to Hoseyn. It appears, for example, in Qā'āni's elegy:

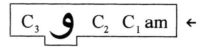

Hoseyn is the innocent victim (11) ظ ل م مظلوم of Omayyad tyranny *ẓolm*. In everyday language a "sweet, harmless, meek, and docile" person is *maẓlum* (Najafi 1999).

Chapter X notes how C_1 ā C_2 C_3 forms emerge in writing about independent action or people in positions of power. By contrast, when writers address victimization in Persian, certain maC_1 C_2 u C_3 terms are likely to appear. When Shahrokh Meskoob (1972:82) describes Shi'is' sense of grievance about Karbala, he uses the phrase *maẓlumi-e pākān* or "the victimization of the immaculate ones" مظلومی پاکان. Children and the childlike are often *ṭefl-e maˁṣum* or—even more helpless—*ṭeflak-e maˁṣum* (with the diminutive suffix *-k*):

	diminutive ك
طفل معصوم	طفلك معصوم
[Pezhvāk 1998:180]	[Jamālzādeh 1964:27]

The use of *maˁṣum* after a noun of little power like *ṭefl* is so customary that when the poet E. Khu'i uses it to describe the despotic, the effect is jarring: "the hands of the innocent tyrannous" *dasthā-ye setam-kār-e maˁṣum* دستهای ستمکار معصوم (*Ṣedā-ye Sheˁr-e Emruz* 135). Finally, when the topic is the loss of Persian identity through the uncritical embrace of western culture, another ma C_1 C_2 u C_3 term applies. The seminal critic of deracination among Iranians, F. Shādmān, once remarked (ˁA. Milāni 1999:139), "Some of us have become captivated by Europe" *barkhi az mā maftun-e farang shodah-im*:

برخی از ما مفتونِ فرنگ شده ایم.

have become Europe captivated us of some ←

In this phrase the captive Persians are bound to their captivators by *eḍāfeh*.

Chapter XIII

Us/Them

Arabs and Persian

Every language contains expressions that reveal attitudes of the majority of its users (us) toward ethnic and religious minorities (them). The topic of language and ethnicity is not new to this book. In Chapter II, the term *ˁajami*, in addition to introducing the letter *ˁeyn*, serves as a token of the relationship between language and ethnicity. When Arabs became rulers of Iran in the seventh century, عـجـمـی , literally "stutterer," came to refer to Persians because they could not pronounce Arabic sounds as native speakers did. Naturally, the privileging of Arabic and Arab religious practices and customs at the time provoked counter-prejudices in Persian.

Certain idioms preserve these prejudices. For example, *az bikh ˁarab shodan* از بـیـخ عرب شدن "to become Arab to the core" (Haim 1956:21) refers to someone who denies everything or pretends not to understand Persian to avoid responding to awkward questions. The language also becomes markedly anti-Arab when it is most nativisitic. In the latter part of the nineteenth century the writer Mirzā Aqā Khān Kermāni (1853-96) defamed Arabs in terms that still haunt Persian *rāhzanān-e berehneh va ˁoryān, mush-khᵛārān-e bi-khānamān...sharirtarin-e jānavarān, jamāˁati-e dozd-o shotor-charān*:

راهزنان برهنه و عریان، موش خواران بی خانمان ...

شریرترین جانواران، جماعتی دزد و شترچران..

"Nude and naked bandits, rat-eating tramps,... vilest of creatures, band of thieves and camelboys..." (Kermāni 1991:77). The redundant "nude and naked" in the first phrase is an example of the rhetorical paring of Arabic (*ʕoryān*) and Persian (*berehneh*) synonyms, introduced in Chapter III.

The principal minorities in the Persian world are not Arabs. They are Jews and Christians, the so-called People of the Book, ***ahl-e ketāb*** اهل کتاب (for the revelations in the Torah and the Bible) and Zoroastrians (by extension). The texts in this chapter are about identity in Persian. They contain many expressions the majority, *aksariat*, use to define the minority, *aqalliat*. These expressions map the social boundaries between Persian-using Moslems and the Jews and Christians that live among them.

Us

The majority of Persian users consider themselves Aryans آریان ها or آریائی ها . The term is not only an ethnicity, it also applies to part of the geography of Central Asia. The name "Iran" may have originated in the phrase "land of the Aryans" *sarzamin-e āriā'i* سرزمین آریائی ها . Linguists have posited the existence an ancient people called Aryans, who lived in Central Asia and used a language that may be the common ancestor of modern Indo-European languages. Some time in the second millennium B.C. these people left their Central Asian homelands and came to India and Iran. The language they spoke mixed with others to produce modern Persian .

The Persian identification with Aryans has played a role in modern history. Before World War II when Reza Pahlavi was Shah of Iran, the British and Russians vied for influence in the country. The Shah, who "was an enthusiastic admirer of the goose-stepping new German state" (Farman Farmaian 1992:73), counter-balanced the influence of England and Russia by inviting hundreds of German advisors to Iran. As war came to the nominally neutral country, some Persian users even identified (or affected to identify, see Dāneshvar 1974:52-3) Hitler as the long-awaited Lord of the Age, *ṣāḥeb-e zamān* صاحب زمان , the Twelfth Imam, who would rid them of the British and Russians forever. Hitler, in turn, recognized Persians as fellow Aryans. Not only was this consistent with Nazi racial policies, it served his strategic purposes; control of Iran and Afghanistan was vital to the eventual conquest of British India.

During WWII, the tug of Aryanism was so strong in Iran that it attracted non-Aryan minorities. Moḥammad Bahman Beygi (1992:153-58), a member of the Turkish-speaking Qashqai قشقایی tribe, was a schoolboy during the war. He was also an unabashed patriot or "country-worshipper" *vaṭan-parast* وطن. پرست The spectacular German victories over Iran's chief tormentors, the Russians and British, were so encouraging to him and many of his fellow Qashqais that they became instant Aryans. The excerpts from Bahman Beygi's writing describe the young man's naive admiration of the Germans, whose army he predicts would "liberate" the Middle East from the yoke of British colonialism.

In this version of Bahman Beygi's writing, expressions of nativism and chauvinism are outlined in Persian and italicized in English translation. Transcription: *jang-e jahāni-e dovvom dar jariān bud. piruzi-hā-ye sepāhiān-e ālmān omid-hā-ye farāvān dar del-e vaṭan-parastāni az noʕ-e man bar angikhteh bud....man doshmanān-e vaṭan-rā beh khubi mi-shenākhtam. joz rus-o englis nabudand. ālmān har do-rā beh zānu dar āvardeh bud. doshman-e moshtarak-e ānān bud. dar jang-e jahāni-e avval chonin bud. dust-e dirin-o ṭabiʕi-e mā bud. ʕeshq beh ālmān morādef bud bā ʕeshq beh irān. ālmān shamshir-e qahr-e elāhi bud. orupā gharq-e khun sākhteh bud......māhi nabud keh keshvari-rā nagoshāyad va tāj az sar-e pādeshāhi narobāyad. qoshun-e mottafaqin-rā dar donkerk beh āb rikhteh bud. faqaṭ kānāl-e kam-ʕarḍ-e mānsh māndeh bud....enqerāḍ emperāṭuri nazdik beh naẓar mi-rasid. ṣedā-ye pā-ye sardārān-e ālmāni dar savāḥel-e nil shenideh mi-shod. parcham-hā-ye ṣalib-e shekasteh az ḥowmeh-hā-ye moskow tā qolleh-hā-ye qafqāz dar ehtezāz bud. vaṭan-parastān-e irāni bā shur-o showq chashm beh rāh-e vorud-e yārān-e dirin-e khod budand vali bakht yāri nakard va beh jā-ye ānān sepāhiān-e doshmanān budand keh dast-e dusti beh ham dādand va khāk-e ˤaziz-e mihan-e mā-rā zir-e pā ghoḏashtand....man-o rafiq-am dar bāreh-ye ˤaẓamat-e nezhād-e bartar-e ārāyi dāstān-hā mi-sorudim. ālmān-rā dar orupā va irān-rā dar āsiā namāyandegān-e bar-gozideh-ye in nezhād mi-shemordim. ḥaqq-e ḥayāt-o ḥokumat māl-e mā bud. digarān joz farmānbari va gholāmi rāh-e digari nadāshtand. naqsheh-hā-ye joghrāfiā-rā dar ham mi-rikhtim va az irān keshvari bozorg ḥattā bozorgtar az āncheh dar dowrān-e hakhāmaneshi bud mi-škhtim....qoshun-e fāteḥ va ẓafarmand-e ālmān-rā az do jebheh beh irān mi-āvardim: dar yak jebheh az kuh-hā-ye qafqāz forud mi-āmadand. chāh-hā-ye naft-rā dar ekhtiār mi-gereftand. az rud-e aras mi-goḏashtand va shahr-hā-ye az dast rafteh-rā taqdim-e mām-e mihan mi-kardand. dar jebheh-ye digar fildmārshāl romel, savāḥel-e su'ez-rā posht-e sar mi-nehād. khāvar-e miāneh-rā dowr mi-zad, ˤerāq-rā az baghdād tā baṣreh zir-e pā mi-gaḏasht va ziāratgāh-hā-ye moqaddas-rā taḥvil-e shiˤiān-e irān mi-dād. ashk dar dideh-hā jamˤ mi-shod va ˤeddeh-i az vaṭan-parastān-o mosalmān-e ˤashāyeri chonān shād-o khorsand mi-shodand keh az jā bar mi-khāstand va bā vojud-e kambud-e fashang tir-hā-ye shādi beh havā mi-andākhtand.*

جنگ جهانی دوم در جریان بود. پیروزی های سپاهیان آلمان امیدهای فراوان در دل وطن پرستانی از نوع من برانگیخته بود. ... من دشمنان وطن را به خوبی می شناختم. جز روس و انگلیس نبودند. آلمان هر دورا به زانو در آورده بود. دشمن مشترك آنان بود. در جنگ جهانی اول نیز چنین بود. دوست دیرین و طبیعی ما بود.

عشق به آلمان مرادف بود با عشق به ایران.

آلمان شمشیر قهر الهی بود. اروپارا غرق خون ساخته بود. ... ماهی نبود که کشوری را نگشاید و تاج از سر پادشاهی نرباید. قشون متفقین را در دونکرك به آب ریخته بود. فقط کانال کم عرض مانش مانده بود.... انقراض امپراطوری نزدیك به نظر می رسید.

صدای پای سرداران آلمانی در سواحل نیل شنیده می شد. پرچم های صلیب شکسته از حومه های مسکو تا قله های قفقاز در اهتزاز بود.

وطن پرستان ایرانی با شور و شوق چشم به راه ورود یاران دیرین خود بودند ولی بخت یاری نکرد و به جای آنان سپاهیان دشمنان بودند که دست دوستی به هم دادند وخاك عزیز میهن مارا زیر پا گذاشتند....

من و رفیقم در بارهٔ عظمت نژاد برتر آریایی داستان ها می سرودیم. آلمان را در اروپا و ایران را در آسیا نمایندگان بر گزیدهٔ این نژاد می شمردیم. حق حیات و حکومت مال ما بود. دیگران جز فرمانبری و غلامی راه دیگری نداشتند. نقشه های جغرافیارا در هم می ریختیم و از ایران کشوری بزرگ حتی بزرگ تر از آنچه در دوران هخامنشی بود می ساختیم ....

قشون فاتح و ظفرمند آلمان را از دو جبهه به ایران می آوردیم: در یك جبهه از کوه های قفقاز فرود می آمدند. چاه های نفت را در اختیار می گرفتند. از رود ارس می گذشتند وشهرهای از دست رفته را تقدیم مام

میهن می کردند.

در جبههٔ دیگر فیلدمارشال رمل، سواحل سوئزرا پشت سر می نهاد. خاورمیانه را دور می زد، عراق را از بغداد تا بصره زیر پا می گذاشت وزیارتگاه های مقدس را تحویل شیعیان ایران می داد. اشك در دیده ها جمع می شد و عده ای ازوطن پرستان و مسلمانان عشایری چنان شاد و خرسند می شدند که از جا بر می خاستند و با وجود کمبود فشنگ تیرهای شادی به هوا می انداختند.

World War II was under way. The victories of the German armies had raised countless hopes in the hearts of *patriots* of my ilk....I knew *the enemies of the land* well. They were none but the Russians and the English. Germany had brought both to their knees. It was their common enemy. This was also so during the First World War. Germany was our age-old and natural ally. Love of Germany was synonymous with *love for Iran.*

Germany was the sword of the wrath of God. It had drowned Euope in blood....Not a month passed when it didn't snatch the crown from some king's head. It had driven allied troops into the sea at Dunkirk. Only the slim English Channel remained...The fall of the Empire was near.

The sound of German officers' footsteps was heard on the shores of the Nile. Swatstika flags were flying from the outskirts of Moscow to the peaks of the Caucasus Mts.

Iranian *patriots* eagerly awaited the arrival of their old allies, but fate did not prove friendly, and, instead of them, the armies of the enemy joined hands in friendship and trampled *the soil of our beloved homeland* under foot.

My friend and I would spin tales about the grandeur of

> the superior race. We considered Germany *the chosen representative of this race* in Europe and Iran [its repesentative] in Asia. *The right to life and rule was ours.* Others had no choice but submission and slavery. We discarded the old maps and remade Iran into a country larger than what it was in Achaemenian times....
>
> We had the conquering and triumphant German troops invade Iran from two fronts. On one front they would descend from the Caucasus Mountains and take control of the oil wells. They would cross the Aras River and return *the cities had had been lost to the motherland.*
>
> On the other front Field Marshal Rommel would put the shores of Suez behind him. He would go about the Middle East, march through Iraq from Baghdad to Basra and present the *sacred pilgrimage sites* to the Shi'i of Iran. Tears would well up in our eyes, and *patriots and tribal Moslems* would become so happy and gratified that they would rise up and, despite a shortage of ammunition, fire bullets of joy into the air.

The rhetoric of patriotism in this passage evokes some of the terms found in the poem "O Realm full of Jewels" (Chapter X). In Bahman Beygi's memoir, the Germans do not restore lost territory to just Iran, they give it to the "motherland"; likewise, Farrokhzād does not just receive an identity card, but is admitted to the "loving embrace of the motherland." In the two phrases, Arabic *vaṭan* and Persian *mihan* (lines 31-2) are interchangable:

Farrokhzād	Bahman Beygi
آغوش مهربان مام وطن	مام میهن

Mihan and *vaṭan* also admit the suffix to form Persian synonyms meaning "patriot." The passage contains another word that conveys "land, country," *keshvar*, but the word *keshvar-parast* is impossible in this context:

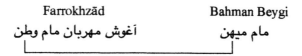

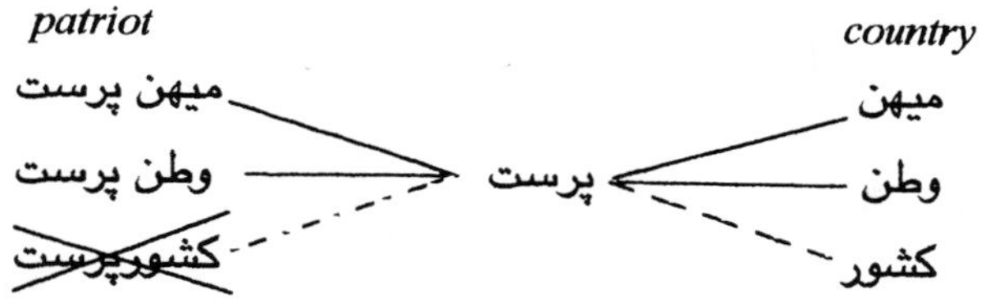

Bahman Beygi's youthful Aryanism is a odd mix of Nazi racism and Persian nostalgia for a greater Iran. Not only does he embrace the idea of a superior race, he also predicts that the Germans will restore Iran's full territorial integrity; in fact he dreams of a homeland that exceeds the boundaries of Persia's greatest empire. The religious narrative of Karbala (see the previous chapter) also plays a role in his Aryanism. In his vision of the future, General Rommel would remove the British from the martyr ground and, out of the goodness of his Aryan heart, bestow the pilgrimage shrines upon the grateful Shi'i masses.

The verbs of Bahman Beygi's writing are also worth studying. Because he describes on-going events in the past—the Nazis *were conquering* territory, *deposing* kings, he and his friend *were redrawing* the map, etc.—the writing is full of examples of the Persian past continuous (see Chapter VIII). As the translation shows, the past continuous can also have a habitual sense, in which case "would" is often the English rendering. When Bahman Beygi describes his and his friend's vision of German troops invading Iran on two fronts or of greater Iran, the past continuous does double duty as the subjunctive "contrary to fact." In other words, these were events that, though hoped for, did not actually happen, because, as he writes, "fate did not prove friendly" (line 18). Bahman Beygi's subjunctive hopes were disappointed when the Russians and English occupied Iran to make it the main conduit for American lend-lease matériel.

Them (I): Jews

In Persian, Jews are *jahud* جهود , *yahudi* یهودی (from Hebrew יהודי), and *kalimi* کلیمی (because the Prophet Moses was "conversant with God" *kalimollāh* کلیم الله). Idiomatic language with these expressions reveals attitudes toward Jews that one often encounters in Persian society. The Shylock Jew of legend (Gross 1994), for example, emerges in the vulgar expression *jahud-bāzi* جهود بازی "Jew-play" (Najafi 1999) or "pretending to be servile and miserly." Persian Shylock comes in the first line of a short story from a collection that changed Persian prose forever, turning it into a modern literary language, *ʿādat ham ḥaqiqatan methl-e gedā-ye sāmereh va gorbeh-ye khānegi va yahudi-e ṭalabkār...* (Jamālzādeh 1964:111):

عادت هم حقیقةً مثل گدای سامره و گربهٔ خانگی و یهودی طلبکار...

"Habit truly is like a beggar from Samaria or a pet cat or a Jew owed money..."

The association of Jewry and money is common in modern popular fiction also. When one character in the novel "Tehran Nights" asks another whether a woman they both know has remarried, the response is: *bā pesar-e ṣāḥeb-e kafsh-e melli, fekr konam jahud ast* با پسر صاحب کفش ملی، فکر کنم جهودست "to the son of the owner of National Shoe, I think he's Jewish" (ʿAlizādeh 1999:329). Why the groom's religion is relevant, other than its evocation of wealth, is not clear from the context.

The money-worshipping Jew is a stock figure in the discourse of the Islamic Republican political elite. ʿAli Akbar Hāshemi Rafsanjāni, who served as President from 1989 to 1997, addressed a clandestine gathering on November 16, 1968. The subject of his sermon was the "Jewish" interpretation of *ruz-e maʿād*, the "Day of Return" or Judgement Day. According to Rafsanjāni (1997:757), instead of being patriotic, *vaṭan-parast*, Jews are slaves to material and money *yahudi-hā mādi va pul-parast hastand*:

یهودی ها مادی و پول پرست هستند

are worshipper money and material Jews

So blinded by their infatuation with profits are Rafsanjāni Jews that they do not concern themselves with the punishments of Judgement Day.

Anti-semitism, *yahud-āzāri*, in modern Persian tends to rise with the prominence of Jews in current events. Rafsanjāni may have been reacting to the success of Israel in the 1967 War. Four years before his sermon, the writer Jalāl Āl-e Aḥmad (1994), who popularized the term *gharbzadegi*, demonized the name of the Jewish state—*esrā'il* in Persian—by calling it *ʿazrā'il*, the name of the angel of death:

عزرائیل ◄——*demonization*—— اسرائیل

Āl-e Aḥmad toured Israel as the guest of the government for two weeks in February of 1963. If the purpose of the trip was to win friends for Israel among Persian intellectuals, it did not work. Āl-e Aḥmad concluded that the Jewish state was the creation of a guilt-ridden European bourgeoisie, a bridgehead for Western interests in the Middle East, and the scourge of any Arab state that opposed those interests (1994:90).

As a minority whose presence, at times, the non-Jewish majority barely tolerates, Jews have learned to keep a low profile. Though often portrayed as wine-makers (e.g., Dāneshvar 1974:76), Jews have rarely shared intoxicants with Muslims to whom they are forbidden; hence, "Jewish wine" *sharāb-e yahudi* شرابِ یهودی is a very rare vintage (LN). Such stereotypes cannot be dismissed as relics of the medieval past. The Moslem dissident ʿAli Akbar Saʿidi Sirjāni, who was tortured and killed in an Islamic Republican prison, described Jews as a "wandering and perpetually terrified minority" *aqalliat-e sargardān-o dā'eman dar vaḥshat.* اقلیت سرگردان و دائما در وحشت (Saʿidi Sirjāni 1983:*yak*). Terrified of what?

A good beating, for one thing. In the next excerpt, Ṣadr al-Din Elahi (1997:143-46) remembers an incident from his school days at Badr Junior High in Tehran. Famous for "knowing" French, he and a few of his classmates represented their school at a city-wide test of language competence. "Jew-killing," *jahud-koshi*, tells how Jewish students, who attended a private school run by the Alliance française, recklessly raised their profiles by being better at French than the Moslem majority. The Badr boys decided to avenge the slight to the honor of their teacher and school by hammering the victors back into anonymity. The Jewish boys, in turn, re-lowered their profiles by refusing to defend themselves.

In the following version of *jahud-koshi*, terms of Persian and Jewish identity are outlined in Persian and italicized in translation. Transcription: *kelās-e hashtom-rā dar madraseh-ye badr dāshtim tamām mi-kardim keh āqā-ye kāshāni moʿallem-e farānseh mozhdeh dād qarār ast yak mosābaqeh-ye farānseh-dāni miān-e...madraseh-ye mā...va etteḥād...ṣurat be-girad. madraseh-ye etteḥād sākhtemān-e nowi dāsht va mi-goftand māl-e ālyāns farānseh ast va aksariat-e qarib beh ettefāq-e shāgerdān-ash yahudi hastand, chun mosalmān-hā rāgheb nistand keh bachcheh-hā-ye khod-rā ānjā be-ferestand. panj nafar az behtarin-hā-ye kelās-e shānzdeh hafdeh nafari-e farānseh entekhāb shodand keh beh mosābaqeh ferestādeh shavand. man ham yaki az ānhā budam keh--beh eʿtebār-e farānseh-dāni va farānseh-khᵛāni-e pedar...ravāneh-ye majles-e mosābaqeh shodam. tar-o tamizi-e madraseh va in keh beh divār-e rāhrow-hā-yash khaṭṭ-e medād-rangi nakashideh va ru-ye miz-hā-yash-rā bā tigh yadgāri nakandeh budand va dar mostarāḥ-hā-yash, beh dar-o divār, ḥarf-e zesht naneveshteh va ʿaks-e bad nakashideh budand, hameh-ye mā bachcheh-ye mosalmān-hā-rā beh ḥeyrat andākht. emteḥān mānandi bud shabih-e emteḥān-e nehāyi-e sheshom-e ebtedāyi....yak sāʿat baʿd az shoruʿ-e do sāʿat-e vaqt-e mosābaqeh, bachcheh-hā-ye* *etteḥād varaqeh-hā-rā dādand va raftand. hafteh-ye baʕd vaqti āqā-ye kāshāni beh kelās āmad, dahān-ash por bud az malāmat...shomā keh moʕallemi methl-e man dārid, nah tanhā khod-etān balkeh ma-rā ham beyn-e moʕallem-e farānseh-hā sar shekasteh kardid. chun baʕd az madraseh-ye pahlavi...keh shāgerdān-ash beh tanbali shohreh-ye shahr-and, nur-e chashmi-hā-ye badr az ākher dovvom shodeh-and. bad-tar az hameh in keh shagerdān-e etteḥād maqām-e avval beh dast āvardand....sāʕat ākher-e ruz-rā shimi dāshtim....tim-e farānseh-kh^{v}ān-hā tah-e kelās jamʕ shodeh bud tā taṣmim be-girad. sāʕat-e chahār-o robʕ baʕd az ẓohr lashkar-e salm-o tur sar-e sar-chashmeh istādeh bud--bā zanjir-o panjeh-boks--keh enteqām-e in rosvāyi-e ʕelmi-rā az owlād-e musā keh asbāb-e sar-shekastegi-e ānhā shodeh-and be-girad. bachcheh-hā-ye madraseh-ye etteḥād dasteh-jamʕi az sar-chashmeh beh ṭaraf-e maḥalleh sarāzir shodand. dar miān ānhā maʕlum nabud aṣlan farānseh-kh^{v}āni-hā hast yā nah. amā mā-rā cheh gham keh āmadeh budim enteqām-e badr-rā az etteḥād be-girim. do seh-tāi-e bi-savād-e tanbal dāshtim keh gardan-koloft va chāqu-kash-namā budand. ānhā jelow-ye galleh-ye bachcheh-hā-ye etteḥād-rā gereftand va shoruʕ beh foḥsh dadan kardand....ṭeflaki-hā fahmidand havā kheyli pas ast, rizeh-hā-ishān az zir dast-o pā gorikhtand. man az tars-e in keh ʕeynak-am be-shekenad va pedar--keh qasam khordeh bud sāli do ʕeynak-e bishtar barā-yam nakh^{v}āhad kharid--vādār-am konad keh dasteh-ye shekasteh-rā bā nakh posht-e gush-am biāvizam, va niz az ānjā keh kotak-kāri balad na-budam, beh ettefāq-e...do-tā bachcheh-ye tarsu va dars-kh^{v}ān--kār-e chirlider-hā-ye futbāl injā-rā mi-kardim. ānhā mi-zadand va mā hurā mi-kashidim. va tā vaqti keh do seh-tā kāseb va yaki do-tā jāhel-e sar-chashmeh pā beh meydān nagodashtand, inhā zadand va ānhā khordand va ʕajabā keh ānhā barā-ye defāʕ az khod yā zadan-e inhā ḥattā dast az āstin birun nayāvardand. beh ṭaraf-e khāneh keh rāh oftādim, sāʕat-e panj-o nim-e baʕd az ẓohr bud. in dir āmadan dar khāneh-ye pedar-e sakhtgir va mādar-e del-vāpas bakhshidani* *nabud....salāmi-e dozdāneh beh pedar kardim va vaqti u dorosht-o sakht porsid keh kodām guri budeh-im, methl-e nāpole'un bonāpārt...goftim: rafteh budim sar-e sar-chashmeh jahud-koshi, tā khordan zadim-eshān...pedar amā methl-e dig-e dolmeh poq poq mi-kard, angosht-ash gāz mi-gereft va sāket bud. in khaṭarnāk-tarin ḥāl-e in mard-e kutāh-andām-e sabz-chashm bud. har vaqt beh in ḥāl mi-oftād, mi-dānestim keh taṣmim-e sangini gerefteh ast. ṣobḥ ruz-e baʿd keh madraseh labriz az ḥekāyāt-e shojāʿāneh-ye farānseh-khᵛān-hā bud,...pedar vāred-e ḥeyāṭ-e madraseh shod va yak-rāst beh daftar-e modir raft....mā methl-e maḥkumin beh eʿdām dar otāq-e modir budim...va pedar...mi-ghorid...man beh tuleh sag-ā-ye digeh kāri nadāram, vali hamin zang-e tafriḥ-e baʿd, in korreh-khar-u jelow-ye ṣaff tanbih mi-konin va tā unjā keh jā dāreh kaf-e dast-ash mi-zanin enqadar keh nākhon-ash berizeh va digeh az in ghalaṭ-ā nakoneh! in bachcheh-ye khunevādeh-i keh pedar-bozorg-ash vaṣi-e yahudi-ā-ye maḥal mi-shod keh māl-eshun-u ākhond-ā bālā nakashan va beh esm-e sarparasti az ṣeghār-e khuneh va zendagi-eshun-u nefleh nakonan.in bāyad hamin emruz befahmeh cheh ghalaṭi kardeh keh digeh nakoneh! beh hameh be-gin keh cherā dāreh chub mi-khoreh!...dast-hā-yam bād kardeh bud, amā ashk-am dar nami-āmad. āqā-ye shafāi bi-raḥmāneh mi-zad va man mi-shemordam. kaf-e dast-am tof mi-andākhtam, zir-e baghal mi-bordam keh garm shavad va dard-rā kamtar eḥsās konam. vaqti ʿadad-e chub-hā beh panjāh rasid, āqā-ye shafāi morakhkhaṣ kard. kāẓem ḥājj-moḥammad jaʿfar chālmeydāni, ham-kelāsi-am keh jozv-e goruh-e fedāiyān-e eslām bud, dasti beh shāneh-ye man zad va goft, raḥmat beh shir-at keh meth shir vā-isādi-o chub khordi-o dam nazadi-o geryeh nakardi. faqaṭ negāh-ash kardam va goftam, ḥaqq-am bud. ḥaqq-am bud.*

جهود کُشی

کلاس هشتم را در مدرسهٔ بدر داشتیم تمام می کردیم

که آقای کاشانی معلم فرانسه مژده داد قرار است یك

مسابقهٔ فرانسه دانی میان ... مدرسهٔ ما ... و اتحاد... صورت بگیرد. مدرسه اتحاد ساختمان نوی داشت و می گفتند مال آلیانس فرانسه است و اکثریت قریب به اتفاق شاگردانش یهودی هستند، چون مسلمانها راغب نیستند که بچه های خودرا آنجا بفرستند.

پنج نفر از بهترینهای کلاس شانزده هفده نفری فرانسه انتخاب شدند که به مسابقه فرستاده شوند. من هم یکی از آنها بودم که—به اعتبار فرانسه دانی و فرانسه خوانی پدر...روانهٔ مجلس مسابقه شدم. تر و تمیزی مدرسه و این که به دیوار راهروهایش خط مدادرنگی نکشیده و روی میزهایش را با تیغ یادگاری نکنده بودند و در مستراحهایش، به در و دیوار، حرف زشت ننوشته و عکس بد نکشیده بودند، همهٔ ما بچه مسلمانهارا به حیرت انداخت. امتحان مانندی بود شبیه امتحان نهایی ششم ابتدایی...یك ساعت بعد از شروع دو ساعت وقت مسابقه، بچه های اتحاد ورقه هارا دادند و رفتند.

هفتهٔ بعد وقتی آقای کاشانی به کلاس آمد، دهانش پر بود از ملامت...«شما که معلمی مثل من دارید، نه تنها خودتان بلکه مرا هم بین معلم فرانسه ها سرشکسته کردید!» چون بعد از مدرسهٔ پهلوی ... که شاگردانش به تنبلی شهرهٔ شهرند، نورچشمیهای بدر از آخر دوم شده اند. بدتر از همه این که شاگردان اتحاد مقام اول را به دست آوردند.... ساعت آخر روزرا شیمی داشتیم....تیم فرانسه خوانها ته کلاس جمع شده بود تا تصمیم بگیرد.

ساعت چهار و ربع بعد از ظهر لشکر سلم و تور سر

سرچشمه ایستاده بود—با زنجیر و پنجه بوکس--که انتقام این رسوایی علمی را از اولاد موسی که اسباب سر شکستگی آنها شده اند بگیرد. بچه های مدرسهٔ اتحاد دسته جمعی از سر چشمه به طرف محله سرازیر شدند. در میان آنها معلوم نبود اصلاً فرانسه خوانی هست یا نه. اما مارا چه غم که آمده بودیم انتقام بدررا از اتحاد بگیریم. دو سه تایی بیسواد تنبل داشتیم که گردن کلفت و چاقوکش نما بودند. آنها جلوی گلّهٔ بچه های اتحادرا گرفتند و شروع به فحش دادن کردند.... طفلکی ها فهمیدند هوا خیلی پس است، ریزه هایشان از زیر دست و پا گریختند. من از ترس این که عینکم بشکند و پدر--که قسم خورده بود سالی دو عینك بیشتر برایم نخواهد خرید—وادارم کند که دستهٔ شکسته را با نخ پشت گوشم بیاویزم، و نیز از آنجا که کتك کاری بلد نبودم، به اتفاق...دو تا بچهٔ ترسو و درسخوان—کار «چیرلیدرِ» های فوتبال اینجارا می کردیم. آنها می زدند و ما هورا می کشیدیم. و تا وقتی که دو سه تا کاسب و یکی دو تا جاهل سرچشمه پا به میدان نگذاشتند، اینها زدند و آنها خوردند و عجبا که آنها برای دفاع از خود یا زدن اینها حتی دست از آستین بیرون نیاوردند.

به طرف خانه که راه افتادیم، ساعت پنج و نیم بعد از ظهر بود. این دیر آمدن در خانهٔ پدر سختگیر و مادر دلواپس بخشیدنی نبود.... سلامی دزدانه به پدر کردیم و وقتی او درشت و سخت پرسید که کدام گوری بوده ایم، مثل ناپلئون بناپارت... گفتیم: «رفته بودیم سر سرچشمه

جهودکُشی، تا خوردن زدیمشون!» ... پدر اما مثل دیگ دلمه پُق پُق می کرد، انگشتش را گاز می گرفت و ساکت بود. این خطرناکترین حال این مرد کوتاه اندام سبز چشم بود. هر وقت به این حال می افتاد، می دانستیم که تصمیم سنگینی گرفته است.

صبح روز بعد که مدرسه لبریز از حکایات شجاعانهٔ فرانسه خوانها بود، ... پدر وارد حیاط مدرسه شد و یکراست به دفتر مدیر رفت.... ما مثل محکومین به اعدام در اتاق مدیر بودیم ... و پدر ... می غرید ...: «من به توله سگای دیگه کاری ندارم، ولی همین زنگ تفریح بعد، این کره خرو جلوی صف تنبیه میکنین و تا اونجا که جا داره کف دستش میزنین. انقدر که ناخنش بریزه و دیگه از این غلطا نکنه! این بچهٔ خونواده ایه که پدر بزرگش وصی یهودیای محل میشد که مالشونو آخوندا بالا نکشن و به اسم سرپرستی از صِغار خونه و زندگیشونو نفله نکنن. این باید همین امروز بفهمه چه غلطی کرده که دیگه نکنه! به همه هم بگین که چرا داره چوب میخوره!» ...

دستهایم باد کرده بود، اما اشکم در نمی آمد. آقای شفایی بیرحمانه می زد و من می شمردم. کف دستم تف می انداختم، زیر بغل می بردم که گرم شود و دردرا کمتر احساس کنم. وقتی عدد چوبها به پنجاه رسید، آقای شفایی مرخص کرد. کاظم حاج محمد جعفر چالمیدانی، همکلاسی ام که جزو گروه فداییان اسلام بود، دستی به شانهٔ من زد و گفت: «رحمت به شیرت که مث شیر وایسادی و چوب خوردی و دم نزدی و گریه نکردی.» فقط

نگاهش کردم و گفتم: «حقم بود. حقم بود.»

Jew-Killing

We were about to complete the eighth year at Badr School, when Mr. Kāshāni, the French teacher told us the good news that a French contest between our school and Etteḥād had been arranged. Etteḥād school had a new building, which they said, belonged to the Alliance française, and almost all of its students were *Jewish* since *Moslems* were not eager to send their children there.

Five of the best students from the sixteen or seventeen in the French class were chosen to be sent to the competition. By virtue of my father's spoken and written knowledge of French..., I was dispatched to where the contestants gathered. The school was spic and span; there were no pencil-colored graffiti on the hallway walls, nor mementos dug into desk-tops with razor blades, nor dirty words scrawled nor pictures drawn on the restroom doors and walls. All of this astonished us *Moslem* boys. [The contest] was a kind of test like the one given at the end of sixth grade....An hour into the two-hour contest, the Etteḥād boys submitted their papers and left.

The next week Mr. Kāshāni came to class, with nothing but blame, "You, who have a teacher like me, have not only disgraced yourselves but also me among the other French teachers!" For after the Pahlavi school...whose students were notorious thoughout the city for their stupidity, the apple of the eyes at Badr had come in second to last. Worst of all was that the Etteḥād students had taken first place....We had chemistry last period....The French team gathered at the back of class to decide [what to do].

At five fifteen in the afternoon, the *army of Salm and Tur* stood at the head of Sar Chashmeh, with chains and brass knuckles, to take revenge on the *sons of Moses* for the loss of academic face that caused of their disgrace. The Ettehād boys were in a group heading from Sar-Chashmeh to their quarter. It wasn't clear whether there were any French scholars among them or not. But what did we care—we were there to take Badr's revenge on Ettehād. We had a few illiterates who were thugs and looked like they could handle a knife. They blocked the herd of Ettehād boys' way and started to curse them.... The poor kids realized that things were very bad, and the smaller ones fled between arms and legs. Fearing that my glasses would break—father had sworn that he would buy no more than two pairs a year, forcing me to suspend the broken pair behind my ears with a string—and also not knowing how to fight, I and two or three cowards and scholars played the role of cheerleaders at that football game. They would hit and we would cheer. And before a couple of shopkeepers and oafs from Sar-Chashmeh intervened, they kept on beating and the others kept taking it, and amazingly never raised a hand to defend themselves against the blows or even to strike back. It was five-thirty when we started for home. Coming home late to a home with a strict father and an anxious mother was inexcusable.... We said a sheepish hello to father and, when he sternly asked, where the hell we'd been, like Napoleon Bonaparte we said, "We went to the head of Sar-Chashmeh to kill some *Jews* and, boy, did we give it to them!" But father only fumed like a pot and quietly began to bite his finger. This was the most dangerous state for this short-statured, blue-eyed man. Whenever he entered it, we knew he was making a serious decision.

The next morning when the school was overflowing with tales of the French team's valor,...father entered the compound and headed straight to the principal's office. We were gathered there like those condemned to death....Father...roared, "I don't care about the other young pups, but as soon as the next recess, you will punish this

> little ass and beat his palms as much as it takes. So much that his fingernails drop off and he'll never screw up like this again. The child is from a family with a grandfather who served as trustee for the *Jews* in the neighborhood to keep the Mullas from taking their property and, in the name of defending the rights of the little ones in the house, beggar their lives. This one has to understand what terrible thing he's done, so he'll never do it again. And for this reason you'll tell everybody why he's being beaten!"...
>
> My hands swelled up, but the tears didn't come. Mr.Shafā'i struck mercilessly as I counted. I spat on my hands and tucked them under my arms to warm them and lessen the pain. When the count reached fifty, Mr.Shafā'i dismissed me. Kāẓem Ḥājj-Moḥammad Ja'far Chālmeydāni, my classmate who was a member of the Islamic Fedā'i slapped me on the shoulder and said, "You stood up and took it like a lion—bless the milk you had as a child—you didn't snitch or cry." I just stared at him and said, "I deserved it. I deserved it."

In reporting his father's speech, Elahi is faithful to common variations found in the colloquial Persian of Tehran. Examples of the most common substitutions the irate parent makes are:

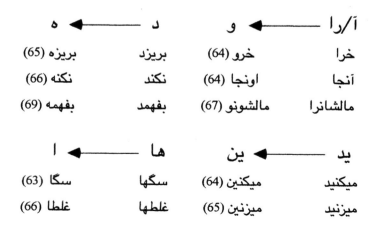

ه ◄——	د	و ◄——	آ/را
(65) بریزه	بریزد	(64) خرو	خرا
(66) نکنه	نکند	(64) اونجا	آنجا
(69) بفهمه	بفهمد	(67) مالشونو	مالشانرا

ا ◄——	ها	ین ◄——	ید
(63) سگا	سگها	(64) میکنین	میکنید
(66) غلطا	غلطها	(65) میزنین	میزنید

یهودیا (67)	یهودیها	بگویین (70)	بگویید
ه ◄——	ر	ن ◄——	ند
دیگه (63, 65, 69)	دیگر	نکشن (67)	نکشند
		نکن (68)	نکنند

E. Golestān makes many of the same substitutions when reproducing the speech of the farmer that is all mouth and no wit (see Chapter VI).

"Jew-Killing" is also a homage to pluralism in Persian. While the idioms, preaching, and other examples introduced earlier in this chapter suggest that the language documents an unrelieved record of bigotry and xenophobia, the opposite is the case. The ancestor Elahi's father extols is not exceptional. He is one in a long line of exemplary Persians that stretches at least as far back to the time when apocalyptic biblical narratives came into being (ca. 2nd century B.C.; Gottwald 1985:590). The Achaemenian (the ***hakhāmaneshiān*** the Bahman Beygi [line27] mentions) kings Cyrus, Darius, and Xerxes were particularly philo-Semitic (*yahud-dust*). The ancient Hebrew and modern Persian names of these great kings are quite close; the English names come to us through Greek and Latin.

هخامنشیان یهوددوست

ruled, *B.C.*	*Hebrew*	*Persian*	*English*
559-529	כורש	کوروش	Cyrus
522-486	דריוש	داریوش	Darius I
486-465	אחשורוש	خشیارشا	Xerxes I

According to the Bible, Kurush, the founder of the dynasty, enabled Jews to return to Jerusalem, build a temple there, embellish it with precious metals and stock it with sacrificial animals (Ezra 1:2). While it is true that Dāryush threw Daniel to the lions, the

Jewish Prophet became the most accomplished administrator in the Achaemenian Empire during his reign (Daniel 6:2-5). Khashayārshā, under whom the Jewish populations throughout the Persian Empire prospered, married the beautiful Esther, who saved Iranian Jews from slaughter (Esther 2:10).

As was the case in the "us" passage, the excerpt from Elahi's writing expresses ethnic identity in both Islamic and pre-Islamic terms. The Badr students are uniformly Moslem, while the Etteḥād students are almost entirely Jewish, because the Moslems are loathe to send their children to a *yahudi* school (lines 7-8). The Badr boys exact their vengeance from the "sons of Moses" *owlād-e musā* (line 30). When Elahi describes the Moslem gang-members, however, he calls them "the army of Salm and Tur" *lashkar-e salm-o tur* (line 28), a reference to the sons of the mythical Iranian king Faridun. These evil siblings killed their other brother Iraj, because they were jealous of the land he inherited from Faridun.

Three Uses of final ی

The voluminous excerpt from "Jew-Killing" is useful to this book because reviews lexical and grammatical material presented in other chapters. Chapter VIII explains why the Jewish boys "eat" (line 47)—as opposed to "suffer"—the enhanced punches of the Moslems, and why Elahi's classmate praises him for "eating wood" (line 78) rather than for "being beaten with a rod." The previous chapter shows why when Elahi's father's swears that he will buy him only two pairs of glasses a year (lines 40-1), he uses the *kh*^{v}*āhad* future (see the previous chapter).

"Jew-Killing" also illustrates important features of Persian ی. In the novel *The Map of Love*, diacritics explode from the tail of a well-formed Arabic *yā'* (see Chapter IV). Though this rarely happens in Persian, final ی has at least three important functions. First, a stressed final ی forms nouns of action. This noun-forming suffix appears in Chapter XI in the term *ham-āghushi*, literally "the act of mutual embrace." Second, an unstressed final ی shows that a noun is indefinte. Elahi's writing contains many examples of both as well as an instructive contrast between the two. *Tar-o tamiz* is an adjective meaning "clean." It appears on line 13 with a final ی to mean "cleanliness." Likewise the adjective *tanbal* "lazy" becomes noun *tanbali* "laziness" (line24). An example of the indefinite-making final ی is *mo*^{ʕ}*allemi* (line 21), "a teacher."

unstressed	*stressed*
معلم + ی ← معلمی	تر و تمیز + ی ← تروتمیزی
a teacher	ness clean

Since stress in rarely marked in writing and the two یs are among the most common features of Persian, they are often a source of confusion. For example, how should one read *farānseh-kh*^{v}*āni*, which appears on lines 11 and 33? Only context tells us that the ی on the end of the first is stressed, while the one on the second is not.

unstressed	*stressed*
فرانسه خوانی	فرانسه خوانی
a French student	study of French

The third function of final ی is to turn infinitives into words expressing "worthiness" or "suitability" (Ṣādeqi 1993b:18). Elahi says (line 51) that his coming home late would not be *bakhshidani* or "excusable." The word is formed from the infinistive *bakhshidan* "to forgive" and a stressed final ی. Other common words formed this way are:

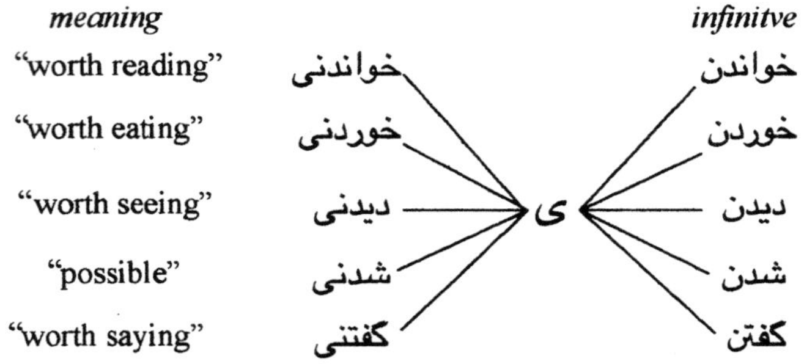

Them (II): Christians

Christians are generally termed *masiḥi* in Persian after the word for Messiah. Most of the Christians in the Persian world are Armenians ارمنی ها and Nestorians نصرانی ها who have lived in Azerbaijan, a province in northwestern Iran, for centuries. There is also a sizable Armenian community in Julfa, a Christian ward of Esfahan that dates back to the early Safavid period (end of the sixteenth century). In the nineteenth century, the Qajar government asked the British to protect the Armenians of Azerbaijan, primarily because the migration of the industrious and skilled minority to Czarist Russia would have severely depleted the human capital of Iran (Wright 1977:45). As a result, the contemporary Armenian communities of Iran, especially under the Pahlavi Shahs, enjoyed some immunity from persecution, predation, and forced conversion. They could be Christians in public: attend church *keliseh* کلیسه on Sundays, pray, and hold a kind of church fair called *bāzār-e makkāreh* بازار مَکاره . More recently, however, confiscation of property and other types of persecution of Armenians have resumed (Melikiān 2001:191-96).

The next excerpts in this chapter come from ʿAbbās Maʿrufi's novel "Symphony of the Dead" (1997:226-27; 281-82). They describes the routines of Sabbath life and marriage in the Armenian community of Tabriz around the time of Reza Shah's abdication (1941). In the following versions, terms related to Christian and

Moslem identity are outlined in Persian and italicized in translation.

Transcription: *ruz-hā-ye yakshanbeh armani-hā-ye shahr yā aṭrāf dasteh dasteh beh keliseh mi-āmadand, do*^{ʕ}*āyi mi-kh*^{v}*āndand, naḏr-o niāz-ash-eshān-rā mi-dādand va dar ḥeyāṭ-e bā ṣafā va por az gol-o derakht-e keliseh nāhār mi-khordand. va* ^{ʕ}*aṣr bar mi-gashtand...ruz-hā-ye yakshanbeh* ^{ʕ}*elāveh bar zā'erān-e mo'men, dast-forush-hā ham besāṭ-eshān-rā aṭrāf-e keliseh, kucheh-ye armanestān va maḥalleh-ye gāzrān pahn mi-kardand, va tamāmi-e ān maḥalleh-ye khalvat-rā beh bāzār-e makkāreh-i mobaddal mi-sākhtand. maḥalleh por mi-shod az ruznāmeh-forush-hā, labuyi-hā, bāqelā-paz-hā, sabzi-forush-hā, lebās-forush-hā, ṣābun-sāz-hā-ye dehāt-e aṭrāf, asbāb-bāzi-forush-hā-ye daghal-bāzi keh sar-e bachcheh-hā shireh mi-mālidand, salmāni-hā-ye dowreh-gardi keh chāi va dārchin ham mi-dādand, va sham*^{ʕ}*-forush-hā-ye keh mi-kh*^{v}*āstand kharj-e yak-sāl-eshān-rā az in gheyr-e mosalmān-hā dar biāvarand.*

روزهای یکشنبه ارمنی های شهر یا اطراف دسته دسته به کلیسا می آمدند، دعایی می خواندند، نذر و نیازشان را می دادند و در حیاط با صفا و پر از گل و درخت کلیسا ناهار می خوردند. و عصر بر می گشتند.... روزهای یکشنبه علاوه بر زائران مؤمن، دستفروشها هم بساطشان را اطراف کلیسا، کوچه ارمنستان و محلهٔ گازران پهن می کردند، و تمامی آن محلهٔ خلوت را به بازار مکاره ای مبدل می ساختند. محله پر می شد از روزنامه فروشها، لبویی ها، باقلا پزها، سبزی فروشها، لباس فروشها، صابون سازهای دهات اطراف، اسباب بازی فروش های دغلبازی که سر بچه ها شیره می مالیدند، سلمانی های دوره گردی که چای و دارچین هم

می دادند، و شمع فروشهایی که می خواستند خرج
یکسالشان را از این غیر مسلمان ها دربیاورند...

> On Sundays the *Armenians* of the city and its environs would come in groups to *church*, say their prayers and make their vows. They would have lunch in the *church* compound, a serene garden full of flowers and trees and would return in the evening....
>
> On Sundays, in addition to the observant pilgrims, vendors would also spread their wares around the church, along Armenia Lane and throughout the Gāzrān neighborhood, turning the whole of the quiet quarter into a *bāzār-e makkāreh*. The neighborhood would fill with newspaper-sellers, cooked-beet men, broad-bean-vendors, green-grocers, clothes-sellers, soap-makers from the surrounding villages, toy merchants who kept the children amused with their tricks, itinerant barbers who also served tea and cinnamon, and candle-makers who hoped to earn their annual expenses from these *non-Muslims*...

Like other members of the official minorities, Armenians generally convert to Islam before they marry Muslims. Chapter VII, Marriage and Mating, states part of the law on interfaith marriage: "The marriage of a female Muslim with a non-Muslim is not permitted." The next excerpt is about the converse: an Armenian bride named Aydā (the narrator) and her Muslim groom called Aydin . The couple first go to the church mentioned in the previous excerpt to carry out the Christian ceremony and, the next day, enter the official presence of a Moslem clergyman, who converts the bride to Islam.

Transcription: *va mā rāh oftādim. ˁeddeh-i az hamsāyeh-hā jelow-ye dar-e keliseh montaẓer-e mā budand. baˁd keh mā rasidim, hameh kaf zadand. ānvaqt beh darun-e keliseh raftim, jelow-ye meḥrāb istādim va kashesh mā-rā ˁaqd kard. ruz-e baˁd ham beh maḥḍar raftim. mādar-bozorg, pedar-bozorg va* *ʕamu gāluset ham budand. āqā-ye ʕemāmeh-sefidi neshasteh bud posht-e miz va dāsht shenāsnāmeh-hā-rā mi-kh^{v}ānd. goft: bebakhshid, shomā masiḥi hastid?. goftam: baleh. goft: āqā-ye dāmād chi? ishān keh mosalmānand ensha'llāh. aydin goft: baleh. man mosalmān-am. āqā goft: nami-shavad keh. nami-shavad ʕaqd kard. goftam: pas cheh konim? āqā goft: mosalmān be-shavid. goftam: mi-shavam. goft: be-gu ashhad an lā elāh ellā-l-lāh. va man goftam. goft: be-gu ashhad anna moḥammad rasulo-l-lāh. goftam. goft: be-gu ashhad anna ʕali valiyo-l-lāh. va man goftam. goft: mobārak ast. va baʕd khoṭbeh-ye ʕaqd-rā kh^{v}ānd.*

و ما راه افتادیم. عده ای از همسایه ها جلو در کلیسا منتظر ما بودند. بعد که ما رسیدیم، همه کف زدند. آنوقت به درون کلیسا رفتیم، جلو محراب ایستادیم و کشیش مارا عقد کرد.

روز بعد هم به محضر رفتیم. مادر بزرگ، پدر بزرگ و عمو گالوست هم بودند. آقای عمامه سفیدی نشسته بود پشت میز و داشت شناسنامه هارا می خواند. گفت: «ببخشید، شما مسیحی هستید؟»

گفتم: «بله.»

گفت: «آقای داماد چی؟ ایشان که مسلمانند انشاء الله.»

آیدین گفت: «بله. من مسلمانم.»

آقا گفت: «نمی شود که. نمی شود عقد کرد.»

گفتم: «پس چه کنیم؟»

آقا گفت: «مسلمان بشوید.»

گفتم: «می شوم.»

گفت: «بگو اشهد ان لا اله الا الله.» و من گفتم. گفت: «بگو اشهد انّ محمدً رسول الله.» گفتم. گفت: «بگو اشهد انّ علیً ولی الله.» و من گفتم. گفت: «مبارک است.» و بعد خطبهٔ عقدرا خواند.

We left. A number of neighbors were waiting for us before at the entrance to the church. When we arrived, everyone applauded. Then we went inside the church, stood before the altar, and the priest married us.

The following day we also entered the office [of the mollā]. Grandmother, grandfather, and Uncle Gāluset were also there. The white-turban man was sitting behind a desk and was reading the identity papers. He said, "Excuse me, "Are you *Christian*?"

I said, "Yes."

He said, "And the groom? He is *Moslem*, God willing."

Aydin said, "Yes. I am Moslem.

The man said, "It can't happen. The marriage cannot take place."

I said, "What should we do?"

The man said, "Become *Moslem*."

I said, "I will."

He said, "Say: '*I attest that there is no God but Allah*'" And I said it. He said, "Say: '*I attest that Mohammad is the Prophet of God*.'" I said it. He said, "Say: '*I attest that ʕAli is the Valiy* [Ally] *of God*. And I said it. He said, "Congratulations," and then he read the declaration of marriage.

The dividing line between Moslem and the religious minorities is clear from the two excerpts. The Moslem candle-makers profit considerably from non-Moslems *gheyr-e mosalmān*. The turbaned clergyman knows Aydin's ethnicity from her identity card. She cannot get married before she leaves the category of non-Moslem.

Moslems	*non-Moslems*
مسلمانان	غیر مسلمانان
شعیان سنیان	میسیحیان یهودیان زردشتیان
	zardoshtiān = Zoroastrians

She does this by reciting two standard articles of faith in Arabic; the first affirms her monotheism and the second her acceptance of Mohammad as the Prophet of God. But Aydā does not become just any Moslem, she becomes Shi'i as she must attest to ʿAli's special relationship to God, as His *valiy* or "friend, ally." By contrast, Sunnis accept the first two articles, but not the third.

The two excerpts from "Symphony of the Dead" present a useful contrast in verb usage. The first passage describes what the Armenians of Tabriz would do Sundays *ruz-hā-ye yakshanbeh*. The dominant verb form, then, is past continuous (see Chapter VIII). The second excerpt is about a particular day, thus most of the verbs are in the simple past (see Chapter VII).

Wedding Day	*Sundays*
به درون کلیسه رفتیم (3)	به کلیسه می آمدند (2)
Ø continuous marker	continuous marker

Idiomatic Persian related to Christians differs from that about the other two minorities in this chapter. For example, one cannot "play the Christian" in Persian, nor be "Christian to the core," nor can one drink "Christian wine." While both Jews and Christians have been and are subject to discrimination in all senses of the word, and both use ceremonial wine, modern Persian is more particular about Jews than it is about Christians.

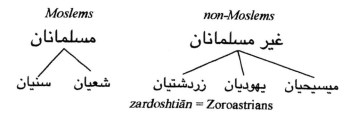

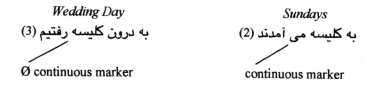

Prosthetic u

In 1981 Cynthia Helms, wife of former U. S. ambassador to Iran Richard Helms (1973-77), published a memoir of her stay in the country. At one point (p. 195) *An Ambassador's Wife in Iran* describes a tour of Esfahan's cathedral mosques. When describing the ornate part of the mosque that indicates the direction of prayer, the book has ***quiblah*** instead of the more faithful-to-the-original Arabic *qiblah*.

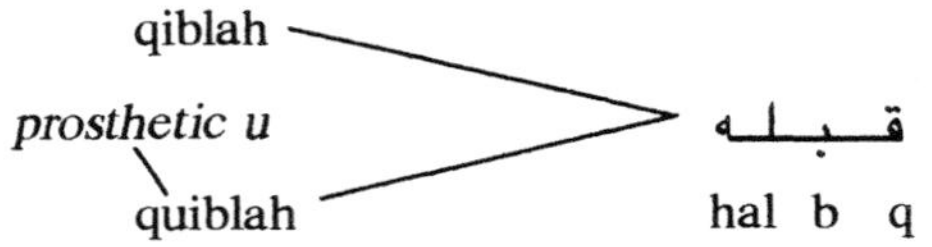

The addition of a "prosthetic" u would be of little consequence, were it not for the fact that one sees this misromanization in many other contexts and on many other texts in languages that use the Arabic writing system. For example, when English-using bookbinders put the romanized titles of Arabic, Persian, and Urdu works on the spines of library books, they almost always write u after q. No matter how many times librarians send the works back with the unnecessary letters marked in irate red, they invariably return as they exited. The binders are so conditioned to putting u after q that even if one removes the offending u, another diligently restores it.

Though technically superfluous, prosthetic u somehow domesticates the unfamiliar. It provides the outsider with a touch of orthographic home. In *An Ambassador's Wife in Iran*, it allows the author or her editors and proofreaders to approach foreign *qiblah* on friendly terms. Prosthetic u makes one part of an alien landscape conform to the English-using observer's alphabetic expectations.

The process of seeing what is not there, adding what is not to be added and thereby making the strange congenial, is very human. Such professional observers as anthropologists and cultural historians constantly have to steel themselves against false visions. Nevertheless, even the most rigorous scholars of the foreign are not immune to prosthetic u syndrome. In a heavily footnoted essay called "The Ecology of Early Food Production in Mesopotamia," Kent V. Flannery (1969:290) succumbs. His romanization of the Perso-Turkish term for "place for wintering" is *quishlaq*, with a useless u. This spelling probably passed muster with several editors, proofreaders, and the author himself. Somewhere along the line *qishlaq* or *qeshlaq*, if they had been considered at all, were rejected as incomplete, missing some vital part, without provenance in an English text.

Transliteration, translating, traveling from one alphabet to another, one syntax to another, challenge conditioned behavior. As I type the italicized, romanized Persian in this book, my mind gropes for the image of the Persian keyboard. But the two templates, Persian and English (marked with an American flag on my word processor) conflict. Before I know it, a meaningless meta-language covers the screen. *Language and Culture in Persian* outlines some to the features of Persian that are analogous to the prosthetic u, utterances and writing that emerges before users "know them." The book studies Persianizations, haphazard, scientific, and ulteriorly motivated. It establishes the tie between dotting and dyslexia, beauty and the alphabet, *kabāb* and sex. It analyzes the language of maturation, minorities, and mating for what it says about a shared Persian culture. Does it assert that Persian-users are what they write, think in certain conditioned ways just because their alphabet looks like: الـــــــفــــبـــــا? Hardly. *Language and Culture in Persian* only begins to catalog certain words, phrases, grammatical structures that emerge when users consider rich topics.

Bibliography

Adib Solṭāni, Mir Shams al-Din 1986

میر شمس الدین ادیب سلطانی. *راهنمای آماده ساختن کتاب*. تهران: سازمان انتشارات و آموزش انقلاب اسلامی، ۱۳۶۵.

Afshār 1965

ایرج افشار. *سواد و بیاض*. تهران: دهخدا، ۱۳۴۴.

Aḥmadi Givi 1994

حسن احمدی گیوی. *ادب و نگارش*. تهران: نشر قطره، ۱۳۷۳.

Agar 1994 Michael Agar. *Language Shock: Understanding the Culture of Conversation.* NY: William Morrow.

Akhavān-Thāleth 1976

مهدی اخوان ثالث. *ارغنون: مجموعهٔ شعرهائی در شیوهٔ کهن*. چاپ سوم. تهران: انتشارات مروارید، ۲۵۳۵.

Al-e Aḥmad 1964

جلال آل احمد. *یك چاه و دو چاله و شرح احوالات*. تهران: رواق، ۱۳۴۳.

__________ 1964a

جلال آل احمد. غربزدگی. چاپ ۲. تهران: رواق، ۱۳۴۳.

__________ 1978

جلال آل احمد. *نون و قلم*. تهران: امیر کبیر، ۱۳۵۷.

__________ 1994

جلال آل احمد. *سفر به عزرائیل*. تهران: مجید، ۱۳۷۳.

__________ 1997

جلال آل احمد. *گزارش ها*، زیر نظر شمس آل احمد، پژوهش و ویرایش مصطفی زمانی نیا. تهران: کتاب سیامك، ۱۳۷۶.

ʿAlizādeh 1999

غزاله علیزاده. *شب های تهران*. تهران: توس، ۱۳۷۸.

Amirshahi 1995

مهشید امیرشاهی. *در حضر*. لوس آنجلس: انتشارات شرکت کتاب، ۱۹۹۵.

__________ 1995a

مهشید امیرشاهی. *در سفر*. لوس آنجلس: انتشارات شرکت کتاب، ۱۹۹۵.

__________ 1999

مهشید امیرشاهی. *مادران و دختران*. کتاب دوم: دده قدم خیر. سوئد: نشر باران، ۱۹۹۹.

Amuzegār 1995

جهانگیر آموزگار. «اقتصاد ایران برسر دوراهی» *ایران نامه*، شماره های ۱-۲، زمستان ۱۳۷۳، بهار ۱۳۷٤، ص ۲۲۹-۲٤۹.

The Arabian Nights

كتاب ألف اليلة و ليلة من أصوله العربية الأولى. حققه و قدم له محسن مهدي. ليدن: ا. ى. بريل، ١٩٨٤.

The Arabian Nights, trans. Husain Haddawy. New York: W.W. Norton, 1990.

Arjomand 1988 Said Amir Arjomand. *The Turban for the Crown: The Islamic Revolution in Iran*. New York: Oxford University Press.

Aryanpur 1974

زمینهٔ جامعه شناسی تألیف آگ برن و نیم کوف، اقتباس ا. ح. آرین پور. چاپ هفتم. تهران: جیبی، ۱۳۵۳.

Based on W. F. Ogburn and M. F. Nimkoff, *Sociology*. Boston, 1958.

Aryanpur Kashani 1986

فرهنگ نوین پیوسته: *فارسی–انگلیسی و انگلیسی–فارسی* عباس آرین پور کاشانی،منوچهر آرین پور کاشانی. Lexington, KY: Mazda, 1986

Ashuri 1993

داریوش آشوری. *بازاندیشی زبان فارسی*. چاپ اول. تهران: نشر مرکز تهران، ۱۳۷۲.

Aṭlas 1996

اطلس کامل گیتاشناسی دورهٔ دوم: سیاسی، طبیعی، اقتصادی. چاپ هشتم. تهران: سازمان جغرافیائی و کارتوگرافی گیتاشناسی، ۱۳۷۵.

Bahār 1976

مهدی بهار. *میراث خوار استعمار*. چاپ چهاردهم. تهران: امیر کبیر، ۲۵۳۵.

Bahman Beygi 1989

محمد بهمن بیگی. *بخارای من ایل من*. چاپ اول. تهران: آگاه، ۱۳٦۸.

__________ 1992

محمد بهمن بیگی. «تلفات» *کلك*، شمارهٔ ۳۱، مهر ۱۳۷۱. ص ۱۵۳-۱٦۲.

Bahrampur 2000 Tara Bahrampur. *To See and See Again*. NY, NY: Farrar, Straus, Giroux.

Bāshgāh-e Ketāb

«باشگاه کتاب، اینترنت و فروش کتاب» بخارا، سال اول، شماره‌ء دوم، مهر و آبان ۱۳۷۷، ص ۳۷۴-۳۷۵.

Bāṭeni 1970

محمد رضا باطنی *زبان و تفکر*. تهران :انتشارات شرکت کتاب، ۱۹۹۵.

__________ 1975

محمد رضا باطنی، *مسائل زبانشناسی نوین*. تهران :انتشارات آگاه، ۱۳۵٤.

Batmanglij 1992 Najmieh Khalili Batmanglij. *New Food of Life: A Book of Ancient Persian and Modern Iranian Cooking and Ceremonies.* Washington, D.C.: Mage.

Beeman 1986 William O. Beeman. *Language, Status and Power in Iran.* Bloomington, IN: Indiana University Press, 1986.

Begdelu 2001

رضا بیگدلو. *باستانگرایی در تاریخ معاصر ایران*. تهران: نشر مرکز، ۱۳۸۰.

Behāḏin 1970

م. ا. به آذین. *مهمان این آقایان*. Inter Compos: Paris ، ۱۳٤۹.

__________ 1973

م. ا. به آذین. مجوعه‌ٔ منتخب. تهران: توس، ۱۳۵۱.

Behbahāni 1996

سمین بهبهانی. *با قلب خود چه خریدم؟*. تهران: انتشارات سخن، ۱۳۷۵.

__________ 1999 Simin Behbahani. *A Cup of Sin: Selected Poems*, ed. and trans. Farzaneh Milani and Kaveh Safa. Syracuse, NY: Syracuse, 1999.

Behruz 1931

ذبیح الله بهروز. گنج باد آورد. بسعی و اهتمام پروفسور بنیامین شل کن هاین. بی نام، کاملاً بی جا، ۱۹۱۰

Behzādi 1993

ماندانا صدیق بهزادی. «ناهماهنگیهای ضبط نامهای بیگانه در فارسی». *فرهنگ*، کتاب سیزدهم، زمستان ۱۳۷۱، ص ۱۰۳-۱۱۸.

Browne 1969 Edward G. Browne. *A Literary History of*

Persia. 4 vol. Cambridge, UK: Cambridge U.

Canterbury 1977 *The Passion of Our Lord according to St. Matthew*. Canterbury, UK: Canterbury Choral Society.

Celce-Murcia 1983 Marianne Celce-Murcia, Diane Larsen-Freeman. *The Grammar Book*. Cambridge, MA: Newbury House.

Chubak 1990

صادق چوبك. سنگ صبور. چاپ جدید. Ketab Corp.

Cockburn 1999 Andrew Cockburn and Patrick Cockburn. *Out of the Ashes: The Resurrection of Saddam Hussein.* NY: HarperCollins.

Dabir-Moghaddam 1992 Mohammad Dabir-Moghaddam. "On the (In)dependence of Syntax and Pragmatics: Evidence from the Postposition *-ra* in Persian" in *Cooperating with Written Texts: the Pragmatics and Comprehension of Written Texts,* ed. Dieter Stein. Berlin & NY: Mouton de Gruyter, 1992, pp. 549-554.

Dā'erat al-Maʕāref

دائرة المعارف بزرگ *اسلامی*، زیر نظر کاظم موسوی بجنوردی. تهران:
مرکز دائرة المعارف بزرگ اسلامی، ۱۳۷۰–.

Dāneshvar 1974

سیمین دانشور. *سو شون*. چاپ ششم. تهران: خوارزمی، ۱۳۵۲.

A Persian Requiem, trans. Roxane Zand. NY: Braziller, 1992. *Savushun: A Novel About Modern Iran,* trans. M.R. Ghanoonparvar. Washington, D.C.: Mage, 1990.

Daryābandari 1974

برتراند راسل. *تاریخ فلسفهٔ غرب*، ترجمهٔ نجف دریابندری.
تهران: جیبی، ۱۳۵۲.

Translation of *The History of Western Philosophy* by Bertand Russell.

__________ 1989

نجف دریابندری. «زبان فارسی، زبان مشترک» *ایران نامه*، سال هفتم، تابستان

۱۳٦۸ ص ٦۷٤-٦۷۸.

Dashti 1971

علی دشتی. *ایام محبس*. چاپ پنجم. تهران: ابن سینا، ۱۳۳۹.

__________ 1976

علی دشتی. *عقلا بر خلاف عقل*. چاپ دوم. تهران: انتشارات جاویدان، ۱۳۵۵.

__________ 1983

علی دشتی. *کاخ ابداع: اندیشه های گوناگون حافظ*. چاپ پنجم. تهران: انتشارات جاویدان، ۱۳٦۲.

__________ n.d.

علی دشتی. *۲۳ سال*. چاپ چهارم. بی جا: بی نام، بی تاریخ.

Dāvodi 1997

حسین داودی. *راهنمای درس املا و دستورالعمل تصحیح آن برای دوره های ابتدایی، راهنمایی، متوسطه و مراکز تربیت معلم*. تهران: سازمان پژوهش و برنامه ریزی آموزشی، ۱۳۷٦.

Dehkhodā 1973

علی اکبر دهخدا. *امثال و حکم*. چهار جلد. تهران: امیر کبیر، ۱۳۵۲.

Dowlatābādi 1973a

محمود دولت آبادی. سفر. چاپ دوم. تهران: گلشایی، ۱۳۵۲.

__________ 1973b

محمود دولت آبادی. *لایه های بیابانی*. تهران: گلشایی، ۱۳۵۲.

Dustdār 1991

آرامش دوستدار. *درخششهای تیره*. کلن: اندیشه آزاد، ۱۳۷۰.

Ebn Qotayba 1966

ابن قتیبة. *الشعر و الشعراء*، تحقیق و شرح أحمد محمد شاکر. (قاهرة): دار المعارف، ۱۹٦٦.

Elahi 1993

صدر الدین الهی. «با صادق چوبك در باغ یادها» *ایران شناسی*، سال پنجم، شمارهٔ ۲، تابستان ۱۳۷۲.

__________ 1997

صدر الدین الهی. «بچه مسلمون ناف محله» *یهودیان ایرانی در تاریخ معاصر*. جلد دوم. امریکا: مرکز تاریخ شفاهی یهودیان ایرانی.

Emdàdi-ye Asl 1996

بهروز امدادی اصل. *نامه هایی از تهران (۱۳۷۳-۱۳٦۷)*. پاریس: چشم انداز، ۱۳۷۵.

Enjil

انجیل عیسی مسیح (عهد جدید). Bartlesville, OK: VOM, 1999.

Eqbāl 1971

عباس اقبال آشتیانی. مجموعهٔ *مقالات عباس اقبال آشتیانی*، با مقدمه و تصحیح محمد دبیر سیاقی. تهران: خیام، ١٣٥٠.

Ershādi 1993

بابك میر خلیل زادهٔ ارشادی. «مقایسهٔ تنوع نامهای زنان و مردان ایرانی» *مجلهٔ زبانشناسی*، سال دهم، شماره دوم، پاییز و زمستان ١٣٧٢.

Fakhrā'i 1975

ابراهیم فخرائی. *سردار جنگل میرزا کوچك خان*. چاپ ٥. تهران: جاویدان، ١٣٥٤.

Fardust 1989

حسین فردوست. *ظهور و سقوط سلطنت پهلوی: خاطرات ارتشبد حسین فردوست*. چاپ ٢. بخش ١. تهران: انتشارات اطلاعات، ١٣٦٨.

Farman Farmanian 1992 Sattareh Farman Farmaian with Dona Munker. *Daughter of Persia: A Woman's Journey from her Father's Harem through the Islamic Revolution.* NY: Anchor.

Farrokh 1995

مهرزاد فرخ. *یادداشت های بعد از انقلاب*. چاپ ١. پاریس: بدون ناشر، ١٣٧٤.

Farrokhzād 1967

فروغ فرخزاد. برگزیده *اشعار*. تهران: مروارید، ١٣٤٦.

__________ 1968

فروغ فرخزاد. *جاودانه فروغ فرخزاد*. ت. امیر اسماعیلی، ابوالقاسم صدارت. چاپ ٢. تهران: مرجان، ١٣٤٧.

__________ 1982 Forugh Farrokhzad. *A Bride of Acacias: Selected Poems*, trans. Jascha Kessler with Amin Banani. Delmar, NY: Caravan Books.

Farshidvard 1993

خسرو فرشیدورد. «ساختمان دستوری و تحلیل معنایی اصطلاحات علمی و فنی» در *مجموعه مقالات سمینار زبان فارسی*. تهران: مرکز نشر دانشگاهی، ١٣٧٢ ص ٣٤٥-٣٥٥.

Fārsi-e Avval-e Dabestān 2001

فارسی اول دبستان. تهران: اداره‌ٔ کل چاپ و توزیع کتاب های درسی، ۱۳۸۰.

Farzāneh 1993

م. ف. فرزانه. *آشنایی با صادق هدایت*: ج. ۱ آنچه صادق هدایت به من گفت؛ ج. ۲ *صادق هدایت چه میگفت و پرونده چند یادبود*. تهران: نشر مرکز، ۱۳۷۲.

Faṣiḥ 1983

اسماعیل فصیح. *ثریا در اغما*. تهران: نشر نو، ۱۳۶۲.

__________ 1989

اسماعیل فصیح. *زمستان ۶۲*. تهران: سینا، ۱۳۶۸.

__________ 1998

اسماعیل فصیح. *پارس: تراژدی کمدی*. چاپ اول. تهران: نشر البرز، ۱۳۷۷.

Ferdowsi *Shahnameh*. Abu'l-Qasem Ferdowsi. *The Shahnameh (Book of Kings)*, ed. Khaleghi-Motlagh, vol. 1. New York: Bibliotheca Persica, 1988.

Ferdowsi 1998

علی فردوسی. «هوس خام: انقلاب در بامداد خمار» *ایران نامه*، سال شانزدهم، شماره‌ٔ ۴، پائیز ۱۳۷۷، ص ۶۴۱-۶۷۸.

Fihrist *The Fihrist of al-Nadim: A Tenth-Century Survey of Muslim Culture*, edited and translated by Bayard Dodge. New York: Columbia U, 1970.

Flannery 1969 Kent V. Flannery. "The Ecology of Early Food Production in Mesopotamia" in *Environment and Cultural Behavior: Ecological Studies in Anthropology*, ed Andrew P. Vayda. Austin, TX: U of Texas.

Ganji 2000

اکبر گنجی. *تاریخانه‌ٔ اشباح: آسیب شناسی گذار به دولت دمکراتیك توسعه گرا*. تهران: طرح نو، ۱۳۷۹.

Ghani, C. 1998 Cyrus Ghani. *Iran and the Rise of Reza Shah: From Qajar Collapse to Pahlavi Rule*. London: Tauris.

Ghani 1961

قاسم غنی. بحث در *آثار و افکار و احوال حافظ*. چاپ ۲. جلد دوم، قسمت اول.

تهران: زوار، ۱۳٤۰.

__________ 1982

قاسم غنی. *یادداشتها*. لندن: سیروس غنی، ۱۹۸۲.

Ghanoonparvar 1982 M. R. Ghanoonparvar. *Persian Cuisine*, Book One: Traditional Foods. Lexington, KY: Mazda.

Gheissari 1998 Ali Gheissari. *Iranian Intellectuals in the 20th Century*. Austin: University of Texas.

Gheyby 1997

بیژن غیبی. *هفت طرح و نو شعر*. Bielefeld, Germany: آنتشارات نمودار.

Golābdarreh'i 1985

محمود گلابدره یی. *سرنوشت بچه ی شمرون*. تهران: رئوف، ۱۳٦٤.

__________ 1986

محمود گلابدره یی. *لحظه ها*. تهران: کیهان، ۱۳٦٥.

Goldziher 1977 Ignaz Goldziher. *Muslim Studies*, ed. S. M. Stern, trans. C. R. Barber and S. M. Stern. Albany, NY: SUNY Press.

Golestān 1994

ابراهیم گلستان. *اسرار گنج درهٔ جنی*. چاپ ۳. نیوجرسی: روزن، ۱۹۹٤.

__________ 1996

ابراهیم گلستان. «از یك مقاله و چند استاد» *دنیای سخن*، شمارهٔ ٦۹، خرداد و تیر، ۱۳۷٥، ص ۱٤–۲۷.

__________ 1998

ابراهیم گلستان. *گفته ها*. نیوجرسی: روزن، ۱۹۹۸.

Golshiri 1971

هوشنگ گلشیری. *شاهزده احتجاب*. تهران: زمان، ۱۳٥۰.

__________ 1977

سال بلو. «ویرانگر» ترجمهٔ احمد گلشیری *الفبا*، جلد ششم، ص ۲۳۰–۲٤۳.

Gottwald 1985 Norman K. Gottwald. *The Hebrew Bible: A Social-Literary Introduction*. Philadelphia, PA: Fortress Press.

Gross 1994 John Gross. *Shylock: A Legend and Its Legacy*. NY: Touchstone.

Hafez 1983

خواجه شمس الدین محمد. *دیوان حافظ* به تصحیح پرویز ناتل خانلری. چاپ دوم. تهران: انتشارات خوارزمی، ۱۳۶۲.

Haeri 1989 Shahla Haeri. *Law of Desire*. Syracuse, NY: Syracuse University Press.

Ḥā'eri, ˁA. 1988

عبد الهادی حائری. *نخستین رویاروییهای اندیشه گران ایران با دو رویهء تمدن بورژوازی غرب*. تهران: امیر کبیر، ۱۳۶۷.

__________ 1993

عبد الهادی حائری. *آنچه گذشت...نقشی از نیم قرن تکاپو*. تهران: معین، ۱۳۷۲.

Haim 1956 S. Haïm. *Persian-English Proverbs: Together with Idioms, Phrases, Glossarial Notes, Mother Stories, etc.* Tehran: B. & D. Beroukihim Booksellers.

Ḥājj Seyyed Javādi 1998

فتانه حاج سید جوادی. *بامداد خمار*. چاپ هفدهم. تهران: پیکان، ۱۳۷۷.

Ḥālat 1997

ابو القاسم حالت. مجموعهٔ *آثار طنز*. دو جلد. تهران: کوتنبرگ، ۱۳۷۶.

Halliday 2000 Fred Halliday. *Nation and Religion in the Middle East*. Boulder, CO: Lynne Rienner.

Hamgām 1978

همگام با شعارها در انقلاب اسلامی ایران. تهران: انتشارات سپاه پاسدار، ۱۳۵۷.

Ḥaqiqat 1999

سوسن حقیقت. *خیال های خط خطی*: خوشنویسی به زبان ساده. تهران: نشر چشمه، ۱۳۷۸.

Ḥaqqshenās 1991

علی محمد حق شناس. *مقالات ادبی، زبانشناسی*. تهران: انتشارات نیلوفر، ۱۳۷۰.

Hāshemi Rafsanjāni 1997

علی اکبر هاشمی رفسنجانی. *دوران مبارزه، خاطرات، تصویرها، اسناد، گاه شمار*. جلد اول. تهران: دفتر نشر معارف انقلاب، ۱۳۷۶.

Hedāyat sd

{صادق هدایت}. *توپ مرواری*. بی جا: بی نام، بی تاریخ.

__________ 1965

صادق هدایت. مجموعه نوشته های پراکنده. چاپ دوم. تهران: امیر کبیر، ۱۳٤٤.

__________ 1965a

صادق هدایت. بوف کور. چاپ یازدهم. تهران: پرستو، ۱۳٤٤.

Hegland 1983 Mary Hegland. "Two Images of Husain: Accommodation and Revolution in an Iranian Village" in *Religion and Poitics in Iran: Shi'ism from Quietism to Revolution*, ed. Nikki R. Keddie. New Haven, CT: Yale UP.

Heine 1991 Bernd Heine, Ulrike Claudi, Friederike Hünnemeyer. *Grammaticalization: A Conceptual Framework.* Chicago: University of Chicago Press.

Helms 1981 Cynthia Helms. *An Ambassador's Wife in Iran.* NY: Dodd, Meade.

Homāyun Pur 2000

هرمز همایون پور، «سائول بلو، در ۸٤ سالگی، دختری نوزاد، کتابی جدید» *بخارا*، سال دوم، شمارهٔ دوازدهم، خرداد و تیر ۱۳۷۹، ص ۳۸۸-۳۹۰.

Irāni 1987

ناصر ایرانی. «مردن از فرط خوشی» نشر *دانش*، سال هفتم، شمارهٔ پنجم، مرداد و شهریور ۱۳٦٦، ص ۲۲-۳۱.

__________ 1989

ناصر ایرانی. «نقش رسانه های همگانی در شکل کیری افکار عمومی» نشر *دانش*، سال نهم، شمارهٔ ششم، مهر و آبان ۱۳٦۷، ص ۲۹-۳۵.

__________ 1989a

رابرتسون دیویس. «رمان و دین» ترممهء ناصر ایرانی، نشر *دانش*، سال نهم، شمارهٔ دوم، بهمن و اسفند ۱۳٦۷، ص ۱۲-۱۹.

__________ 1992

ناصر ایرانی. «داستان ملی شدن نفت ایران» نشر *دانش*، سال دوازدهم، شمارهٔ ششم، مهر و آبان ۱۳۷۱، ص ۲٤-۳۷.

Jafri 1976 S. Husain M. Jafri. *Origins and Early Development of Shi'a Islam.* Beirut: American University of Beirut.

Jamālzādeh 1964

محمد علی جمالزاده. *یکی بود یکی نبود*. تهران: کانون معرفت، ۱۳۴۳.

Kadkani 1971

محمد رضا شفیعی کدکنی. *صور خیال در شعر فارسی*. تهران: انتشارات نیل، ۱۳۵۰.

Kaḥḥālzādeh 1984

میرزا ابو القاسم خان کحالزاده. *دیده ها و شنیده ها: خاطرات..درباره مشکلات ایران در جنگ بین المللی ۱۹۱۸-۱۹۱۴*، به کوشش مرتضی کامران. تهران: نشر فرهنگ، ۱۳۶۳.

Karimi 1991

سیمین کریمی. «نقد مقاله "پیرامون <را> در زبان فارسی"» *مجله زبانشناسی*، سال هشتم، شماره اول و دوم، ۱۳۷۰، ص ۲۳-۴۱. زمستان ۱۳۶۶، ص ۱۷۱-۱۹۹.

Karimi-Hakkak 1989 Ahmad Karimi-Hakkak. "Language Reform Movement and its Language: The Case of Persian" in *The Politics of Language Purism*, ed. Björn H. Jernudd, Michael Shapiro. Berlin, New York: Mouton de Gruyter.

Karimpur Shirāzi 1998

حسن کریم پور شیرازی. *در ماندگان عشق*. چاپ چهارم. تهران: نشر اوحدی، ۱۳۷۷.

__________ 1999

حسن کریم پور شیرازی. *باغ مارشال*. چاپ نهم. تهران: نشر اوحدی، ۱۳۷۸.

Kasravi 1973

احمد کسروی. *کاروند کسروی*، به کوشش یحیی ذکاء. تهران: کتابهای جیبی، ۱۳۵۲.

__________ 1976

احمد کسروی. *زندگانی من، ده سال در عدلیه، چرا از عدلیه بیرون آمدم*. تهران: نشرو پخش کتاب، ۲۵۳۵.

Katirāyi 1969

محمود کتیرایی. *از خشت تا خشت*. تهران: دانشگاه تهران، ۱۳۴۸.

Kermāni 1991

میرزا آقا خان کرمانی. *مکتوب شاهزاده کمال الدوله به شاهزاده جلال الدوله (سه مکتوب)*، به تصحیح بهرام چوبینه. بی جا: مرد امروز، ۱۳۷۰.

Khaleghi Motlagh 1996

جلال خالقی مطلق. «تن کامه سرایی در ادب پارسی» *ایران شناسی*، سال هشتم، شماره ٔ ۱، بهار ۱۳۷۵، ص ٥٤-١٥.

Khalkhāli (2001)

صادق خلخالی (آیت الله حاج شیخ). *خاطرات*. چاپ چهارم. تهران:نشر سایه، ۱۳۸۰.

Khānlari 1944

پرویز ناتل خانلری. «دفاع از زبان فارسی»، *مجله ٔ سخن*، سال دوم، شماره ٔ سوم، اسفند ۱۳۲۳، ص ١٦١-١٦٦.

__________ 1945

پرویز ناتل خانلری. «مسئله اصلاح خط فارسی»، *مجله ٔ سخن*، دوره ٔ دوم، شماره ٔ چهارم، فروردین ١٣٢٤، ص ٢٤٢-٢٤٧.

__________ 1973

پرویز ناتل خانلری. *دستور زبان فارسی*. تهران: بنیاد فرهنگ ایران، ۱۳۵۱.

__________ 1975

پرویز ناتل خانلری. *تاریخ زبان فارسی*. چاپ ششم. تهران: انتشارات بنیاد فرهنگ ایران، ١٣٥٤.

Kimiāyi 2001

مسعود کیمیایی. *جسدهای شیشه ای؟* ویرایش جمشید ارجمند. تهران: نشر آتیه، ۱۳۸۰.

Klein 1987 Ernest Klein. *A Comprehensive Etymological Dictionary of the Hebrew Language for Readers of English*. Jerusalem: Carta.

Kushān 1991

منصور کوشان. *خواب صبوحی و تبعیدی ها* . تهران: نشر شیوا، ۱۳۷۰.

Langaroodi 1998

شمس لنگرودی. *تاریخ تحلیلی شعر نو*. تهران: نشر مرکز، -۱۳۷۰.

Lazard 1964 Gilbert Lazard. *Les premiers poetes persans (IXe-Xe siècles): Fragments rassemblés, édités et traduits*. Tome II: Textes persians. Paris: Maisonneuve.

LN

لغت نامه ، تالیف علی اکبر دهخدا، زیر نظر محمد معین. تهران: دانشگاه تهران، - ١٣٣٤.

Madani 1982

سید جلال الدین مدنی. *تاریخ معاصر ایران* . دو جلد. تهران: دفتر انتشارات اسلامی، ۱۳۶۲.

Mahootian 1997 Shahrzad Mahootian. *Persian*, with assistance of Lewis Gebhardt. London: Routledge.

Makki 1983

حسین مکی. *تاریخ بیست ساله ایران*. شش جلد. تهران: نشر ناشر، ۱۳۶۲.

Manguel 1997 Alberto Manguel. *A History of Reading*. NY, NY: Penguin.

Maʕrufi 1997

عباس معروفی. سمفونی مردگان. چاپ یکم در تبعید. کلن، آلمان، ۱۳۷۶.

Marzieh 199- *Marzieh* (CD). Paris: Culture en Liberté, 199-.

Matini 1982

جلال متینی. «زبان فارسی سند استقلال و قبالهٔ بقای ملت» *ایران نامه*، سال ۱، زمستان ۱۳۶۱، ص ۱۲۷-۱۴۲.

__________ 1988

جلال متینی. «در بارهٔ Farsi Language» *ایران نامه*، سال ششم، شمارهٔ ۲، زمستان ۱۳۶۶، ص ۱۷۱-۱۹۹.

__________ 1995

جلال متینی. «زبان و خط ما» *ایران شناسی*، سال هفتم، شمارهٔ ۲، تابستان ۱۳۷۴، ص ۲۳۵-۲۵۱.

__________ 1999

جلال متینی. «ما مار گزیدگان» *ایران شناسی*، سال یازدهم، شمارهٔ ۲، تابستان ۱۳۷۸، ص ۲۳۷-۲۵۲.

Maẓāheri 1970

علی مظاهری. *این لحظه ها*.... اصفهان: کتابفروشی تأیید، ۱۳۴۹.

Mehrābi 1992

مسعود محرابی. *تاریخ سینمای ایران ۱۳۷۱-۱۳۰۵: پوسترهای فیلم*. تهران: راد، ۱۳۷۱.

Melikiān 2001

آرتاواز ملیکیان. «سرنوشت ارامنهٔ ایران» *ایران نامه*، سال نوزدهم، شمارهء ۱-۲، زمستان ۱۳۷۹، بهار ۱۳۸۰، ص ۱۸۹-۱۹۶.

Meskoob 1972

شاهرخ مسکوب. *سوگ سیاوش: در مرگ و رستاخیز*. چاپ دوم. تهران:

خوارزمی، ۱۳۵۱.

__________ 1994

شاهرخ مسکوب. *هویت ایرانی و زبان فارسی*، تهران: باغ آینه، ۱۳۷۳.

Iranian Nationality and the Persian Language, trans. Michael C. Hillmann. Washington, D.C.: Mage Publishers, 1993.

Milāni 1999

عباس میلانی. *تجدد و تجدد ستیزی در ایران*. کلن: انتشارات گردون.

Mir ʿAbedini 1998

حسن میر عابدینی. *صد سال داستان نویسی ایران*. تهران: نشر چشمه، ۱۳۷۷.

Mir Ṣādeqi 1968

جلال میر صادقی. *شب های تماشا و گل زرد*. تهران: نیل، ۱۳۴۷.

Mohājerāni 1997

سید عطاء الله مهاجرانی. نقد توطئه *آیات شیطانی*. چاپ یازدهم. تهران: انتشارات اطلاعات، ۱۳۷۶.

Mohajeri 1982 Masih Mohajeri. *Islamic Revolution: Future Path of the Nations*. Tehran: External Liason Section of the Jihad-e Sazandegi.

Moḥammadi 1987

منوچهر محمدی. *تحلیلی بر انقلاب اسلامی*. چاپ دوم. تهران: امیر کبیر، ۱۳۶۶.

Moḥammadi Malāyeri 1996

محمد محمدی ملایری. *تاریخ و فرهنگ ایران در دوران انتقال از عصر ساسانی به عصر اسلامی*. جلد دوم دل ایرانشهر: بخش اول. تهران: انتشارات توس، ۱۳۷۵.

Moʿin 1976

محمد معین. *فرهنگ فارسی متوسط*. تهران: امیر کبیر، ۲۵۳۵.

Momen 1985 Moojan Momen. *An Introduction to Shi'i Islam*. New Haven and London: Yale University

Moṣāḥeb 1966

دایرة المعارف فارسی، به سرپرست غلامحسین مصاحب، جلد اول. تهران: مؤسسه ی انتشارات فرانکلین، ۱۳۴۵.

Musavi Garmārudi 1989

موسوی گرمارودی. «مغموم» *صدای شعر امروز* به کوشش بهمن مه آبادی و احمد منطقی تبریزی. تبریز: تلاش، ۱۳۶۸.

Nāderpur 1969

نادر نادرپور. سرمه ٔ خورشید. چاپ دوم. تهران: مروارید، ۱۳٤۸.

__________ 1992

نادر نادرپور. «مشرق در غربت و غربت در مغرب» *ایران نامه*، سال ۱۰، شماره‌ء ۲، تهار ۱۳۷۱، ص ۲۵۱-۲٦٤.

Naipaul 1998 V.S. Naipaul. *Beyond Belief: Islamic Excursions Among the Converted Peoples*. New York: Vintage.

Najafi 1987

ابو الحسن نجفی، *غلط ننویسیم*. تهران: مرکز نشر دانشگاهی، ۱۳٦٦.

__________ 1999

ابو الحسن نجفی، *فرهنگ فارسی عامیانه*. تهران: مرکز نیلوفر، ۱۳۷۸.

Naqavi 1971 Sayyed Ali Reza Naqavi. *Family Laws of Iran*. Islamabad: Islamic Research Institute.

Narāqi 1976a

احسان نراقی. *آنچه خود داشت...*. تهران: امیر کبیر، ۲٥۳٥.

__________ 1976b

احسان نراقی. غربت غرب. چاپ ۳. تهران: امیر کبیر، ۲٥۳٥.

Nashr-e Dānesh 1986

نشر *دانش*. «یادداشت در باره ٔ خط فارسی» سال ششم، شماره ٔ ششم، مهر و آبان ۱۳٦٥، ص ۲-۳.

Netton 1996 Richard Netton. *Text and Trauma: An East-West Primer*. Surrey, Great Britain: Curzon Press.

Neysari 1995

نسیم نیساری. *دستور خط فارسی: پژوهشی درباره ٔ پیوستگی خط فارسی با زبان فارسی*. تهران: وزارت فرهنگ و ارشاد اسلامی، ۱۳۷٤.

Nodushan 1973

محمد علی اسلامی ندوشن. صفیر *سیمرغ: یادداشت های سفر*. تهران: انتشارات توس، ۱۳٥۲.

Nuri ʕAlā' 1969

اسماعیل نوری علاء. *با مردم شب: مجموعه ی شعر*. چاپ اول. تهران: انتشارات بامداد، ۱۳٤۸.

Pahlavān 1991

چنگیز پهلوان. «کپی رایت: روشنفکران، دولت و مصلحت فرهنگ ملی ما» *ارغوان*، سال اول، شمارهٔ پنجم و ششم، مرداد ۱۳۷۰، ص ۸۲-۱۰۷.

Pārsipur 1996

شهرنوش پارسی پور، *خاطرات زندان*. استکهلم: نشر باران، ۱۹۹۶.

__________ 2000

شهرنوش پارسی پور. *شیوا: یك داستان دانش*. سوئد: باران، ۱۳۷۸.

Payām-e Emruz 1998

پیام امروز، شماره ۲۳، ۲۵ اردیبهشت ۱۳۷۷.

Persian Literature 1988 *Persian Literature*, ed. Ehsan Yarshater. Albany, NY: Persian Heritage Foundation.

The Persian Presence *The Persian Presence in the Islamic World*, ed. Richard G. Hovannisian and Georges Sabagh. Cambridge, UK: Cambridge University Press, 1998.

Pezhvāk 1998

ناهید پژواك. *شب سراب*. تهران: انتشارات هدایت، ۱۳۷۷.

Purjavādi 1993

نصرالله پورجوادی و احمد سمیعی. «فرهنگستان و مسئلهٔ واژه های بیگانه» *نشر دانش*، سال سیزدهم، شمارهٔ سوم، فروردین و اردیبهشت ۱۳۷۲، ص ۲-۳.

__________ 2000

نصرالله پورجوادی و. «سفری به لوس آنجلس» *نشر دانش*، سال هفدهم، شمارهٔ دوم، تابستان ۱۳۷۹، ص ۲-۶.

Qazvini 1984

محمد قزوینی. *یادداشتهای قزوینی*، به اهتمام ایرج افشار. تهران:انتشارات علمی، ۱۳۶۳.

Qommi 1980

قاضی میر احمد بن شرف الدین حسین منشی قمی. *گلستان هنر* بتصحیح و اهتمام احمد سهیلی خوانساری. چاپ دوم. تهران: کتابخانه منوچهری، ۱۳۵۹.

Qoran

ترجمة *معاني القرآن الكريم بالانجليزي*. عبد الله يوسف علي، طبعة جديدة. Beltsville, MD: Amana Publications, 1989.

Rabiʕi

ف. ربیعی. «سفری به تهران» *کیهان* چاپ لندن. ۲۲ تیر، ۱۳۷۸.

Rāhjiri 1970

علی راهجیری. *تاریخ مختصر خط و سیر خوشنویسی در ایران*. تهران: مشغل آزادی، ۱۳۴۹.

Rahnamā 1966

زین العابدین رهنما. پیامبر: زندگی حضرت *رسول اکرم*. سه جلد. تهران: جیبی، ۱۳۴۵.

__________ 1970

زین العابدین رهنما. زندگانی *امام* حسین. چاپ ششم. تهران: پرستو، ۱۳۴۹.

Rāhsepār 2000

جمشید راهسپار. «در جستجوی لحظه های صمیمیت» *تطاووس*، شمارهٔ دوم زمستان، ۱۳۷۸.

Rumi 1971

جلال الدین مولوی محمد بن حسین رومی. مثنوی معنوی، به تصحیح رینولد الین نیکلسون. تهران: امیر کبیر، ۱۳۵۰.

__________ 1976

مولانا جلال الدین محمد مشهور به مولوی. *کلیات شمس: دیوان کبیر*، به تصحیح بدیع الزمان فروزانفر. تهران: امیر کبیر، ۲۵۳۵.

Ruznāmeh

روزنامهٔ اخبار مشروطیت و انقلاب ایران: یادداشتهای حاجی میرزا سید احمد تفرشی حسینی در *سالهای ۱۳۲۱تا ۱۳۲۸* قمری به کوشش ایرج افشار. تهران: امیر کبیر، ۱۳۵۱.

Saʕādat 1999

اسماعیل سعادت. «"را"ی بعد از "یا"ی نکره» نشر *دانش* ، سال شانزدهم، شمارهٔ ۱، بهار ۱۳۷۸، ص ۱۷-۲۶.

Saberi 2000 Helen Saberi. *Afghan Food & Cookery*. New York: Hippocrene.

Ṣādeqi 1993

علی اشرف صادقی. «شیوه ها و امکانات واژه سازی در زبان فارسی معاصر (۸)» نشر *دانش*، سال یازدهم، شمارهٔ دوم، بهمن و اسفند ۱۳۷۱، ص ۲۲-۲۹.

__________ 1993b

علی اشرف صادقی. «شیوه ها و امکانات واژه سازی در زبان فارسی معاصر (۱۰)» نشر *دانش*، سال سیزدهم، شمارهٔ چهارم، خرداد و تیر ۱۳۷۲، ص ۱۵-

.٢٣

Saʿdi 1984

مصلح بن عبد الله سعدی. *کلیات* ، به اهتمام محمد علی فروغی. چاپ ٤. تهران: امیر کبیر، ١٣٦٣.

Ṣafā 1956

ذبیح الله صفا. *تاریخ ادبیات در ایران*، جلد اول: *از آغاز عهد اسلامی تا دوره سلجوقی*. چاپ دوم. تهران: کتابفروشی ابن سینا، ١٣٣٥.

__________1973

ذبیح الله صفا. *حماسه سرایی در ایران: از قدیمترین عهد تاریخی تا قرن چهارم هجری*. چاپ سوم. تهران: امیر کبیر، ١٣٥٢.

Safadi 1987 Yasin Hamid Safadi. *Islamic Calligraphy*. London, NY: Thames and Hudson.

Saʿidi Sirjāni 1983

علی اکبر سعیدی سیرجانی. *وقایع اتفاقیه: مجموعه گزارشها خفیه نویسان در ولایت جنوبی ایران از سال ١٢٩١ تا ١٣٢٢ قمری*. تهران: انتشارات نوین، ١٣٦٢.

__________ 1990

علی اکبر سعیدی سیرجانی. *ضحاك ماردوش از شاهنامه فردوسی*. تهران: نشر نو، ١٣٦٩.

__________ 1992

علی اکبر سعیدی سیرجانی. *بیچاره اسفندیار* .Bethesda, MD: Iranbooks

__________ 1994

علی اکبر سعیدی سیرجانی. *در آستین مرقع*. .Costa Mesa, CA: Mazda

Samiʿi 1987

احمد سمیعی. «از دستنویس تا چاپ» نشر *دانش*، سال هفتم، شماره چهارم، خرداد و تیر ١٣٦٦، ص ٤٠-٤٦.

__________ 2000

احمد سمیعی. *نگارش و ویرایش*. چاپ ٢. تهران: سازمان مطالعه و تدوین کتب علوم انسانی دانشگاهها، ١٣٧٩.

Sanāpur 2000

حسین سناپور. *نیمه ی غایب*. چاپ ٦. تهران: نشر چشمه، ١٣٧٩.

Ṣayyād 1996

پرویز صیاد. «سینمای جمهوری اسلامی: دو روی یك سکّه قلب» *ایران نامه*، سال چهاردهم، شماره ٣، تابستان ١٣٧٥، ص ٤٣١-٤٥٦.

Schimmel 1975 Annemarie Schimmel. *Mystical Dimensions of Islam*. Chapel Hill, NC: University of North Carolina.

Ṣedā-ye Sheˁr-e Emruz

صدای شعر امروز بکوشش بهمن مه آبادی، احمد منطقی تبریزی. تبریز: بلاش، ۱۳۶۸.

Sepehri 1998

سهراب سپهری. *اطاق آبی*، ویراستار پیروز سیار. چاپ سوم. تهران: سروش، ۱۳۷۶.

Seth 1993 Vikram Seth. *A Suitable Boy*. New York: Harper Collins.

Shamkhāni 2000

محمد شمخانی. «پاپ آرت» *طاووس*، شماره‌ء دوم، زمستان ۱۳۷۸، ص ۱۳۹-۱۳۸.

Soueif 1999 Ahdaf Soueif. *The Map of Love*. New York: Anchor.

Spooner 1994 Brian Spooner. "Are We Teaching Persian? or *farsi*? or *dari*? or *tojiki*?" in *Persian Studies in North America: Studies in Honor of Mohammad Ali Jazayery*, ed. Mehdi Marashi. Bethesda, MD: Iranbooks, 1994, pp. 175-189.

Stories 1991 *Stories from Iran: A Chicago Anthology 1921-1991* ed. by Heshmat Moayyad. Washington, D.C.: Mage, 1991.

Taˁlimāt

تعلیمات اجتماعی، سال دوم، دوره‌ء راهنمایی تحصیلی. تهران: وزارت آموزش و پرورش، ۱۳۶۰.

Tavakkoli 1994

نیرهٔ توکلی. «نکته هایی در بارهٔ ترجمه و نگارش» نشر *دانش*، سال چهادهم، شمارهٔ سوم، فروردین و اردیبهشت ۱۳۷۳، ص ۱۵-۱۶.

Tehrani 1991 Farideh Tehrani. *Negligence and Chaos: Bibliographic Access to Persian-Language Materials in the United States*. Metuchen, N.J. & London: Scarecrow Press.

Vaziri 1993 — Mostafa Vaziri. *Iran as Imagined Nation: The Construction of National Identity*. New York: Paragon House.

Wright 1977 — Denis Wright. *The English Amongst the Persians*. London: Heinemann.

Wulff 1966 — Hans E. Wulff. *The Traditional Crafts of Persia: Their Development, Technology, and Influence on Eastern and Western Civilizations*. Cambridge, MA: M.I.T. Press.

Yazdāniān 1994

صفی یزدانیان «وودی الن» *کلك* آذر و دی ۱۳۷۲ شمارهٔ ٤٦-٤٥، ص ٢٥٤-٢٥٥.

Yunesi 1973

جنبه های رمان، ای ام. فاستر، ترجمه ابراهیم یونسی. تهران: امیر کبیر، ۱۳۵۲.

Translation of E. M. Forster. *Aspects of the Novel*.

Yusofi 1989

غلامحسین یوسفی. «افراط، تفریط، اعتدال در نگارش فارسی» نشر *دانش*، سال نهم، شمارهٔ دوم، بهمن و اسفند ۱۳٦٧، ص ٢-٤.

Zarrinkub 1974

عبد الحسین زرین کوب. *نه شرقی، نه غربی-انسانی: مجموعهٔ مقالات، نقدها، نمایشواره ها*. چاپ اول. تهران: امیر کبیر، ۱۳۵۳.

__________ 1974a

عبد الحسین زرین کوب. *فرار از مدرسه: در بارهٔ زندگی و ندیشهٔ ابو حامد غزالی*. تهران: انجمن آثار ملی، ۱۳۵۳.

Zaryāb Kho'i 1992

عباس زریاب خویی. «نگاهی تازه به مقدمهٔ شاهنامه» *ایران نامه*، سال دهم، شمارهٔ اول، زمستان ۱۳۷۰، ص ١٤-٢٣.

Zibākalām 1998

صادق زیباکلام. «ما چه در عشق و چه در نفرت غرب را نشاخته ایم» گفت و گو با دکتر صادق زیباکلام. *دنیای سخن*، شمارهٔ ۷۸، اسفند و فروردین ۱۳۷۷، ص ۲۸-۳۲.

Index of Technical Terms